T0350651

Beyond Positivism, Behaviorism, and Neoinstitutionalism in Economics

Beyond Positivism, Behaviorism, and Neoinstitutionalism in Economics

DEIRDRE NANSEN MCCLOSKEY

THE UNIVERSITY OF CHICAGO PRESS   CHICAGO AND LONDON

The University of Chicago Press, Chicago 60637
The University of Chicago Press, Ltd., London
© 2022 by The University of Chicago
All rights reserved. No part of this book may be used or reproduced in any manner
whatsoever without written permission, except in the case of brief quotations in critical
articles and reviews. For more information, contact the University of Chicago Press,
1427 E. 60th St., Chicago, IL 60637.
Published 2022
Printed in the United States of America

31 30 29 28 27 26 25 24 23 22   1 2 3 4 5

ISBN-13: 978-0-226-81830-6 (cloth)
ISBN-13: 978-0-226-81944-0 (paper)
ISBN-13: 978-0-226-81831-3 (e-book)
DOI: https://doi.org/10.7208/chicago/9780226818313.001.0001

Library of Congress Cataloging-in-Publication Data

Names: McCloskey, Deirdre N., author.
Title: Beyond positivism, behaviorism, and neoinstitutionalism in economics /
    Deirdre Nansen McCloskey.
Description: Chicago : University of Chicago Press, 2022. | Includes bibliographical
    references and index.
Identifiers: LCCN 2021056675 | ISBN 9780226818306 (cloth) | ISBN 9780226819440
    (paperback) | ISBN 9780226818313 (e-book)
Subjects: LCSH: Economics—Philosophy. | Positivism. | Philosophical behaviorism. |
    New institutionalism (Social sciences)
Classification: LCC HB72.M3295 2022 | DDC 330.01—dc23/eng/20220103
LC record available at https://lccn.loc.gov/2021056675

Contents

The Argument in Brief

I offer here a criticism and then a reshaping of my beloved economic science. The criticism is sometimes harsh, exhibiting indignation against those I conceive to have misshapen it. Adam Smith ([1759] 1790) warned early in *The Theory of Moral Sentiments* (1.1.1.6) that indignation can arouse a paradoxical sympathy for its target. "As we are unacquainted with . . . [the] provocation . . . we cannot . . . conceive anything like the passions which it excites." I worry that my passions, and even my attempts at wit (to which I am addicted), will dispose you to take the part against what aroused my indignation. Let's see, and at the least I acquaint you with the provocation.

The detailed criticism arrives at a recommendation for "humanomics," sketched in part 3 of this book and explained more fully in another book, *Bettering Humanomics: A New, and Old, Approach to Economic Science.* The two books are a pair. The elevator pitch is that to get an adequate economic science we need one that uses broader but nonetheless more rigorous theorizing and broader but nonetheless more serious empiricism than at present.

And we need, as ethical social scientists, to be rigorously modest.[1] The ethics of liberalism, born in the eighteenth century, should be foundational in a good economic science in all senses of "good." Liberalism—which is to say the theory of a society of people liberated from hierarchies—is productive in sciences, whether natural or social or humanistic. Free entry (and exit) is foundational in a science or politics or economy. Slaves can't exit (or enter). Therefore, slaves don't produce innovation, in art or science or the economy. Look at Nazi painting or Soviet department stores. It's no accident that art and science have flourished most in the more liberal societies under roughly liberal economic institutions, what Karl

Popper called the open society.[2] Good science, surely, and most obviously good social science, should be made by good, open, honest, voluntaristic, liberal people, or else it is liable to break bad. (I will use the word *liberal* throughout, you can see, not in is strange American sense since the 1920s but in its original and international meaning, that is, a society composed on nonslaves—liberated adults, *liberi*, not slaves to husbands or masters, to kings or bureaucrats.)

Such a conclusion about economic science was hinted at back in 1994, in *Knowledge and Persuasion in Economics* (McCloskey 1994). Fully twenty-five years later, *Why Liberalism Works: How True Liberal Vales Produce a Freer, More Equal, Prosperous World for All* finally got the politics of it more or less straight. (I am not the swiftest of thinkers.) In particular in the present book I argue that "neoinstitutionalism," and other positivist, anti-ethical, neobehaviorist, manipulative, and illiberal movements over the past few decades in economics don't fit the bill for an ethical and scientific economics suited to liberated adults.

I respond here to various counterclaims implicit in the present-day method and substance of economics. "Responding," understand, is not merely irritated disputation or somehow impolite. It's the only alternative to an authoritarian hierarchy in science of the sort that prevented American geologists from accepting plate tectonics for fifty years and prevented Mayanists from decoding glyphs for thirty years and prevented economists from challenging Keynesianism for twenty years. Responding is what scientists—or citizens or lawyers or marriage partners—should do, every time, as amiably as they can manage. "What's your position? Oh, I see. Hmm. Well, dear, consider my amiable response to your logic and evidence. Maybe we can reach agreement. Let's discuss it. You come too." It's the human conversation of a good science, in the laboratory or the seminar room. So I went to it with a will. (You're welcome.)

We should all try to follow the motto of the philosopher Amélie Oksenberg Rorty, who wrote in 1983 that what is crucial is "our ability to engage in continuous conversation, testing one another, discovering our hidden pre-suppositions, changing our minds because we have listened to the voices of our fellows. Lunatics also change their minds, but their minds change with the tides of the moon and not because they have listened, really listened, to their friends' questions and objections."[3] Listening, really listening, is the "hermeneutic" part of a triad of hermeneutic (listening), rhetorical (speaking), and substantive (philosophizing) criticism.[4] It's how science advances, really advances, whether on little matters such as an econometric β coefficient or on world-shaping claims such as put forward by Newton or Darwin or Marx or Keynes. The procedure is this: By careful listening to the rhetoric, find out what's really being said and how it is argued, and therefore what might be mistaken in an earlier piece of science. If it's mistaken, fix it. The method in a word is *critique*. In 1867 the subtitle of Marx's *Kapital* was *Kritik der politischen Ökonomie*. That's the scientific spirit.

The discoveries I have made through critique about my beloved economics and economic history are two:

1. In the other book, and by implication here, too, I claim that there is emerging a new and more serious and sensible way of doing economic science — quantitatively serious, philosophically serious, historically serious, and ethically serious too. The economist Bart Wilson and a few others nowadays call it humanomics.[5]

2. In this book I give an example in detail of what appears to be wrong with non-humanomical economics. The example is "neoinstitutionalism," put forward over the past few decades by Douglass North and Daron Acemoglu among many other superb economists and political scientists. I claim that neoinstitutionalism is not the way forward in the science or in its policy recommendations. If people as smart as North and Acemoglu and the rest can get our science so wrong, we need to stop to think.

Scientifically speaking, the factual claims of neoinstitutionalism, like those of the other recent fashions — such as neuroeconomics and behavioral finance and happiness studies — are dubious. Like the others, the neoinstitutionalists do not listen, really listen, to the evidence of humans or to their friends' scientific questions and objections. Substantively and rhetorically, they treat creative adults like a flock of little children, three-year-olds to whom we scientists need not listen. We need merely, they say, to "observe" their behavior (omitting for some reason linguistic behavior) and then record the behavior in questionable metrics. Then the children-citizens are to be pushed around with "incentives," the beloved of Samuelsonian economists and econowannabes. From a great height of fatherly expertise in the designing of Max U institutions, the behaviorist looks down with sneering contempt on the merely human actions of liberated adults. It gives me the creeps. It should give you the creeps, too.

The neoinstitutionalism I focus on here, I repeat, is one of many neobehaviorist fashions in economics: a behavioral economics claiming that cognitively we are all little children; field experiments in economics performed unethically on literal little children; a neuroeconomics hitching the little children up to electrodes to detect a brain but not a mind; a happyism for the miserable little children recording meaningless metrics; and, more generally for the past century or so and reaching a climax now, an economic engineering emanating from Washington or London or Brussels adding more and more "policies" to domineer over the pathetic little children.[6] For their own good, you understand. Creeping creepiness. The US federal government has in place over a million regulations. One million. The Democrats say, "Add more bureaucrats domineering over prescription drugs instead of letting adult Americans buy them freely abroad." The Republicans say, "Add more police domineering over northeast Baltimore instead of letting adult Baltimoreans find employment at a wage that businesses are willing to pay."

The neobehaviorist fashions go in the wrong direction, adopting an implausible and illiberal hypothesis that Economic Daddy Knows Best, treating grown-up people as less than fully dignified.[7] (I say "most of" them because a few economists try, and to some extent succeed, in humanizing behaviorism: Morris Altman's recent *Why Ethical Behavior Is Good for the Economy* [2020] is a glittering example, and Richard Langlois and certain others, who recognize that humans are actually human, want to hold on to more behaviorism than I or Arjo Klamer or Bart Wilson or George DeMartino or a few others do.[8]) But the vaunted empiricism of neobehaviorism turns out to be startlingly hollow. It's rather like the broken-windows policy that in 1982 the political scientists George L. Kelling and James Q. Wilson recommended, which had wholly unpredicted, and vicious, results.[9] To overcome the illiberalism and to fill up the empirical hollows, we need a better economics, a bettering humanomics — an economics with the humans left in.

Whether or not you are an academic economist, you should care about the future of the field. Madmen in authority, it has been said, who hear voices in the air are distilling their frenzy from some academic scribbler a few years back. The distilled products are the gallons of Kool-Aid imbibed by the Politburo, the Council of the European Union, the Federal Reserve Bank, the Chinese Communist Party, the US Treasury, the IMF, the World Bank, the federal and state and local governments, Joseph Stiglitz, Paul Krugman, Elizabeth Warren, Marianna Mazzucato. The distillation's recipe calls for more and more policies and regulations devised by saintly and omnicompetent masters to govern the pathetic little lives of the misled, stupid, irrational little children. That's you, dears. You should care if such a distillation will demean and then kill you.

Still, the main implied reader here is a professional economist, or a fellow traveler among sociologists, philosophers, law professors, and political scientists. I've been an economist and economic historian most of my life, and I love and admire economics and the economists. Mostly. Paul Samuelson and Milton Friedman, Geoff Harcourt and Harry Johnson, Bob Fogel and Albert Hirschman, Harold Demsetz and Joan Robinson, Friedrich Hayek and Bob Heilbroner. Hurrah for the ideas of opportunity cost, of supply and demand, of general equilibrium, of entry and exit, and all of their mathematical and statistical expressions. Three cheers for the accounting of national income and the wheel of wealth, especially in their historical implementations. The Lord's blessings on cooperation and competition, their analysis and their analysts. Yes, I said, yes I will yes.

But if the distillation is not to demean and then kill you and me and pretty much everyone from Boston to Beijing, we economists need to rethink the recipe, devising a new one that nonetheless does not throw away what's known from good old economic science. (A careless throwing away has long typified proposals for this or that "new" economics, from quite a few of the Marxists and Keynesians and institutionalists to all of the Modern Monetary Theorists.) In a word, serious economists need a serious rethinking of their *scientism*, that is, their imitation of how they imagine physics works, their proud ignorance of science studies since Kuhn, their "cargo-cult" pretense of quantification, their contempt for the humanities, their sneering dismissal of ethics, their scorn for the bulk of human knowledge and behavior, their illiberalism even when claiming the honorable title of liberal.

"Cargo cult" may need explanation. It's the label the physicist Richard Feynman assigned to projects having the external look of science but that are actually make-believe.[10] His metaphor refers to the highlanders of New Guinea after World War II, who set up coconut-shell lamps and runway-like clearings in the cultish hope that the big wartime planes with their enriching cargo would come back. The planes didn't actually come back. Similarly, much of what passes for high-level evidence in economics *looks* like quantification, or at any rate mathematics, but doesn't relevantly quantify or yield actual truths about how the economy works. And likewise, much of what passes for high-level theorizing in economics *looks* like insight into the world's work but doesn't yield that either.

The "sneering dismissal of ethics, and the scorn for most of human knowledge," doesn't need explanation. You see it in action daily. The very word *science*, when used in ignorance of the actual history, philosophy, and sociology of science, is deployed by the proudly ignorant—among them, sadly, many economic scientists—to ignore ethics and to exclude other ways of knowing. "No ethics, please, and certainly no evidence beyond cargo-cult econometrics: We're scientists."

"Scientism," to put it another way, is the belief that you are only scientific if you follow a method of science laid down by an amateur philosopher fifty or a hundred or four hundred years ago. In Samuelsonian economics everything is supposed to be quantitative, or at any rate mathematical, because then we're scientists. (I once believed this, so I know.) In science, as the word has been understood in English from the middle of the nineteenth century, the method is supposed to be Baconian, from the last man in England to use torture for official purposes, Francis Bacon (1551–1626). It was expressed in 1886 by Sherlock Holmes in *A Study in Scarlet*: "It is a capital mistake to theorize before you have all the evidence. It biases the judgment."[11] Never mind that what "evidence" is depends every time on some tentative theory of the matter. The theory poses a question relevant to who the murderer is, such as the question of how high the lethal gun was shot from, a question that the evidence of blood spatter or of embedded slugs can answer. In historical science the Baconian method was celebrated by Leopold von Ranke's maiden book of scientific history, in 1824—*wie es eigentlich gewesen* (as it [the past] actually was). And in American history from the 1880s to the 1960s it was celebrated as "that noble dream" of an objective historical science.[12]

By the 1930s in economics a little more sophisticated method—of "observable implications" of the theory of the gun shot—came from Lionel Robbins, influenced by Viennese logical positivism. Logical positivism was a school already then under devastating attack by philosophers such as Ludwig Wittgenstein and Karl Popper in Britain and Austria, then in the United States by philosophers such as Willard Van Orman Quine and eventually Hilary Putnam, and then by historians and sociologists and rhetoricians looking into how science is actually done. Logical positivism was illogical on numerous points—being for example a metaphysical dogma arrayed against metaphysical dogma. And it was factually mistaken on numerous other points—such as positing simple entailment when complex entailment is the life of science. It never did fit how economic science actually persuades.[13] Yet logical positivism was enthusiastically seconded by Paul Samuelson in the 1940s and by Milton Friedman in the 1950s. In the minds of most economists, that's where method has remained.

The method was given its final form in the constitution of Samuelsonian economics, drafted by Tjalling Koopmans in 1957, *Three Essays on the State of Economic Science*. Koopmans (whose name, by the way, means in his native Dutch "salesmen") recommended a theoretical-empirical specialization, which he believed was characteristic of the physics in which he was educated. He recommended that theorists up on the top floor spend their time gathering a "card file" of *qualitative* theorems, attaching a sequence of axioms A', A'', A''', and so forth, to a sequence of conclusions C', C'', C''', and so on, *separated from* the empirical work "for the protection [note the word, you students of free trade] of both."[14] Then the empirical econometricians, the bench scientists down in the basement, would get to work to see whether in the actual world A' leads to C' or to C''.

The official method of economics would be all right as a useful portion of scientific persuasion (though it leaves out most of what actually persuades in any science), but only if the economic theorems were not merely *qualitative*. In 1941 the twenty-six-year-old Paul Anthony Samuelson, in his modestly titled PhD thesis at Harvard, "The Foundations of Economic Analysis" (published, to justified acclaim, in 1947), laid down the rule that the theorems would mostly be qualia, not quanta. One could have no objection if they instead took the quantitative form of the mathematics used by physicists or geologists. Then the duller wits like McCloskey the economic historian could be assigned to mere boring observation, filling in the quantitative blanks in the theory. But the trouble is that chronically in post-Koopmans economics *there are no blanks to fill in*, no how-much questions asked, especially in the sort of theory that the top economists admire and that absorbs much of their waking hours.

Consider for example the theory of abstract general equilibrium studied by Arrow and Debreu and Hahn, or the rational-expectations theory of Lucas and Sargent, or the informational-asymmetry theory of Akerlof and Stiglitz. In recent years, thankfully, economics has turned some toward the sort of quantitative simulation that other quantitative sciences use, which had been proposed early in the reign of Koopmans by Barbara Bergman and by my teacher, Guy Orcutt.[15] Praise the Lord. (I cannot praise so warmly, though, the recent shift to ersatz sociology without economic theory—or for that matter without serious engagement with sociology or history—guided only by regression analysis using tests of significance lacking substantive loss functions.)

In its theoretical branch of economics, the excess of liabilities over assets in the Koopmans method is well illustrated by noncooperative game theory. For one thing, as Vernon Smith has long pointed out, experimental economics has shown over and over and over again that the premise of noncooperation is factually mistaken in humans. It is not mistaken in our cousins the gorillas or even in most chimps. But humans massively cooperate.[16] Adam Smith noted that the implicit cooperation in commerce and its division of labor "has in view no such extensive utility" as in fact comes from it. The arm's-length cooperation arises, he said, from a specifically human "propensity to truck, barter, and exchange." Such a propensity is "the necessary consequence of the faculties of reason [which Smith did *not* construe as Mr. Max U] and speech [which is the linguistic behavior set aside in behaviorism]."[17] An economist using noncooperative game theory and ignoring the cooperation explicit in family life or the Good Samaritan and implicit in social life or language would be like a physicist proposing an inverse *cube* law of universal gravitation. He keeps on publishing lovely papers about such a world despite thousands of experiments and observations showing that in fact the correct exponent is an inverse *square*.

And for another, to get technical about it, finite noncooperative games unravel, and infinite games have infinite numbers of solutions. In Yiddish syntax, Some theory! It's empirically false and theoretically inconclusive.

A future economics should on the contrary use the available scientific logic and evidence, all of it—experimental, simulative, introspective, questionnaire, graphical, categorical, statistical, literary, historical, aesthetic, psychological, sociological, political, ethical. To deploy an old joke, the economist drunk on his neobehaviorist distillation should stop assuming that the house keys he lost out in the dark have shown up mysteriously under the lamppost, where, he explains, the light is better. The economist should become seriously quantitative and seriously *qualitative*, too, practicing an entire human science. Get right the numbers *and* the categories. No more cargo cults, dears. Get serious ethically. Search for all the scientifically relevant knowledge out in the dark, where much of it is to be found, not only under the lamppost.

PART I

Economics Is in Scientific Trouble

An Antique, Unethical, and Badly Measured Behaviorism Doesn't Yield Good Economic Science or Good Politics

A leading example of a cargo cult in present-day economics, I here argue, is neoinstitutionalism, the mainly historical branch of recent behaviorist programs in economics. The advocates for neoinstitutionalism—such as the Nobelist and theorist Oliver Williamson and the Nobelist and economic historian Douglass North—declare that "institutions in the economy *matter*." The italics are part of the rhetoric, sliding over the absence of measurement or comparison or causal analysis establishing *how much* they matter.

The neoinstitutionalist idea, articulated most influentially for historical explanations by the amiable North (1920–2015), is that black-letter law provides "the rules of the game." If we change the rules we of course will often change the outcome of the game. Lower the pitcher's mound, and hitters will get more hits. In particular, the neoinstitutionalists in economic history repeatedly claim that in olden days people knew not the rules of property rights and contract law, and therefore when we got such rules, the people got modern economic growth too. In other words, the neoinstitutionalists claim that recently—say in 1689 in England—the rule of law was discovered, to all our joy. A possibly necessary cause is construed as assuredly sufficient. Nowadays, says the World Bank, instructed by North, we add the rule of law and stir, making the poor rich. A snap. Get black-letter rules, such as the Soviet Constitution (1924, 1936, 1977). Job done.

It's called *neo*institutionalism to distinguish it from the old American school of institutionalism of Veblen, Commons, Ayer, and Galbraith, which itself was a chip off the old block of the German Historical School of Schmoller, Weber, Sombart, Lowe, and Polanyi. Contrary to such oldsters, *neo*institutionalism uses enthusiastically (sometimes accompanied by a strange insistence that it does not) the tools of "neoclassical" economics. Especially it uses the subtools featured in what I have already been calling "Samuelsonian" economics, in which modern economists are overtrained—tools such as that same noncooperative game theory and its construal of the human as Mr. Max U, a narcissistic sociopath intent on maximizing his utility subject only to the constraint of the rules of the game. Or not, if he can get away with it.

"Samuelsonian," I note, is historically more accurate than the conventional term, "neoclassical." The crushingly intelligent Paul Anthony Samuelson (1915–2009) laid down the methodological rule that economics must be about individuals who maximize their utility subject to their constraints, that Max U—what I call below *P*-logic or "Prudence Only." The category "neoclassical," by contrast, includes other economists following on the sharp revision of political economy in the 1870s, such as the Austrians and Marshallians and Keynesians and even post-Keynesians (though those last are more properly viewed as classical rather than neoclassical). The non-Samuelsonians do not agree with what the excellent Samuelson laid down as the rule of method. The non-Samuelsonians say, for example, that evolution or an aggregate matters and are willing to start the analysis at that level. The non-Samuelsonians are not obviously mistaken in such a method, and the Samuelsonians are not obviously correct in rejecting it. (Yet I am fond of remarking that in the late twentieth century our economic science had the great advantage over linguistic science, with which it shares many features, that its great MIT Leader was the tolerant, moderate, amiable, and crushingly intelligent Paul Samuelson instead of the dogmatic, extremist, nasty, and crushingly intelligent Noam Chomsky.[1])

Why then does neoinstitutionalism with its Samuelsonian method need to be criticized and replaced by humanomics? I'll give the case in full below, in parts 2 and 3, after this part detailing the wider problems I discern in economic science. But for now, consider the following.

For one thing, neoinstitutionalism, like much of economic thinking, confuses necessary with sufficient conditions, and confuses helpful side conditions with inspiring causal conditions. For example, the idea overused in Samuelsonian economics of the "production function" (which I myself overused for decades after learning it in graduate school) says that a book of alternative recipes for products is necessary. Certainly it is, whether literally written down or not. Put together such and such a tonnage of coke (from coal), iron ore, and limestone into a blast furnace with such and such specifications run by a certain number of laborers with such and such skills, according to page 106 of the book of recipes, and you get a ton of pig iron. Use instead the recipe from page 26, which entails much more labor and is charged instead with charcoal (from wood, instead of coal), and you get the ton of pig iron but with differing opportunity cost of the inputs used. Good to know. But to stop at the recipe book as the "cause" of the pig iron is to confuse the book with the human action sufficient and inspiring that yielded the very book, such as an engineering education and craft traditions and a liberal society encouraging having a go to exercise them. And most basically it ignores the human creativity that suffices for education and craft and betterment, when the society permits.

True, French cuisine still depends to some degree on *Le guide cuisinaire* (1903; also called *L'art culinaire*) by Auguste Escoffier, as for example in its five "mother sauces": béchamel, espagnole, velouté, hollandaise, and tomate. Escoffier's *Guide* is a necessary input, or at least a helpful one, into *Mastering the Art of French Cooking*, and into Julie's 365 days of dinners cooking from it. But the sufficient and inspiring causes of French cuisine are not such items in the present supply chain. They are the social and intellectual arrangements in French kitchens and restaurants that made for the books in the first place, from Guillaume Tirel in the fourteenth century and Catherine de Medici in the sixteenth century down to untold thousands of wives—and then husbands, too—inventing crème caramel and bouillabaisse and the millions of French eaters insisting on getting a good meal—"slow food"—and willing to chat about it endlessly. The "causes" in a sense relevant to serious scientific description, and to proposals for policies to encourage haute cuisine, were not recipes but the *ideas* for the recipes, the human creativity along with the conditions such as *liberté*, and then practice, practice (How do you get to Guy Savoy, Monnaie de Paris, 11?). The causes were not production functions—not the routine, bookable recipes helpfully teaching how to combine ingredients and to practice, practice in chopping potatoes. The sufficient cause under some broadly available necessary conditions, such as the existence of labor and sunlight and Paris, was the human creativity.

Confusing necessary with sufficient conditions—confusing modestly helpful pedagogy with powerfully inspiring conditions for creation, as for example does the economist's "growth theory"—leads away from a proper understanding of economic growth, among lesser topics in economics. Establishing property rights under a rule of law, to instance the neoinstitutionalist's favorite cause, is necessary and helpful, of course, or the life of man, quoth Thomas Hobbes, is solitary, poor, nasty, brutish, and short. You can therefore explain why nations *fail*, and can discern the origins of poverty, by noting the nasty incentives that have led most nations for millennia far enough away from the rule of law and of alienable property rights and the rest to hobble the economy.[2] You can see it, too, in the nationwide discouragement of Black inventors and entrepreneurs after the Tulsa race riot of 1921, or the worldwide discouragement of female inventors and entrepreneurs after Eden. But you can only explain why nations *succeed*, and then discern in a proper economic science the origins of our startling modern prosperity and the comparative liberation of Blacks and women, by noting with Francis Hutcheson of Belfast and Glasgow the sufficient cooperativeness—and noting with his student Adam Smith of Glasgow and Edinburgh—the inspiring liberties, jointly sufficient, that led a few nations such as Holland and Britain early and the US and Sweden and Japan later toward enterprise and betterment. If *Le guide cuisinaire* or *The Foundations of Economic Analysis* had been deeply flawed books, you could explain, too, some outcomes in bad cooking or bad economics. But in any case excellent cooking and excellent economics comes from human creativity liberated—such as exhibited by the admirable Escoffier and the admirable Samuelson. We should seek to know the sufficient conditions for such creativity. That's economic science.

Elevating a necessary condition such as property rights to the cause of modern growth would be like elevating the existence of the tomato in Europe after the Columbian Exchange to the cause of *sauce tomate*. It was necessary, obviously, but not sufficient, equally obviously. The British and the Dutch and the Germans had the necessary tomatoes, too, but did not have the sufficiencies that made for their glorious Italian and then French use. Tomatoes, labor, and capital in France made for French cuisine; in Germany, German. (I rest my case.) Or take pastry. Austria, Denmark, and France, alone among European nations, know how to make superb pastry. If you drive from Copenhagen across the bridge and down to Malmö in Sweden, the pastry shifts from ambrosia to fodder. The Swedish recipe and its Swedish practitioners were not created equal to the Danish.

And the necessary conditions featured in neoinstitutionalism are in fact commonplace, like sunlight. A society wholly without property rights and the rule of law is not a society. The historical truth is that since the beginning of human societies, the enforcement of property rights and civil peace have been more or less universal, with or without the permission of a sovereign, if there was one. The scientific question is "more or less," not "yes or no" or "present or absent." Little bands of hunter-gatherers, with no fixed sovereign, or much of any leader at all, had a vivid sense of ownership, as in a lesser and nonalienable form do many species down to butterflies. The coiner I have mentioned of the word *humanomics*, Bart Wilson, sees in a 2020 book the origins of the uniquely human practice of alienable property in the mental and ethical habits of making compound human tools, such as spears.[3] Prisoners and gold miners without kings devise rules of property.[4] To speak of larger societies, Israel under the judges had fully enforced private property, though the evidence from the Bible is mixed on its exact character, well before the Israelites unwisely demanded that God give them a king—who then in fact compromised their property rights, just as God through Samuel had warned them he would.[5]

Genghis Khan unified the wild horsemen of Mongolia by enforcing fiercely the rule of law, with strict property rights in horses and wives.[6] The resulting *Pax Mongolica* of the thirteenth and fourteenth centuries imposed peaceful property rights on the largest contiguous land empire ever assembled, from Korea to Hungary. An Italian merchant in 1340 declared that the Central Asian routes under Mongol control were "perfectly safe, whether by day or by night."[7] Yet conquest and a kingly government did not yield innovation, aside from Mongol military tactics.

Of an Iceland without kings, *Njàl's Saga* declares, *Með lögum skal land byggja* (With law will the land be built), and so it was.[8] (The quotation is also the first sentence of the Danish Jutland law code of 1241, inscribed to this day on Danish law courts, and it is the motto of the Shetland Islands and of the Icelandic police force.[9]) The motto continues with *en með ólögum eyða* (and with bad laws [the land is] destroyed). The law in the Icelandic case was enforced not by a king but by kin.[10] When Gunnar Hámundarson in *Njáls Saga* killed two members of the family of Gissur the White, Gissur's family was authorized by Icelandic law to kill him in turn, and eventually it did. No one went to the police—in Iceland in the tenth and eleventh centuries there being none. In other words, property rights and laws against murder are necessary, true, but by no means regularly dependent on centralization in kings.

The neoinstitutionalists, that is, are mistaken in their legal centralist theory. Recent experiments by Kimbrough, Smith, and Wilson and by

Wilson, Jaworski, Schurter, and Smyth show property emerging without the legal centralist support that James I of England or Douglass North of Washington University claimed is necessary and sufficient.[11] Nor is there archaeological or historical evidence for the Northian view. "It takes an overly narrow view of human history," Kimbrough, Smith, and Wilson write, "to argue that no property existed prior to the creation of law and the state, for both agriculture and animal husbandry far pre-date the state."[12] Mainly ethics—not mainly law—holds societies together.

Observe: not one of these law-abiding societies yielded modern economic growth until in eighteenth-century Britain and its North American colonies the ancient routine of reasonably good laws was mixed for the first time in agricultural societies with an entirely new idea, an egalitarian liberalism explored first in Dutch cities and theorized in French salons and then applied throughout the Anglosphere. The liberal releasing of human creativity has *sufficed* for growth, when the routine and widespread necessary and helpful conditions have obtained—the existing recipe books, as they routinely do exist, such as property rights, rule of law, capital markets, liquid water, oxygen in the air, absence of an active civil war, the arrow of time, the existence of the universe. Northern Italy, the Ottoman Empire, Northern India, Japan, and China had for centuries all such necessary conditions, as did the Mayan, Roman, and Assyrian empires before. Yet they did not achieve the Great Enrichment emerging from a Dutch-influenced and liberalizing England around 1700 and spreading after 1800 to the world.

Therefore, I say to my beloved colleagues in economics and history: please stop putting forward as an explanation for the shocking betterment since 1800 yet another necessary or helpful (or sometimes in fact obstructive and unhelpful) condition—coal, canals, patents, banking, industrial policy, this or that expanding sector, the rule of law. If you are politically on the right, my dear friends, I suppose you put the rule of law forward because you imagine that the unruly little children should be controlled from above. If you are on the left, my equally dear friends, you put forward industrial policy because you imagine that the stupid little children should be controlled from above. Either way, controlled from above. Realize in a liberal way, dear friends, that the great virtues of commercially tested betterment come mostly from adult human actions independent of state action. State action can wreck them, and often does, with eminent domain and industrial policy and ill-designed taxes. When the state does permit human action—with honest courts and short patents—the rarity is cause for breaking out the champagne.

Look instead for the sufficient and inspiring conditions for adult creativity. You will not usually find them in a nondestructive form in the law and the state, which after all are mostly devoted to enforcing obedience and obstructing creativity (*en með ólögum eyða*). The world possessed plenty of laws and states for millennia before it added an eighteenth-century liberalism making for massive innovation and a Great Enrichment of thousands of percentage points increase of income per person.

A society surely needs a framework of laws and other routines, commonplace though they have been. But it also needs a liberal allowance for breaking them, the way Gandhi broke the Raj's laws of the state salt monopoly and shamed liberal Britain. Otherwise the polity or the economy stagnates, because of course laws are commonly the creatures of special interests. The rule of law is often shameful, such as Jim Crow or apartheid or qualified immunity for the police. Erasing such shames requires a polity in which Ella Baker or Nelson Mandela or Black Lives Matter can disobey, creatively, without in the end being crushed by the rule of law. The same is true of strictly economic laws, which are regularly protections for existing interests. If the interests are to be overcome, and progress assured, rigor is not wise.

* * *

Another criticism of neoinstitutionalism and the other behaviorist fashions is an old technical point, namely, that they exhibit a notable deficiency in measurement and often an absence of quantification altogether. Cargo cults. Much of orthodox economics nowadays, I propose to show, shares the fault. If economics, beyond its scientific goal of true description, is a policy science, as economists have asserted boldly for about a century—which is to say, a social engineering in which brilliant economists make helpful suggestions in line with American progressivism or Fabian socialism to offset "imperfections," such as the externalities or monopolies in markets that mere liberalism had so disgracefully allowed to proliferate—then of course it requires measurement of the effects. Yet economics since first claiming to be a masterful policy science has with rare exceptions undertaken neither the measurement of the damage from the alleged "imperfections" nor the equally essential measurement of the probable if unintended damage from the suggested interventions.

If you are a Samuelsonian economist, you will wax wroth that I say such a crazy thing. After all, the journals are filled with alleged measurements.

But consider. Monopoly or inequality or externality or informational asymmetry "exist," to be sure. A few economists have been vigorous in measuring their local effects, on telephone pricing, say, or the imperfect market for imperfect horses or automobiles.[13] But their national significance has been nothing like established in economic measurements. Consider various impossibility theorems put forward by economic theorists. The best known is Arrow's impossibility theorem on possible cyclic majorities in voting, also known as Condorcet's Paradox. Less well known but of the same character, and also generating a Nobel prize, is the Myerson-Satterthwaite theorem, which says that a seller and a buyer of a house might not arrive at a deal even though both would be better off if they did. Neither has been shown to have factual oomph in the political or the economic world. Yet political scientists and economists go on supposing that such fancies do have oomph, and then they worry, with much thoughtful beard stroking, about a liberal polity and a liberal economy.[14]

It would be as though a physicist concluded from a local study that ignored external sources of energy that the laws of thermodynamics are false. He would then propose as a policy a lovely engine of perpetual motion. Externalities, among other allegedly significant imperfections, have been posited, without serious empirical inquiry, to justify all manner of governmental policies.[15] Listen to the rhetoric that defends a new policy: "We need regulation of this horrible new imperfection I have imagined, and have received a Nobel prize for imagining," though he has not given evidence of its magnitude—just as he supports an evidence-free antitrust policy against allegedly harmful "monopoly" by Amazon or an evidence-free tariff policy against allegedly harmful "dumping" by China.

Meanwhile the highly "imperfect" economy of the world since 1800 has yielded a rise of income for the poorest of us . . . wait for the hot news from economic history . . . *3,000* percent. Listen to it. An economy riven by horrible imperfections has yielded since 1800 a rise by a factor of about thirty in the ability of the poorest among us to buy goods and services, a Great Enrichment. Hmm. In Yiddish syntax again: With such imperfections, who needs perfection?!

The "rare exceptions" I mention to a lack of measurement are to be seen in agricultural economics measuring, say, the effects of tobacco allotments on the price of North Carolina land, or in transportation economics measuring the cost and benefit of high-speed rail between Chicago and St. Louis, or (with markedly less believability) in macroeconomics measuring the trade-off between inflation and employment. Even these measurements seldom ask what the *national* and *long-run* significance is of the entire bundle of problems and programs and policies. That is the scientifically relevant question: is giving the government more and more powers to enforce, say, innovation policy going to result in markedly more, or perhaps much less, innovation? Likewise, breaking up Amazon because it is a "monopoly" is probably a policy that will reduce innovation in retailing. Exceptionally, A. C. Herberger's old and Nobel-worthy estimate of the loss from monopoly did answer the scientifically relevant question.[16] The Lucas Critique in macroeconomics makes a similar point, though not measuring. And I note later that even a scientific and political program that I very much admire, the empirical Austrian economics centered at George Mason University, shares in the Samuelsonian orthodoxy's lack of believable, on-the-whole measurement of national importance.

We've got to do better as economic scientists.

* * *

And finally one needs to ask whether it is *ethical* to intervene the way a behaviorist policy science does, such as the policy of adding institutions and stirring that the World Bank following North has adopted. To put it succinctly, I doubt the policy of policy, and so should you. The French tradition of Louis XIV's controller general, Jean-Baptiste Colbert, carried down to the present in that splendid nation, is to suppose that an economy, unlike art or music or language or numerous other human projects, needs detailed and centralized regulation. The businessmen of Paris were asked by Colbert in 1681 what the government could do to help them. They replied, "Leave us to do it."

I echo them: leave liberated adults to do it. Scientific description, yes; overmastering policy, no. Wise remarks about how the social world is in actual, quantitative fact, yes; calling in the cops to push harmless people around, no. Early intervention in a plague or forest fire or foreign invasion, yes; expanding the state to run most innovation and allocation, no. "The key functions of the legal system," writes the classical-liberal theorist of law Richard Epstein, "can be neatly summarized in four words: aggression no, exchange yes."[17] As the liberal political thinker David Boaz puts it, "In a sense, there have always been but two political philosophies: liberty and power."[18]

Modern economic orthodoxy sets aside the creativity of liberated adults in favor of a mechanical behaviorism depending on "given" books of rigid recipes and the interventionist policies of Daddy Colbert. As the Nobelist Hayek and his followers such as another Nobelist, Vernon Smith, say, economic policy is "constructivist," that is, it implements the rationalist side of the Enlightenment as against the liberty side, France's Enlightenment as against Scotland's.[19] Let us construct the world anew, the constructivists declare. *We* can construct it—we wise and good economists empowered by the government's monopoly of coercion. Economics is simple, they suppose, merely a matter of input and output, structure and accounting, the supply chain, the production function, the book of rigid recipes. An extreme recent example of such simplicity is Marianna Mazzucato's claim that *lo stato* is the leading entrepreneur, and should be.[20]

The term of art used by Austrian economists against such a pervasive constructivism is *discovery*. Discovery is not routine and not simple, or else it is not discovery and does not earn supernormal profit, the free lunch of the Enrichment of the last two centuries. Will the new little grocery store on Printer's Row in Chicago succeed? Don't know, can't know, hard to know. There's no mechanical assurance like a production function, and therefore the usual accounting of the cause of economic growth depending on the notion of a production function is mistaken. Discovery is creative and liberated and adult. It's also scary, admittedly, which leads to the temptations of "protection." But in the end it was massively enriching, the 3,000 percent following from the liberal plan of letting people be adult nonslaves. And therefore it was dignifying. It is the actual "universal basic income," as against the enchanting but unhinged constructivism recently proposed to raise the state to 80 percent mastery of the economy. Discovery should be encouraged, not crushed by orders from Daddy and his planners or by the Sun King and his bureaucrats or by the guildsman and his tariff walls.

An economics without discovery at its center therefore gets the economic science wrong. Neoinstitutionalism and the other behaviorisms get it wrong. Humanomics gets it right. The political scientist and 2009 Nobel laureate in economics Elinor Ostrom (1933–2012), one of a thin stream of practitioners of humanomics before the letter, imitating Adam Smith, wrote in 1990,

> The intellectual trap in relying entirely on models to provide the foundation for policy analysis is that scholars then presume that they are omniscient observers able to comprehend the essentials of how complex, dynamic systems work by creating stylized descriptions of some aspects of those systems. With

the false confidence of presumed omniscience, scholars feel perfectly comfortable in addressing proposals to government that are conceived in their models as omni-competent powers able to rectify the imperfections that exist in all field settings.[21]

The sounder policy is to give up policy, retaining a humane and sensible safety net, and to let human creativity do its work—at which it has, since liberalism came to England, been spectacularly successful. Social engineering is illiberal on its face and is regularly disastrous. Liberalism is what made us very rich and reasonably good, as in the liberal parts of the US economy since 1800 and in the liberal parts of the Chinese economy since 1978 and in the liberal parts of the Indian economy since 1991. Enrichment came from new ideas, nourished by what the economist and philosopher Arthur Diamond in a brilliant book calls "openness to creative destruction."[22] It does not come from the intermediate causes along the supply chain, such as capital or institutions or state intervention. Strategic bombing, which relied on input-output thinking, did not work as expected in the face of creativity by Germans or Soviets or North Vietnamese. The idea of an order at Key West is not engineerable—not in its ghostlier demarcations, keener sounds. It is human creativity unleashed that makes for great enrichment.

The creative idea can be as simple as that of selling goods on a mean street in Baltimore, Maryland. Bubbles in *The Wire*, for example, is an entrepreneur financing his drug habit by buying deodorant and candy bars low and selling them high. Everyone is better off, though not of course when Bubbles gets robbed every day by a tough guy. Or, outside of fiction, Mohamed Bouazizi had the idea of selling goods on the mean streets of Sidi Bouzid, Tunisia, though robbed repeatedly by the police and finally in protest immolating himself and initiating the liberal Arab Spring. No pushing people around. Ideas matter most, and liberated people create them.

Good ideas, contrary to the advocates for state coercion such as Paul Krugman and Marianna Mazzucato, do not come importantly from big government. A persuasive demonstration that the statist belief is mistaken is Thomas Hazlett's recent history of wireless in the United States. Hazlett deals, for example, with the urban myth that the government, or maybe Al Gore, invented the internet. On the contrary, the internet was invented by profit-making entrepreneurs. A bit of the technology came from defense contracts, though mostly held in secret too long. And anyway an economist who understands economics will suspect that private substitutes were often available for Defense Department ideas. That the Amphitheater Parkway outside Google's office in Mountain View was built by the city does not mean that the city caused the search engine. The short-run necessary is not the long-run sufficient.

If substitutes are not available, as the economists who do not understand economics seem to believe, then everything is caused by every moderately necessary condition, from the Mountain View parkway up to God's will. We are left without a scientific understanding of what matters. The mistake may be called the Supply-Chain Fallacy, on full display in Mazzucato's books. Or, in criticism of Samuelsonian economics, it can be called the Production-Function Fallacy. Or, in criticism of Marxian economics, it can be called the Structural Fallacy. True, this or that item in the supply chain or the production function or the present structure can be seen as necessary in the short run. But it's like a mechanical watch. For the watch to work, the gears and face and so forth are of course necessary. But its motive force is the spring, the human action and the conditions that encourage it, such as winding the watch and liberating the spring by its escapement to impart a *primum mobile*. Google needed a road, but Larry Page and Sergey Brin were the springs.

The management theorist P.-C. Spender describes the usual springless theory of management so: "the manager is treated as a decision-making 'black box' automaton rather than the lively entrepreneurial creator of the business.... The manager is ... simply the theory's instrument. His only options are to follow the theory's dictates or to make an error."[23] Economists will recognize here the neoclassical nontheory of the firm in which the firm is the maximizing black box, having no internal structure. It is "the theory's instrument" merely. On the contrary, Spender redefines the entrepreneur "as the person having a particular talent for making good decisions in the absence of the necessary data." Different industries, he notes from his own experience at Rolls Royce and other companies, have different ways of dealing with uncertainty. "What everyone who knows this industry understands" is the industry's "recipe," understood not as rigid production coefficients but rough-and-ready advice on how to deal for this particular industry with the "knowledge absences" of life and of business. That's more like it, and it allows for bettering ideas occurring to a liberated human rather than making the entrepreneur a reaction machine.

It has turned out that good, bettering, productive ideas come most easily from liberated people—at best a people liberated from all human coercion or at least liberated within their corporation or government to try out novelties. In a corporation the CEO/entrepreneur is the star of such a show, but it is said that Toyota gets a million new ideas a year from the suggestion boxes on the factory floors. General Motors routes the suggestion boxes into the circular file. Liberated economies are like Toyota, and big governments are like General Motors. In the fantasy world of social engineering, of course, the governments, even if not very creative, are at least sweet and good. But in fact most governments outside of Estonia and Minnesota are notorious for being obstructive and counterproductive—at the worst by employing thugs in aid of the cousins, or of the Chinese Communist Party, or at the best by using the Progressive/Fabian/socialist faiths of omnipresent externalities and omnicompetent governments to coerce, boss, nudge, push around and therefore impoverish the mere citizens on the west side of Chicago. I say let the people go.

The omnicompetence assumed in a policy science is regularly accompanied by a lack of ethical reflection.[24] I ask, Where do you get off, Ms. Economist, in thinking that you are qualified in science or entitled in justice to "nudge" liberated adults? The tilt of economic policy since the Progressives and the Fabians has been sharply toward centralized, Colbertian, top-down intervention. It is notably antiliberal—even when in the United States, and to a lesser degree elsewhere in the Anglosphere, the policy of coercing adults calls itself, brazenly, "liberalism." Worse yet, the twentieth century saw explicit fascism or communism, revived in the twenty-first century on the right in culpably infantilizing populism proposing to mount up the man on the white horse and on the left in culpably naive populism proposing to "try socialism." The middle-of-the-road regulatory state, too, revives a masterful lordship and a guild mercantilism that long dominated Europe from above before the liberal and enriching era of Smith and Mill.[25] Let's not. Let's be liberal.

Let's not, in other words, reinvent the hierarchy imposed by agricultural societies 8000 BCE to 1800 CE and instead take full advantage of the liberal autonomy and egalitarianism of status built into the genes of our hunter-gatherer ancestors during the few millions of years wandering in small groups. The scientific consensus is that "a core characteristic of documented nomadic foragers is their political egalitarianism. Nomadic foragers have no hierarchical social stratification. . . . Leaders (if they exist) have little authority over group members; rotation of roles and functions occur regularly; people come and go as they please; and no person can command or subject group members to act according to one's political aspirations."[26] Contrast such genes with the hierarchical pushing around characteristic of agricultural societies, and now of modern governments. It ain't natural. (Well . . . love of charismatic leadership seems also to be hardwired in humans.) Our better genes, and angels, combined with the literacy and enrichment and now the internet sophistication of humans, all developing in the past two centuries, imply liberalism, not coercive governments and top-down economics. Now is the time for liberty from policy. Humanomics.

CHAPTER TWO

Economics Needs to Get Serious about Measuring the Economy

How did the illiberal and unscientific line in economics arise? This way: over the last couple of centuries there was a rise to and then a retreat from scientific understanding of the economy, the retreat coming after 1848 from a notable failure to measure the understanding. It's been the main problem in economic science.

Down to 1848 the new field of political economy was gradually coming to understand the system of commercially tested betterment. (It was, lamentably, called by its enemies "capitalism," suggesting that capital accumulation is a sufficient cause of betterment. It is not. A much more scientifically accurate name for the system since liberalism is "innovism.")

After 1848, however, more and more of the economists, as they increasingly called themselves, came to *mis*understand commercially tested betterment and its ideology of liberal innovism. Indeed, the political left and the middle came to treat innovism with angry contempt, such as Thorstein Veblen's blast in 1898 against British economics, with its allegedly necessary assumption of the "hedonistic conception of man . . . of a lightning calculator of pleasures and pains, who oscillates like a homogeneous globule of desire of happiness under the impulse of stimuli."[1] "Imperfections" in the market took center stage in economics, and the understanding that had developed during the century or so of rise up to 1848 was at best forgotten or at worst condemned as "capitalist" propaganda so obviously evil and false that no actual measurement of its evilness or falsity needed to be offered.

The consequence of the gradual retreat from understanding after 1848 is, as I have said, that seldom—and approximately never—has an alleged imperfection in commercially tested betterment been subject to a measurement showing that the imperfection is important enough to abandon the approximations of supply and demand and a liberal economy. The alleged imperfections offered up since 1848 are theoretical, a Koopmans card file of qualitative theorems. Often they are thoughtfully and mathematically expressed, which is good. Nothing is wrong with theorizing or mathematics as such. But theories, whether mathematical or verbal, are not of course proven scientific facts, and to treat concepts without empirical content as facts is a scientific mistake. As Immanuel Kant said, "thoughts without content are empty."[2]

The retreat from understanding of the market economy, in other words, has not been justified scientifically. (Nor, as I will later show, has neoinstitutionalism, partaking in the hue and cry against imperfections, been justified—but here the subject is Samuelsonian economics more broadly.) The imperfections might, that is (to dust off an image used in 1922 by the economic historian John H. Clapham, a student of Marshall), turn out to be "empty economic boxes."[3] The theoretical boxes are empty, Clapham said, because we have not measured their contents. Most scientific justification depends on measurement. The retreat from 1848 has not. It has depended on thoughts, or boxes, as categories without factual content. From the point of view of the sciences depending on measurement, such as geology or history, the course of economic science since 1848 looks strange indeed.

The crux in the retreat from understanding after 1848 was an unhappy choice of rhetoric, the locution *"perfect* competition." It is a rhetorical companion to the lightning calculator of pleasures and pains, Max U, understood as exact.[4] Perfect competition came to be seen by the left and then by the center and even by some on the right as a unicorn, a mythical beast. Economists discovered more and more reasons, they thought, to doubt that such a beast existed, *even approximately*—even, that is, as a dirty little whitish horse with a notable bump on his forehead. The word *approximately* here is crucial. What a descriptive science like economics requires is adequate approximations in which one can state the degree of approximation. That's how other descriptive sciences such as evolutionary biology or military history work. Economics on the whole does not. It's either yes or no, on or off, exact or nothing.

The intellectual history of the science of the economy can therefore be divided into two parts. Before 1848, extending to the 1870s, was the education. The anticommercial darkness of Aristotle began to be overcome by glimmers in Aquinas in the thirteenth century and from the Domini-cans of Salamanca in the sixteenth century, but the dawning light came in France in the early eighteenth century, the full light of day in Scotland in the late eighteenth century, and noon in the early nineteenth. After 1848, and itself brightening after the 1870s, came the reeducation in shadowy "imperfections." Or some would say, as I would, the "de-education."

The economist Joseph Persky's splendid book of 2016, *The Political Economy of Progress: John Stuart Mill and Modern Radicalism*, dates the turning point at Mill's *Principles of Political Economy*, whose first edition was in that revolutionary year of 1848. Persky argues persuasively that Mill expresses the triumph of laissez-faire yet also expresses the begin-ning of the theoretical criticisms of its alleged imperfections. Persky cel-ebrates the criticisms. Like another brilliant student of such matters at the University of Illinois at Chicago—the philosopher Samuel Fleishacker (2014) writing about our blessed Adam Smith—Persky, writing about the amiable Mill, claims his man for the political left.

My brilliant colleagues on the left are surely correct in part. Mill, under the influence of Harriet Taylor and under his own unusual openness to views contrary to his own, became, as Persky says, the original moderate social democrat while also being the culmination of classical liberalism. And Smith, as Fleishacker says, was indeed for his time a radical egalitar-ian, advocating what he called "the liberal plan of [social] equality, [eco-nomic] liberty and [legal] justice."[5] In other words, Mill and Smith were original liberals, advocating leaving people alone to prosper. (Yet Smith was no country-club scorner of the poor. He advocated, for example, Scottish-style elementary education paid for locally.)

The simplest form of the unicorn criticism after 1848 is to note with a smirk that in the world after Eden, of course, no "perfection" can ex-ist. Note the word *exist*, a qualitative absolute. No approximations about it. On or off. Yes or no. The argument is heard daily on both sides of the question whether we live under approximately favorable conditions. The argument depends on a humanistic, pure-mathematics notion of exist or not. Economists think they are doing quantitative, descriptive science when they produce another *possible* failure of commercially tested bet-terment to achieve utopia—even though they do not offer evidence of its factual importance for the system as a whole. It would be like producing a nontectonic model of the rise of mountains yet not offering evidence on the factual oomph of the new model. Mountains rose, say, from the crust "wrinkling." The geological pseudoscientist would be ignoring the magnitude of the central Atlantic rift in the way the economic pseudoscientist ignores the magnitude of the Great Enrichment.

The routine of exist or not infects statistical studies, too, which are supposed in the Koopmans Constitution to give just such evidence of the degree of approximation. The studies depend on a mistaken notion that "significance" (misunderstood as meaning "importance") can be judged from the very numbers themselves as *statistical* significance, yes or no. It lacks a scientific judgment of how big is big. The notion has recently been repudiated even by its longtime sponsor, the American Statistical Association.[6] It's time, perhaps, for economists to take note.

The problem is not, I repeat, the use by economists of mathematics or of statistical theory. The problem is the *kind* of mathematics and statistical theory used, arising from the kind of teachers to whom the young economists apply. Most economists learn their mathematics from the Department of Mathematics, not from the Departments of Engineering or of Physics or of Meteorology. Therefore, they learn to prove mathematical propositions qualitatively rather than to use the propositions to study the world quantitatively. Actual engineers and physical scientists do not care whether the mathematical propositions have been proven back in the Department of Mathematics up to the standard of a Greek-style proof of existence by contradiction, such as the proof of the irrationality of the square root of 2. They care only that the propositions are useable approximations. For example, the square root of 2 can be expressed as a rational number approximately, such as 1.41421 plus or minus 0.000005. The approximations appear to have allowed the bridges built with their aid to continue standing. Calculus, for a later example, was used to study the physical world in all manner of ways during the two centuries after its invention, well before the Department of Mathematics came up with a rigorous proof that it made sense to claim that epsilon was "infinitesimally" small but not zero. Schödinger's wave equation, again, has no axioms that prove it by the rules of the Department of Mathematics. But since 1926 it has been used in physics most energetically.

Yet to enter a leading graduate program in economics nowadays, you need to master the ill-named "real analysis," the calculus on steroids that is the foundational course for an undergraduate majoring in mathematics. It consists of the proofs of exist or not beloved by pure mathematicians but useless for actual science. An economist so educated by pure mathematicians is tempted to linger in the lovely world of exist or not and to eschew the trouble-filled world of factually large or small required for a descriptive economics. She believes (mistakenly, as the physicists could tell her) that a mathematical expression, or an economic theory such as purchasing power parity, is of no use if you cannot arrange a mathematics department proof of its consistency with axioms. The economist believes similarly that you need a proof of the stability of the Italian economy before you can propose mathematical expressions for its movements. She believes that calculus must of course be proven (by real analysis) before you can use it to maximize a function such as utility. She believes, when she turns to what she thinks is an empirical method, that whether a coefficient in a regression equation "is positive" is a meaningful scientific question. Exist or not.

Alan Turing, a great British mathematician, had in 1939 a famous debate with Ludwig Wittgenstein, a great Austrian philosopher trained as an aeronautical engineer. Great against great, but from two worlds of mathematical learning.

WITTGENSTEIN: The question is: Why are people afraid of contradiction? It is easy
    to understand why they should be afraid of contradictions in orders, descrip-
    tions, etc. *outside* mathematics. . . . Why should they be afraid of contradictions
    inside mathematics? Turing says, "Because something may go wrong with the
    application [of the mathematics]." . . . But if something does go wrong . . . then
    your mistake was of the kind of using as wrong natural law.
TURING: You cannot be confident about applying your calculus until you know that
    there is no hidden contradiction. . . .
WITTGENSTEIN: But nothing has ever gone wrong that way yet.[7]

The economists, inhabiting a bridge-building science of description and policy, should be on Wittgenstein's side, using mathematics to measure the economy. Too often they are on Turing's side, yearning and yearning to prove economic theory free of hidden contradictions.

My point, I repeat for the last time (are you listening?), is not antimathematical. But what we need is the mathematics relevant to the actual economic world, such as Fourier series and general-equilibrium simulations and fuzzy logic. Not their proofs. If you can prove that on such and such axioms "there exists" a competitive equilibrium, you have offered nothing of scientific value. I knew slightly the mathematical economist Frank Hahn (1925–2013). I said to him once that theorems about the existence of general competitive equilibrium were useless as descriptive economics or political economy. He replied that if he could show how very many and very strange were the conditions necessary for *perfect* competition he could show "why Margaret Thatcher was wrong." Frank was lingering in the world of thoughts without content for an ethicopolitical purpose. Suppose you agree with him that Thatcher was wrong. To prove it, though, you do not need theorems. You need an empirical demonstration that her (brief) flirtation with liberal free-market policies turned out badly in the actual British world.

Nor is my point antihumanistic, to look at the other side, lest you are made uneasy by the emphasis here on quantification. The humanities study categories, a necessary initial step in any scientific argument. Any and all. The concept "gravity," when expressed mathematically, proved to be wise; "phlogiston" and "the ether" not so much. In 1880 economists and psychologists thought that "utility" was measurable; then after a while not; then maybe, for wagers;[8] and then finally yes again, in measures of declared "happiness." (Criticism from the humanities makes that new happyism look highly doubtful.[9] Thus, measure Jane's happiness as 100 degrees Celsius and John's as 212 degrees Fahrenheit, and conclude that their average happiness is . . . uh . . . 156.)

Yet if you are making a quantitative point, as must happen in a descriptive science like economics, you must, after the humanistic step, proceed to the actual count. Then perhaps you can prove Margaret Thatcher wrong. We are liable in an economics without measures of oomph to be misled by our political passions, as Frank Hahn was. If you know that real income per head has risen in Italy since 1800 by a factor of thirty or more, then your political impulse to condemn "capitalism" as impoverishing is at least disciplined. You may continue to be a socialist, but as a serious scientist you will have to sharpen your argument in some other way than going on and on deploying the alternative false fact of impoverishment.

The unicorn argument against the market depends on a commonsense-sounding piece of nonsense. It depends, to quote again Kant, the theorist of perfection, on the sad truth that "Out of the crooked timber of humanity, no straight thing was made."[10] We know such a proposition a priori. But imperfection by such a nonquantitative standard is not, as Kant also put it, a "synthetic" (i.e., a God-given but empirical) statement. And so, says the left wing of economic politics (the right also offers such evidence-free logic, so I'm being fair to haters of Thatcher), "perfect" competition cannot *exist*. And so commercially tested betterment fails. Despite the factor of thirty. QED. It's being said to fail *categorically*, in Kantian terms, by a "synthetic a priori," which was Kant's personal unicorn. An opening gambit ends the game in four moves. Queen's gambit declined. Concede.

It's a silly argument, though it's heard on all sides. Moderate leftists, such as Paul Samuelson and Joseph Stiglitz and many of their followers, argue (without measurement) that a *perfect* market cannot *exist*, and therefore government intervention is desirable/necessary/good. Moderate rightists, such as Leo XIII and William Buckley and many of their followers, argue (without measurement) that a *perfect* community without hierarchy cannot *exist*, and therefore Church and aristocracy are necessary/holy/good. Liberals, such as Ludwig von Mises and Friedrich Hayek and many of their followers, argue (without measurement) that a *perfect* central plan cannot *exist*, and therefore socialism is impossible/impractical/bad. Notice again that I am being politically fair in the accusation of silliness.

This has got to stop. The unmeasuring silliness has been a persistent feature of economics since Athens or Salamanca or Edinburgh or Cambridge, England or Cambridge, Massachusetts or Chicago. It substitutes an existence theorem for a quantitative judgment, substituting blackboard economics for factual inquiry. No need to measure. Decide on humanistic grounds that the economy falls into this or that qualitative category—the labor-excess category or the irrationality-of-consumers category—and then go home. Or, rather, go to partisan, unscientific politics.

The properly descriptive question in economic science is *how far* actually existing plans or actually existing markets deviate from a pretty good result. The "pretty good" locution comes from the political scientist John Mueller's important book of 1999, *Capitalism, Democracy, and Ralph's Pretty Good Grocery*. He argues that "pretty good" is all we can hope for—which is to say that we seek the approximately good in a sense we can measure. We better not attempt utopia, considering how far from pretty good the attempts at utopia have ranged—from the theocracies of Geneva and Khomeini's Iran to the socialisms of New Harmony and Stalin's Russia and now Maduro's Venezuela.

I myself would judge empirically that central planning, or even its socialism-lite version of heavy regulation as in Italy or the United States, have on the whole in their twentieth-century versions been pretty bad for the poor. The Chinese under the centralizing theories of Mao or the Indians under the centralizing theories of the License Raj were, of course, even more badly treated. I judge that if we want to actually help the poor, as everyone should want, then laissez-faire is a better choice, as indeed the recent liberalizations of the economies of China and India suggest. Add on to laissez-faire a sensible safety net and you have a Christian liberalism. You may disagree. But anyway such a judgment needs to be factual and quantitative, not humanistic and categorical—even though the humanistic and categorical step, I say again, in praise of theory, is necessary to start and can also be calmly debated as qualia among scientists who listen, really listen.

That is, I judge *quantitatively* that the experience of East Germany compared with West Germany, say, shows that thoroughgoing central planning leads to incomes half or less of what can be attained in a more laissez-faire economy, even aside from communism's wretched enslavement of people to the secret police and their informers. The same is shown by Hong Kong (1949–2020, RIP) compared with what used to be called Red China. Thomas Sowell puts the material portion of the argument this way: "While capitalism has a visible cost—profit—that does not exist under socialism, socialism has an invisible cost—inefficiency—that gets weeded out by losses and bankruptcy under capitalism. The fact that most goods are more widely affordable in a capitalist economy implies that profit is less costly than inefficiency. Put differently, profit is a price paid for efficiency."[11] Profit, including land rent, is perhaps 20 percent of national income in the United States.[12] The inefficiency of socialism, never mind its hideous authoritarianism, judging from examples such as East Germany and North Korea and Venezuela, is more like 50 percent. Generously. Case closed, empirically, if one accepts the strictly utilitarian grounds, never mind the additional evil of coercion intrinsic to socialism even in it milder forms. You retort that the case is not closed. All right, but at any rate the numbers speak to what you will agree is a relevant scientific question. The humanistic categories "capitalism" or "socialism" by themselves do not. In some possible worlds, central-planning-and-nationalizing socialism *could* "work." That it doesn't work very well in our actual world is an empirical fact, if true, not to be answered by categories alone.

You may disagree with me on the quantitative judgment. You may argue, for example, in the style of what philosophers of science call Duhem's Dilemma that I have not properly controlled the experiments, such as for the especially tyrannical character of East Germany or North Korea or Venezuela, which can be argued is not in the same humanistic category, if in the milder form, as taxation and regulation backed by police powers in Sweden and the United States. You may say, as many youngsters do nowadays, that the historical cases ranging from monasteries to the dictatorship of the proletariat didn't exhibit the right sort of socialism. Let's try it again. In ignorance of 1917.

But the point remains that when we talk of measurement we have at least initiated a liberal discussion among friends listening, really listening, with some chance of eventual resolution. If we stay with the blackboard economics of exist or not and are not familiar with techniques in the humanities for making progress even in such disputes about qualia, we are liable to argue endlessly and increasingly angrily about what kind of unicorn we scorn, blue or red. The left says that a perfect market is the unicorn, a mythical beast. The liberals say that on the contrary a perfect government is the unicorn, equally mythical. More likely, we will stop listening to the other side and never get to a reasoned, quantitative agreement about description and policy. *Audite et alteram partem* was inscribed over the door of many a medieval city hall. "Listen even to the other side" is a good motto for science too.

The humanities I repeat (for I promise the last time) *are* necessary for a descriptive science: What is the correct definition of "labor's share"? What is the most sensible definition of "externalities"?[13] Does it entail ethical decisions? What is the criterion for the "good" functioning of a market? How does care work figure in the economy?[14] Have we chosen the accounting categories comprehensively?[15]

But categories are the beginning of a policy discussion, not the end. Too many economists think they are the end. John Clapham's complaint in 1922 was that the theorists, as they still do nowadays, were proposing on the basis of a diagram or two that government should subsidize allegedly increasing-returns industries. The economists were silent on how to attain the knowledge of how to do it or how much their nonquantitative advice would actually help an imperfect government to get closer to the perfect society if it started from a pretty good, or pretty bad, actual society. Clapham wrote with irritation that the silence was discouraging to "the student not of categories but of things." (The "'categories" are the humanistic steps in a science; "things" are the next steps, a history with measurement.) He chided A. C. Pigou in particular. One looks, Clapham wrote, into Pigou's *The Economics of Welfare* to find that, in nearly a thousand pages, there is not even one illustration of what industries are in which boxes [that is, in which theoretical categories], though many an argument begins, 'when conditions of diminishing returns prevail' or 'when conditions of increasing returns prevail,' as if everyone knew when that was." Clapham ventriloquized the reply of the theorist imagining without quantitative oomph "those empty economic boxes," a reply heard down to the present with no improvement during the intervening century in its plausibility: "If those who know the facts cannot do the [later econometric] fitting, we [theorists finding grave faults in the economy so easily remedied by our splendid proposals, such as an industrial policy favoring increasing-returns industries] shall regret it. But our doctrine will retain its logical and, may we add, its pedagogic value. And then you know it goes so prettily into graphs and equations."[16]

Long ago I expressed the grave problem with the method of exist or not in a theorem, one that seems to fit the history of disputes in economic science since the beginning. I called it the "A-Prime–C-Prime Theorem," as follows.[17] (I adumbrated it above in criticizing Koopmans and Hahn.) Suppose a set of assumptions A alleged to characterize the economy—including, say, a convex production possibility set—implies a set of conclusions about policy, C, such as that free international trade would then be desirable. With such and such general (or not so general, but anyway categorical, nonquantitative) assumptions A, there exists—strictly implied by A—a state of the world, a conclusion C. A typical statement in economic theory is, "if information is [perfectly] symmetric, a [perfectly desirable] equilibrium of the game exists," or, "if people are [perfectly] rational in their expectations in the following sense, buzz, buzz, buzz, *then* there exists an equilibrium of the economy in which monetary policy is useless." Fine. That's qualia, humanistic, theoretical, categorical work, well worth doing as a first step in a science.

Now imagine an *alternative* set of assumptions about the economy, A', which is to say A prime. Just such a re-imagining is what happened, for example, in the transition from rational expectations to neo-Keynesian macroeconomics, or much earlier from competitive, free-entry to monopolistic, excess-capacity microeconomics. Naturally, if you change assumptions—introduce households that do not operate on lightning calculation, say; or make information a little asymmetric; or introduce any Second Best, such as monopoly or taxation; or admit nonconvexities in production, Pigou's increasing-returns industries—the conclusion is going to change, at any rate in general.

Of course. Remember the pitcher's mound, or noncooperative game theory. There is nothing profound or surprising about such a claim. Changing your assumptions might change your conclusion, a little or quite a lot depending on the world's facts. Call the new conclusion C', which might be that free international trade is under the new assumptions *not* desirable. So we now have both the old and disgracefully liberal A implies C and the fresh, publishable, Nobel-worthy, and splendidly left-wing novelty, A' implies C'.

Yet we can add *another* prime, and, as the mathematicians say, proceed as before, introducing some other possibility for the assumptions, A'', A

double prime, which implies its own C'', and we get still another publication in the *Journal of Economic Theory*. And so forth: A''' implies C''' without limit through any number of primes attached to the assumptions and conclusions. And on and on and on, until the economists get tired and go home, or go to fiercely partisan politics.

Any economist who has lived through the rise and fall on the blackboards of abstract general-equilibrium theorizing or free-lunch Keynesian theorizing or activity analysis theorizing or narcissistic game-theory theorizing or rational-expectations theorizing or neoinstitutional theorizing or behavioral economics theorizing (I am offering predictions about those last two) knows that A-prime, C-prime goes nowhere scientifically.

The A-Prime, C-Prime Theorem

For each and every A mapping into C, there exists an A' or A'', arbitrarily close to A, mapping into C' or C'' or whatever, disjoint with the original C. Proof: Left as an exercise for the reader.

What has been gained scientifically? The A-Prime, C-Prime Theorem is a good description of how economic argument proceeds when it's not seriously tested, as it never is if one stays with tests of statistical significance — that bankrupt method — or in any case if one does not take the quantitative step seriously and inquire into actual magnitudes. It is pure thinking, "thoughts without content," in Kant's phrase — philosophy or theology or pure mathematics or economic theory, excellent fields of study, among my favorites, in three of which I have in fact published a little. Yet none of them is sufficient for a descriptive science. The theorizing of imperfections has not been disciplined by any serious inquiry into How Much, which might involve serious simulations or other serious ways of facing up to the critique of judgment entailed in the issue of how big is big. The theorizing, and the criticism or defenses of market society that it is supposed to support, are at present ordinarily qualia, not quanta. They are not organized to allow actual numbers into the story.

CHAPTER THREE

The Number of Unmeasured "Imperfections" Is Embarrassingly Long

I have claimed that the rise to and retreat from liberalism is a useful, if depressing, framework for the history of economics. I have just claimed, by way of justifying the wider claim, that an error of scientific method, which one can study in the rhetoric of economics, caused the retreat. Consider some details.

Here is a partial list of worrying pessimisms (if you are an economist who knows a little about the history of her field, you will think of additions), each of which has had its day since the time, as the historian of economic thought Anthony Waterman put it, "Malthus' first [1798] *Essay* made land scarcity central. And so began a century-long mutation of 'political economy,' the optimistic science of wealth, to 'economics,' the pessimistic science of scarcity."[1]

1. Malthus worried that workers would proliferate.
2. Ricardo worried that the owners of land would engorge the national product.
3. Marx worried, or celebrated, depending on how one views historical materialism, that owners of capital would at least make a brave attempt to engorge it.
4. Mill worried, or celebrated, depending on how one views the sick hurry of modern life, that the stationary state was around the corner.

Then the economists, many on the left (but some also "liberals" in the correct sense, identified here with an asterisk), in quick succession, 1848 to the present, commenced worrying about numerous other imperfections.

While they were weeping and wringing their hands and suggesting that the state *do* something radical about each imperfection, the innovism they ignored was driving real wages up and up and up by the factor of thirty. The numerous causes for pessimisms the economists discerned concerning "capitalism" included

5. greed, offensive to Christians
6. alienation, offensive to the young Marx
7. the uneducated consumption tastes of the workers, offensive to the clerisy
8. the drinking habits of the workers, also offensive (thus Irving Fisher)
9. infant industries (List in Germany, Carey in the United States)
10. the unique national histories of economies (the German Historical School) as against the analytic egalitarianism assumed in "English" economics[2]
11. the lack of bargaining strength by the workers
12. racial impurity
13. women working
14. immigration of lesser breeds
15. the race to the bottom in wages, considering that there was an easy eugenic solution such as immigration restriction, compulsory sterilization, and the minimum wage (all advocated by most of the American economics profession ca. 1910)
16. neoclassical theory being insufficiently evolutionary (Veblen, Alchian)
17. monopoly and the trusts (Hovenkamp 1990)
18. imperialism, the last stage of capitalism (Lenin, Hobson)
19. imperialism as robbery (vs. *Davis and *Huttenbach 1988)
20. adulterated food if no regulation
21. Veblen effects: demand curve sloping up
22. unemployment (a new word coming into fashion around Beveridge's book of 1909)
23. lack of coordination (in the 1920s to be solved by "rationalization" by cartel)
24. self-interested markets, so obviously bad, unlike the wise and good social engineers in government—the master postulate of modern economics
25. business cycles (eventually Schumpeter, *Hayek, Keynes)
26. underinvestment in increasing-returns industries (as Pigou argued)
27. externalities: the master lemma leading to the master postulate of modern economics
28. British overinvestment abroad (vs. *Edelstein 1982; *McCloskey 1980)
29. underconsumption (dating back to Malthus and the general glut, then Keynes, now the neo-Keynesians and the new Keynesians)

30. monopolistic competition
31. separation of ownership from control (Berle and Means)
32. lack of planning (vs. *Mises)
33. the economy is embedded in society, making prices conventional (Karl Polanyi)
34. price-governing markets are only recent, and optional (Karl Polanyi, Moses Finley)
35. postwar stagnationism (Keynes, Hansen)
36. investment spillovers
37. unbalanced growth
38. capital insufficiency (Harrod/Domar/Solow models vs. *William Easterly, *Mc-Closkey 2010)
39. businesspeople do not price by marginal cost or marginal revenue but by average cost plus markups
40. predatory pricing leads to monopoly
41. few competitors in an "'industry" leads away from price equal to marginal cost
42. absence of entrepreneurs in certain cultures, such as China and India
43. dual labor markets (W. Arthur Lewis)
44. cost-push inflation (Otto Eckstein)
45. capital-market imperfections
46. oligopoly
47. peasant irrationality (vs. *Theodore Schultz)
48. cultural irrationality
49. economic behavior has motives beyond self-interest
50. low-level traps, the cycle of poverty (W. Arthur Lewis, Gunnar Myrdal)
51. the prisoner's dilemma (vs. *Elinor Ostrom)
52. public goods cannot be supplied privately (Samuelson vs. *Coase, *Demsetz)
53. the failure to define property rights (*Alchian, *Demsetz, *Coase)
54. incomplete contracts (*Cheung)
55. overfishing (*H. Scott Gordon [1954] and *Anthony Scott [1955])
56. tragedy of the commons (Garrett Hardin)
57. overpopulation (Hardin's motive)
58. transaction costs (*Coase)
59. public choice, entailing public servants with interests of their own (*Buchanan, *Tullock)
60. regulatory capture (the ICC case being Gabriel Kolko 1965; *Stigler 1971)
61. free riding (*Mancur Olson 1965)
62. sclerosis of institutions (*Mancur Olson 1982)
63. missing markets (George Akerlof 1970; Joseph Stiglitz 1984)
64. the Cambridge capital controversy and the indefinability of capital (Piero Sraffa, Joan Robinson, Geoffrey Harcourt; see above, Ricardo)

65. informational asymmetry (Akerlof)

66. unions as good monopolies (vs. *H. Gregg Lewis, 1955–1980)

67. Third World exploitation (see above, imperialism)

68. advertising (Galbraith 1958)

69. public underinvestment (Galbraith 1958)

70. without fine tuning of the economy, we are doomed

71. large-scale econometric models are the way forward

72. the invisible hand is mere magic unless proven by axioms mathematically

73. the conditions sufficient in logic for pleasant invisible-hand results are unreasonable (Hahn, Arrow, Debreu)

74. false trades out of equilibrium make it impossible to conclude that supply equal to demand is optimal

75. any imperfection throws economic analysis into a hopeless world of second best (Lipsey and Lancaster 1956)

76. all policy arguments, such as the effect of a minimum wages, must be expressed in general equilibrium, or else they are inconclusive

77. most economic propositions, such as downward sloping demand curves, are only provable econometrically

78. without econometrics we have no empirical proofs of anything

79. most econometric results have serious flaws

80. the middle-income trap

81. history is irrelevant: what matters is the future

82. history is decisive: what matters is the past

83. path dependency (Brian Arthur 1994; Paul David 1985)

84. the economy is a complex system, with chaos and catastrophe (Arthur 1994)

85. worker cooperatives are lamentably rare considering that they are always better than corporations or proprietorships

86. the lack of international competitiveness (Michael Porter 1990)

87. consumerism (see above, bad taste of workers; advertising)

88. consumption externalities (Fred Hirsch, Robert Frank)

89. overworking (Schor 1993)

90. unemployment and inefficiency results from menu costs in the product market (neo-Keynesian neoclassicism)

91. knowledge has zero opportunity cost but is expensive to produce (*Paul Romer)

92. irrationality (behavioral economics)

93. irrational entrepreneurs (Schumpeter, Keynes, Akerlof and Schiller)

94. hyperbolic discounting

95. too big to fail

96. environmental degradation

97. absence of considerations of gender in economics (Julie Nelson)

98. underpaying of care workers (Nancy Folbre)

99. GDP is a poor indicator of anything important (Stiglitz and others)

100. prices are influenced by an unjust distribution of income and therefore are irrelevant to policy for a just society

101. profit is against people and social well-being

102. overpayment of CEOs

103. without artificially high wages we will not get labor-saving innovation (Kaldor, Habakkuk, Robert Allen, Robert Reich)

104. the government has innovated most (Mazzucato)

105. any imperfection—orphan drugs, for example—shows that capitalism is bad on balance even if the imperfection is caused by government

106. neoliberalism has impoverished people worldwide

107. neostagnationism (Cowen 2011, 2014; Gordon 2016)

108. rising inequality, soon (Thomas Piketty).

Every nineteen months or so after 1848 an economist discerned yet another disastrous imperfection in the economy. I submit that such a list of imperfections, all of them lacking serious measurement of their economy-wide effects, has been for economics a scientific disaster.

Thomas Piketty's book *Capital in the Twenty-First Century* (French 2010, English 2014), worrying that the rich might someday get richer, expresses only the latest, you see, of the leftish (and some liberal) worries about imperfections in "capitalism." One can line up the later items in the list, and some of the earlier ones revived à la Krugman, with particular Nobel Memorial Prizes in economic science. I will not name the men (all men, in sharp contrast to the method of Elinor Ostrom, Nobel 2009; though Esther Duflo, Nobel 2019, reverted) but can reveal here the formula. First, discover or rediscover a necessary or sufficient condition for *perfect* competition or a *perfect* world (in Piketty's case, for example, a more perfect equality of income, the perfection supposed to be equal incomes for everyone regardless of talents). Then assert without evidence (here Piketty does very much better than the usual practice) but with suitable mathematical ornamentation (again, he is restrained in such ornamentation) that the condition might be imperfectly realized or the world might not develop in a perfect way. Perfection, after all, is a unicorn. Then conclude with a flourish (here however Piketty joins the usual low scientific standard) that "capitalism" is doomed unless we experts intervene with a sweet use of the monopoly of coercion by the state to implement antitrust against malefactors of great wealth or subsidies to diminishing-returns industries or foreign aid to splendidly honest governments or protection for obviously infant industries or nudging of sadly childlike consumers or, Piketty says, a tax miraculously arranged worldwide on inequality-causing financial capital.

What is bizarre about the history of imperfection finding — and, from the left, the proposed statist corrections — I have said, is that never does the economic thinker feel it necessary to offer evidence that this or that proposed intervention by the state will work as it is supposed to. And never does he feel it necessary to offer evidence that the imperfectly attained necessary or sufficient condition for perfection is large enough in the actual world that its imperfect fulfillment reduces by much the performance of the economy in aggregate.[3] Meanwhile, since 1848, I say again, the real income of the formerly poor such as the ancestors of you and me has exploded.

As the amiable Joe Stiglitz, prize student of the amiable Paul Samuelson (Paul being only the first of two Nobels raised in Gary, Indiana, Joe being the other one), put it, "Whenever there are externalities — where the actions of an individual have impacts on others for which they do not pay or for which they are not compensated — markets will not work well. But recent research has shown that these externalities are pervasive, whenever there is imperfect information or imperfect risk markets."[4] The '"recent research" Joe has in mind, showing that imperfect information is relevantly "pervasive" and that markets at risk are "imperfect," is "research" on the blackboard. No one has offered a criterion short of perfection for "will not work well." No one has measured how "pervasive" within explicit error bounds the externalities arising from imperfection are. No oomph. Nada.

The number of the briefly fashionable but seldom or never measured "imperfections," fully 108 here, has taught young economists to believe, by the figure of rhetoric called by the Romans *copia* (i.e., the sheer abundance of named though unmeasured imperfections), that commercially tested betterment has worked disgracefully badly. They believe it even though all the quantitative instruments agree that innovism has worked since 1800 spectacularly well. The youngsters are taught for a week or so at the beginning of the course about the optimality of supply equaling demand — the portentously named First and Second Theorems of Welfare Economics — and then in the rest of the course are taught the 108 imperfections. They innocently suppose that their elders such as Stiglitz or Samuelson or Pigou *must* have found some actual facts behind what goes so prettily into graphs and equations. The youngsters therefore become huffy and scornful when some doltish economic historian such as Clapham or McCloskey asks them for actual scientific evidence.

A rare exception to the record of not checking out what oomph might characterize an alleged imperfection was the book of 1966 by the Marxists Paul Baran and Paul Sweezy, *Monopoly Capital*, which actually tried (and honorably failed) to measure the extent of monopoly overall in the American economy.[5] For most of the other worries on the list and the corresponding statist solutions—such as that externalities obviously require government intervention (as in historical succession; Pigou, Samuelson, Stiglitz)—the economists have supposed that for this or that reason the economy is horribly malfunctioning and obviously needs immediate, massive intervention by the state, advised by wise heads such as Pigou, Samuelson, and Stiglitz. The economic scientists have not felt it worth their scientific while to show that the malfunctioning matters.

By contrast, the economists of liberalism (I repeat, by the international definition of the word), such as Arnold C. Harberger and Gordon Tullock and H. Gregg Lewis and Deirdre Nansen McCloskey—claiming that the economy works pretty well through a commercially tested betterment inspired by equality before the law and equal permission to have a go—have sometimes actually done the factual inquiry or have at least suggested how it might be done.[6] The performance of Pigou, Samuelson, Stiglitz, and the rest on the left would be as though an astronomer proposed, based on some qualitative assumptions, that the hydrogen in the sun would run out very, very soon (as in fact Lord Kelvin did proposed, to show how wrong Darwin was in the great length of time he needed for evolution), requiring urgent intervention by the Galactic Empire, but then didn't bother to find out with serious observations and serious quantitative simulations and serious applied mathematics roughly how soon the sad event was going to happen.

An old instance in economics is Robert Solow's influential assertion in the late 1950s that saving rates do not affect the rate of growth . . . in the steady state.[7] Down to the present the growth theorists conjure with the steady state despite the calculation made soon after Solow by a Japanese economist, Ryuko Sato, that concluded that to get back to 90 percent of the steady state after a rise or fall in the savings rate would take . . . about a century.[8] Mostly in economic theory it has sufficed to show the mere *direction* of an imperfection on a blackboard, the qualitative theorems recommended by Samuelson in 1941, and then await the telephone call from the Swedish Academy quite early on a Monday in early October.

One begins to suspect that the typical leftist—most of the graver worries about innovism have come from thereabouts, naturally enough, though perhaps not so naturally considering the enormous payoff for the working class from such a "capitalism" in the Great Enrichment—starts with a root conviction that commercially tested betterment is seriously defective. The conviction is acquired at about age sixteen, when the protoleftist discovers his neighbor's poverty but has no intellectual tools to understand its source. I myself followed such a pattern and therefore became for a time a Joan Baez socialist, singing labor-union songs, with guitar accompaniment. Then the lifelong "good social democrat," as he describes himself (and as I for a while described myself), when he has started to become a professional economist, looks around, in support of the now deep-rooted conviction innocently acquired, for any qualia that in some imagined world would make the conviction true, without bothering to find numbers drawn from our actual world that show it to have scientific oomph, economy wide. An instance, examined in detail through a survey of economists by Jason Briggeman, is the widespread belief that the Food and Drug Administration is justified in requiring that drugs be subject to "pre-market testing for efficacy." None of the economists Briggeman asked, up to and including the excellent Kenneth Arrow, could offer factual evidence for the claim that such a policy improves consumer welfare, considering the probability of a Type II error.[9] The pattern is the utopianism of good-hearted leftward folk who say, "Surely this wretched society, in which some people are richer and more powerful than others, can be greatly improved. We can do *so much* better!" The utopianism springs from the dialectical logic of stage theories, conceived in the eighteenth century as a tool with which to fight traditional society, as in *The Spirit of the Laws* and *The Wealth of Nations* among lesser books. "Surely," the leftists say indignantly, "Francis Fukuyama—that 'conservative'—is wrong that liberal democracy is the 'end of history.' *Excelsior!*"[10]

True, the actual conservatives and even the true classical liberals such as Fukuyama and me can sometimes be accused of utopianism as well. Liberal utopianism has its own adolescent air, asserting without evidence that we live already in the best of all possible worlds. Some of the older-model Austrian economists, and some of the Chicago School who have lost their taste for engaging in serious testing of their truths, act so. Yet admitting that there is a good deal of blame to spread around in economics for developing a cargo-cult pseudoscience without measurement, the leftward refusal to quantify as a whole about the system they hate seems more prevalent and more dangerous.

I have a beloved and extremely intelligent Marxist friend who says to me, "I *hate* markets!" I reply, "But Jack, you delight in searching for antique furniture *in markets.*" "I don't care. I *hate* markets!" The Marxists such as Jack have their own specialized collection of empty economic boxes. They have worried in sequence that the typical European worker would be immiserated, for which they had little evidence, then that he would be alienated, for which they had little evidence, then that the Third World worker in the periphery would be exploited to benefit the worker in the core, for which they had little evidence. Recently the Marxists (and admittedly much of the rest of the society, educated in elementary school to worship the forest) have commenced worrying about the environment—on what the historian Eric Hobsbawm called, with a certain distaste natural in an *old* Marxist, "a much more middle-class basis."[11] We await their evidence, and their proposals for what to do about it, short of having us all return to Walden Pond and the life of 1854 or having us all commit suicide and leave the world to less evil species.

Long ago I had a nightmare. I am not much subject to them, and this one was vivid. It was an economist's nightmare, a Samuelsonian one. What if *every single* action, I dreamt, had to be performed *exactly* optimally? Maximize Utility subject to Constraints. Max U s.t. *C. Precisely.* Suppose, in other words, that you had to reach the *exact* peak of the hill of happiness subject to constraints with *every single* reaching for the coffee cup or *every single* step on the sidewalk. You would of course fail in the assignment repeatedly, frozen in fear of the slightest deviation from optimality. In the irrational way of nightmares, it was a chilling vision of what economists call rationality. A recognition of the impossibility of *exact* perfection lies behind Herbert Simon's satisficing, Ronald Coase's transaction costs, Steven N. S. Cheung's contractual incompleteness, George Shackle's and Israel Kirzner's reaffirmation of the wisdom of the baseball player and coach Yogi Berra: "It's hard to predict, especially about the future."[12]

We young American economists and social engineers in the 1960s, innocent as babes, were sure we could attain down in Washington predictable perfection. "Fine tuning" we called it. It failed, as exact perfection always must. Unicorns. John Mueller's "pretty good" would require some fact-based estimate that the economy was not terribly far from optimality in, say, Garrison Keillor's imagined Lake Wobegon, Minnesota, in which

Ralph's Pretty Good Grocery is in its advertising comically modest and Scandinavian ("If you can't find it at Ralph's, you probably don't need it"). Or the fact-based estimate might conclude that the economy *is* in fact far from optimality: actual empirical results sometimes run irritatingly contrary to one's ideological hopes.

Mueller and I reckon, though, that innovism and democracy as they actually, imperfectly exist in places like Europe or its offshoots or now their eastern imitators are pretty good. Or they *might* be pretty good. We don't actually know until we've made the estimates of how far from perfection all the imaginable imperfections take us. Mueller and I reckon that the failures to reach perfection in, say, the behavior of Congress or the equality of the US distribution of income are probably not large enough to matter all that much to the performance of the polity or the economy. After all, we are immensely more liberated legally and more rich economically than our ancestors in 1800. The Great Enrichment is a powerful empirical test, I have said, justifying optimism about democracy and commercially tested betterment. Or not, you say. But if you say not, you as a scientist will want to provide contrary evidence and not rely merely on lofty sneering.

* * *

The result of the ever-lengthening list of imperfections has been that young economists do not feel that they need to study the history of economic thought—or "price theory" as understood by economists such as Armen Alchian or George Stigler or Steven Cheung—even up to the level of grasping what the political economists of 1848 understood about how commercially tested betterment functioned.

You will perhaps challenge me on the point. Surely economists who can master Mas-Collel-Whinston-Green can handle anything that such primitives as Mill or Marshall or Friedman knew. Surely. But, alas, no. Because of the abstraction of exist or not and the long, long list of imperfections, the young economists, and many of the elderly ones, rush on to splendid versions of Max U and instrumental variables before they understand . . . well . . . economics. They do not understand the wisdom of 1848. They are therefore singularly ill equipped to criticize it.

A startling example of the left not understanding what it is criticizing is the way Thomas Piketty botches the response of supply to increasing scarcity on the bottom of page 6 of the English translation of *Capital in the Twenty-First Century*. If you don't understand that increasing scarcity entices new entrants into an industry, you do not understand much about a market economy at the level of 1848.[13] A good many economists—because they rush on to higher technicalities, such as the accounting of surplus value or the existence of competitive equilibrium—do not understand the less elevated technicalities. For example, they do not understand that the balance of payments is of no consequence, or that national income equals national expenditure, or that trade benefits both sides (thus on all counts Trump's advisor Peter Navarro). Or that shortage yields responses of supply (thus Piketty).

I give a good many talks to audiences of well-meaning and well-educated lay people, many of whom have had a course or two in academic economics. I write a good many reviews of books by well-meaning scholars without PhDs in economics, such as Robert Reich and Michael Sandel.[14] I engage in a good many academic disputes with well-meaning scholars *with* PhDs in economics, such as Thomas Piketty and Marianna Mazzucato. None of these fine people has the slightest understanding of elementary economics.

The fact is surprising and depressing. When I make elementary points, such as that profit guides investment or that prices come from supply and demand or that there are no massive free lunches lying about, my audiences are regularly amazed, puzzled, astonished, and often enough angry, indignant, scornful. It would be like a mathematician noting that prime numbers are unbounded but then facing an audience amazed and then scornful. Or an archaeologist noting that all *Homo sapiens* once lived in Africa and had black skins and facing an audience amazed and then scornful.

Something is wrong. It seems to arise, I have said, from the *copia*, the sheer number, of alleged but unquantified "imperfections" taught to people inside and outside courses in economics, which then spill into the public discourse about the economy.

CHAPTER FOUR

Historical Economics Can Measure Them, Showing Them to Be Small

W̶hat is to be done?

Answer: follow the scientific standard of physics or geology or history and refrain from offering up an alleged imperfection in a market or in markets in general—or to the contrary offering up an assertion that markets are gratifyingly flawless—without an empirical demonstration that the alleged effect, good or bad, is quantitatively important. At the very least the economist should show the oomph of the good or bad quanta in the particular market under consideration, and at the best—the truly relevant scientific calculation—in the economy as a whole. Only then will she have given a sufficient reason to turn then to the governmental policy backed by coercion (or in the other case *not* so to turn). And instead of merely assuming that governments are wonderfully wise and honest, she should then offer quanta about the government's capacity to actually help. It's only scientific.

Let me give as an example an empty economic box—number 17 in the list of imperfections above, the alleged prevalence and especially the *increasing* prevalence of enterprise monopoly. Many economists, and more of the general public, believe that the power of monopolies has increased steadily since, say, 1800 or 1900 or 1950 or whenever. They look at any large company such as Google or Facebook and, illogically, conclude that the company must be a "monopoly." They see a high share of a market and, illogically, conclude that the monopoly must be permanent and very damaging, lacking any threat of entry by competitors, and therefore justifying immediate application of antitrust and other trust busting.

The belief in the proliferating history of private monopoly buttresses many other of the entries in the list of 108 imperfections, such as adulterated food from monopolies in meatpacking ca. 1910 if not regulated; the lack of coordination (or the opportunity for it, thinking of syndicalism) during the 1920s; the monopolistic competition studied in the 1930s by my teacher Edward Chamberlain; the cost-push inflation from monopolized industries studied in the 1950s by another teacher of mine, Otto Eckstein; the regulatory capture by the very monopolies, as argued by my colleagues in the 1970s at the University of Chicago; the advertising and planned obsolescence à la Galbraith; the overpayment of CEOs; the oligopoly allegedly addressed by game theory; the too big to fail in banking; and now the cry against allegedly rising inequality. All are said in part or in whole to derive from proliferating monopoly.

I note here briefly the contrary Chicago School line — a line developed on the basis of massive evidence collected from economic history, a line with which, if you care, I pretty much agree — namely, that the government itself is actually the main source of sustained monopoly. The savants of the Chicago School claim that without governmental intervention some new entry — a supply response — is usually vigorous and that a new Bill Gates is usually working in a new garage right now to overturn the old Bill Gates. The empirical evidence for the "usually" in the last sentence seems on its face strong. The evidence is strong, for example, that long-term monopolies have been created by the ever-extending system of state-enforced patents and copyrights, devices for monopoly invented many centuries ago by the governing elite in Venice (no friend of liberal competition). Consider, too, how governmental prohibitions, regulations, licenses, corruptions, patents, and protections clotted the radio and related technologies for decades.[1] And on and on.

After all, creative *destruction* of temporarily dominant technologies made the Great Enrichment. Once upon a time, for example, many little local fortunes were based on a local monopoly of a department store, a welfare-improving model of retailing invented in the late nineteenth century. Marshall Field's motto for his department store in Chicago was "Give the lady what she wants." Yet the department store model, and the shopping malls that depended on it when the local chains had merged, has long faded, and with it the supernormal rents making such fortunes. The fading is to our common good, producing the equality of real comfort between rich and poor that characterizes the modern world. The Nobelist William Nordhaus has calculated that in recent times the original inventor retains only 2 percent of the social value of her invention, the rest going to the consumers by way of entry.[2] To you and me.

But the Chicago School line is not my main point here. My point is a simple empirical test of how important monopoly is for the economy as a whole (by a criterion that can be justified by the theory of the core originated by Edgeworth in 1881).[3] It is this: How many competing suppliers did the typical consumer face in 1800, and how many now, weighted by the importance of the item consumed in the consumer's budget? How many competing labor demanders, likewise, did the typical worker face in 1800 and in the present for her services? In other words, how many coalitions (to use the terms in the theory of the core; distinct from game theory, note) did buyers and sellers have available? How big?

I think it is obvious—I would like to hear why it is not—that the number of such suppliers or demanders has enormously increased since 1800 or 1900 or 1950 or whatever date during the last two centuries you wish to specify. It has increased especially among a substantial margin of customers located between two alternate suppliers or demanders. That is to say, monopoly/monopsony has *decreased* dramatically, not increased. We are now much closer, factually speaking, to a pretty good competitive economy than we were in 1800 or 1900 or 1950. To put it another way, we are closer to Pareto optimality—not further away, as is mistakenly implied by the sequence of imagined imperfections that economists have piled up since 1848. We are much closer now than we were formerly to the pretty good outcome that Mueller and I see in the economy—just as the polity has been moved closer to the liberal ideal by improved education, wider majority voting, and the breakdown of social hierarchy.

The central reason for declining monopoly of course is falling transport/transaction costs. In 1800—even in a country quite rich by the wretched standards of the time, such as Holland or England—the average consumer of bread faced very few suppliers, or very few suppliers of the flour and yeast to make it. She could not get across town easily to take advantage of the price differential between her local monopolist baker and the new and cheaper entrant over at Zeedyk. Her husband could not venture to the next town to find employment and continued therefore to labor at low wages for the local chair maker. It's a simple matter of transport/transaction costs.

In a wider field, to get out to the frontier of settlement in the United States—or Argentina or Australia, or at any rate escaping the low land/labor ratios of much of Europe compared with the frontiers—in the old days cost many months of nonemployment on a sailing ship and many weeks of saving out of paid employment at home to get steerage passage even in a much-improved steamship. It's why immigrants to the new worlds were

commonly, when not convicts or slaves, a little richer than their countrymen stopping at home to face hunger. Nowadays an airfare to the United
States costs a couple of weeks' wages even in a poor country, and the flight
takes hours rather than weeks of time out of work to complete.

Europeans in those lovely olden days were well and truly stuck. True,
they were less stuck in 1800 than in the Middle Ages (and by the way there
is a good case to be made that even in 1800, and especially in the European Middle Ages, people in China were less stuck). But stuck they were,
partially walled off from competitive offers to sell or buy goods or labor in
their locale by transportation costs and state-sponsored monopolies and
high transaction costs such as serfdom and guilds and tariffs.

I do not claim that trade did not occur across regions in the European Middle Ages. On the contrary, even in a Europe riven by tariffs and
mountains and guilds, not to mention its unusually violent and persistent
warfare, there was sufficient competition by marginal buyers and sellers
across locales to bring prices of many goods and services and of labor and
capital closer and closer by arbitrage to the prices in other places. Arbitrage in wheat and even in labor improved a great deal from the Middle
Ages to Early Modern times.[4] Asserting it did was one of Adam Smith's
(few) unique analytic contributions, backing it up, as he characteristically
did, with canny factual observations. But I do claim about the olden days
that inside the margin of, so to speak, the gold points, many a consumer
or employee had by recent standards few options. The suppliers or demanders she faced had an ability, considering the high transactions costs
of resale of goods or labor, to search for the terms of trade favorable to
themselves. Monopoly. Monopsony.

And I further claim that a long, long series of innovations in transport
and transaction costs since 1800 has radically reduced the ability of the
monos to do so. Consider (I invite quantitative suggestions or contradictions—it would make a very useful PhD thesis to provide them): proliferating turnpikes in the eighteenth and early nineteenth centuries (as Klein
and Fielding 1992; Klein and Majewski n.d.; and others have shown); the
rise of nonstate supplied local roads (ancient, but improved in the nineteenth century; still common in Sweden), metaled roads between towns by
McAdam, and stage coaches (see Charles Dickens) rushing along them;
river and port betterment; canal transport (especially in Holland, as Jan de
Vries has shown, but then also in Britain and in the United States, notably
the Erie Canal); the breakdown of guilds, as for example by Napoleon's
conquering armies (see Ogilvie 2019); the breakdown of local tariffs, as on

the Rhine, again by Napoleon; paving of roads in town; gas illumination of towns; policing of roads, in town and out (highwaymen disappeared in Western Europe); the telegraph, giving information on prices instantly; steamboats on the western rivers (see Mark Twain, *Life on the Mississippi*, 1883); above all the railway, pushing into every big village in England and every substantial town in the United States; faster sailing vessels, such as China clippers, eventually steel hulled; the steam ship, connecting markets worldwide and leading to passenger liners and a sharp fall in transatlantic fares; liberation of serfs, servants, slaves, allowing people to move and to sell (indentured servitude was before the nineteenth century in fact a way of financing the movement of labor; liberation of slaves as of course limited then by, say, Jim Crow or apartheid); liberation of women, again allowing movement; the street car, first pulled by horses, then by steam plants pulling cable cars (in the 1880s Chicago had the world's longest cable car network); then electric trolleys, making the department store with its price-breaking bon marché (see Zola, *The Ladies' Paradise*, 1883); and especially the bicycle, at first an expensive toy for gentlemen, eventually a breaker of monopoly and monopsony for working people on good urban roads; reliable postal service on the railways (my great-grandfather sorted mail on the route into Chicago from Indianapolis); and then the mail-order firms, such as in the United States Montgomery Ward and Sears, Roebuck; subways, first steam and then (1890 in London) electric; the telephone, at first also an expensive toy then a ubiquitous tool for dealing and information; above all, the automobile, yet again at first a toy of the rich but at length even the Joad family in Steinbeck's *The Grapes of Wrath* would flee starvation by auto; the self-service grocery store, invented in Memphis in 1916; and the motor truck, cheapening delivery and competing eventually with the railways; the Good Roads Movement, paving even outside of towns the dirt tracks of, for example, Route 66 from Chicago to Los Angeles, and eventually making delivery cheap by truck of even slaughtered cattle; buying on time in the 1920s (Olney 1991); the Sears, Roebuck regional brick-and-mortar stores after World War II; widespread checking accounts, eventually for women; breakdown of gender restrictions on women entering occupations (offset post-WWII by a large increase in state licensure); the interstate system of highways, thanks (for a refreshing change) to the government; the supermarket, enabled by the automobile; the commercial strip outside every US town, competing with downtowns, an innovation prevented by interested zoning in most European towns; the shopping mall, with a department store anchor, again

resisted for a long time in Europe by the machinations of High Street landlords; credit cards widespread; falling tariffs, enforced by the World Trade
Organization, making the world a single market in, say, automobiles; and
eventually routine air transport; deregulation of air and truck and rail
transport; breakdown of noncompeting groups because of discrimination
against, say, Jews (that against Blacks was retained); the breakdown of governmental postal and telephone monopolies worldwide; the breakdown
of restrictions on retailing, such as those against evening or Sunday trading, yet again slow to happen in Europe; the ending of resale price mainte-
nance and other Depression-era schemes to restrict competition; discount
stores, such as Walmart; and especially the internet, giving low-cost information about alternative deals; cell phones; then Yelp and other surveys
of reputation by the internet; and then Amazon.com reinventing the mail
order.

In other words, it would seem that since 1800 or 1900 or whenever,
competition in the sense of multiple sources of supply and demand has
increased greatly, and the power of monopolies ("the international corporations" the left says, with a shiver) has declined. During the 1950s Americans spoke of having "three and a half" suppliers of automobiles, namely,
Ford, Chrysler, General Motors, and American Motors. Then the tariffs
on imported autos were slashed, with transitional episodes of quotas on
Japanese autos to enrich auto workers at the annual cost of $200,000 in
higher prices to the amassed auto buyers for every $20,000 job saved in
Detroit. Now an American consumer faces four times or so more suppliers of autos, such as Toyota, GM, Volkswagen, Hyundai, Ford, Nissan, Fiat-
Chrysler, Honda, Suzuki, Groupe PSA, Renault, BMW, SAIC, Daimler,
Mazda, Dongfeng, Mitsubishi, Changan, Tata, and the rest. There is now
more reason, not less, to expect commercially tested betterment to work
in the way the political economists by 1848 had realized it might, leading
to the Bourgeois Deal: Let the bourgeoisie, such as the manufacturers of
autos, try out betterments for profit, and assure free entry, and in the long
run the bourgeoisie will enrich us all.[5]

The scientific point here is that if monopoly is typical of the list of imperfections—and as I said monopoly undergirds many of its items—it is a
scientifically feeble list. And there are in fact good economic and historical reasons to think that the case against the significance of monopoly is
not a singleton. Informational asymmetry such as George Akerlof's Lem-
ons Problem is lessened by universal education, by autos for comparison shopping, by telephones ("Let your fingers do the walking" was the

motto of the Yellow Pages in the United States, now creatively destroyed by the internet), by cell phones, and now by Yelp and the like. That is, there is good reason to think that informational asymmetry is a *lessening* problem—noting that there was no scientific showing in any case that it was a *big* problem to begin with, speaking of the economy as a whole, and speaking of the economy's closeness, or not, to a pretty good outcome of neoclassical supply and demand and, especially, its ability to yield a Great Enrichment out of creativity. That last is the main point of the Austrians: that information asymmetry is not a defect but a feature of innovism. Informational asymmetry, and its disequilibrium, causes innovation. James Watt knew, or reckoned he knew, that a separate condenser would improve the efficiency of a steam engine. Other people did not. Result: Watt's invention, and his monopoly patent, after which in due course arrived the age of steam.

The empirical showing on the list of imperfections, I have said, is nil. I await testing refutations, but it seems to me on the basis of existing empirical studies, especially by economic historians, that the following propositions are factually true. Inequality since 1800 has fallen, not risen, if one focuses on equality of real comfort instead of on Liliane Bettencourt's undoubtedly most vulgar jewelry box. Imperialism was not profitable for the countries conquering others, however gratifying to jingoism and however devastating to its victims. Unemployment is caused as much by government intervention, such as interference in the wage bargain, as it is by inherent flaws in market economies. Stagnationism has been asserted by every second generation of economists, to be refuted in the economic history of the next. Nonlinear dynamics, though attractive to the engineering mind, cannot be shown factually to be typical of market economies. If industrial policy and other central planning were good ideas, the economists proposing them could have made private fortunes exploiting the imperfection justifying them, and centrally planned economies would have been sterling triumphs instead of miserable failures. That consumers are irrational does not imply that markets are. The middle-income trap confuses absolute with comparative advantage. If advertising had magical powers, it would not be merely 2 percent of national income, much of it informative, and aimed at experts. If free riding were insoluble we would have a war of all against all, and the life of humans solitary, poor, nasty, brutish, and short, which increasingly since 1800 it is not. Overpopulation did not happen. Peak oil didn't happen. China and India broke out of the vicious and allegedly unbreakable circle of poverty. Foreign aid has not saved the poor of the world but has enriched elites and financed impoverishing projects. Inflation is everywhere and always a monetary phenomenon, and to think otherwise is to mistake relative for absolute prices. Capital accumulation has not been the cause of commercially tested betterment but its consequence. Monopolistic competition assumes that suppliers do not acknowledge interaction when it is obvious that they can and should.[6] Immigrants were not lesser breeds. Global warming is a crisis but not an existential one. The landlords did not engorge the national product, and monopoly capitalists were competed away by entry—as I said, by falling transport and transaction costs.

*   *   *

The hunt for imperfections in the form of A-prime, C-prime assertions of exist or not, in short, has been great fun, but it has been a scientific mistake. We need to dust off and then test the soft priors of 1848 using our by now superior abilities in measuring to get back to a descriptive science—as indeed applied economists (with low scientific prestige) are forced to do when they actually advise the prince. Richard Feynman declared in 1965 that "it does not make any difference how beautiful your guess [at a scientific law] is. It does not make any difference how smart you are.... If it disagrees with experiment [or observation] it is wrong.... Guessing, computing consequences, and comparing with experiment [and observation] is all there is to science."[7] Note: "*computing* consequences." How big? Oomph?

Such a science, I predict, will discover what the undoubted magnitude of the Great Enrichment suggests: that we've done amazingly well, and that a free-market economy left pretty much to its own devices worked astoundingly well for the poor, who are your ancestors and mine, especially by calling out from the mass of ordinary people, when they were suddenly permitted and encouraged by the new liberalism to have a go, the commercially tested betterments that explain most of economic growth despite a hundred and more confidently alleged but on the whole unimportant imperfections piled up in libraries since 1848 by the economists dealing in thought without content.

Time to get back to serious science after a century and a half of playing with those empty economic boxes.

CHAPTER FIVE

The Worst of Orthodox Positivism Lacks Ethics and Measurement

L et me give a little concrete example of how very badly Scientism works. A paper in 2017 by the business lecturer Werner H. Erhard (he of the "est" movement) and by the maven of positivist finance Michael C. Jensen is admirably ambitious. But it commits three related errors, adding up to exceptionally bad ethics and exceptionally bad science. The errors are not peculiar to Erhard and Jensen but worse in their paper than is usual even in run-of-the-mill Samuelsonian economics, which makes it a good proof text. If we economists are going to get serious about ethics and about science, we should stop committing gross errors in ethical and epistemological philosophy and in quantitative science.

Bad ethics first. Erhard and Jensen suppose that economics, or any science, not to mention any social science, can arrive at judgments of good or bad without ethics. They think they are avoiding ethics, getting to the good "with no normative aspects whatsoever."

You can see that there is something strange in such a program. The strangeness comes from the ethics and epistemology that economists catch in graduate school and that some of them never recover from. Erhard and Jensen draw on the vocabulary of "positive" as against "normative," which is the reduced ethical theory that the typical economist takes as the last word in philosophy. As they write, "Because in the current economic mindset 'integrity' automatically occurs as normative, most economists will dismiss it out-of-hand." That's certainly correct as sociology. The dismissal is a Nouvelle Chicago School/junior high school dogma, enforced with more and more enthusiasm as the 1970s wore on.

But the positive-normative distinction comes out of a (justifiably) obsolete philosophy of ethics and of science. A central dogma in the positivism of the early twentieth century was that "good" and "bad" are merely opinion, "preaching" (with an anticlerical attitude assumed against preaching). It is called the "hurrah-boo" theory of ethics, or "emotivism." Emotivism was believed by very many twentieth-century people, some under the influence of logical positivism, more under the influence of a falling away from religious faith, and most it would seem (from the parallel evidence in the visual, literary, and musical arts) from people grown despairing and cynical from the horrors of the Great War and its follow-ons. It is "the doctrine that all evaluative judgments and more specifically all moral judgments are *nothing but* expressions of preference."[1] Or as Thomas Hobbes, a fount of emotivism long before the letter, wrote in 1651, "Good and evil are names that signify our appetites and aversions."[2] (Emotivism, observe, taken as a doctrine that one *should* believe, is of course self-contradictory, since preaching against preaching is preaching. But noncontradictory logic is not the strong point of logical positivism or of those who have fallen away from religious faith or are despairing.)

Undergraduates and many of their professors become uneasy and start giggling when an ethical question arises. They regard such questions as having mainly to do with sex—thank *you* fundamentalists of the late twentieth century—or with unargued authority, such as the Baltimore Catechism and the nuns to enforce it, or with the Party Line and the cadres to enforce it. I was chatting with a leftish colleague during the Tiananmen Square debacle in 1989 and expressed my ethical disapproval of the thuggish, if usual, behavior of the Chinese Communist Party. To my astonishment, she replied that she didn't know what to think about it until she had time to consult the Party Line, such as an editorial in *The Nation*.

The agreement to disagree that ended the wars of religion in Europe can be traced in the unease and in the stock expressions of it: "That's just a matter of opinion." "Religion should not be mentioned in polite conversation." "If we disagree about ends it is a case of thy blood against mine."[3] "What does the Party say?" "The only methods for reconciling different normative value judgments are political elections or shooting it out at the barricades."[4] According to the emotivist theory, to be caught making ethical statements is to be caught in meaningless burbling. Shame on you. That's why Erhard and Jensen are so proud they have achieved "no normative aspect whatever."

Yet we cannot in science or business do without ethics, which we need to think through ourselves, and neither can Erhard and Jensen. Their laboriously axiomatized "model," therefore, will have to sneak in its ethics unobserved. Of course. You can't get "good" results, in business or in science itself, both of which Erhard and Jensen seek, without having some idea of goodness.

The way forward is to realize that most scientific issues are both positive and normative. Therefore, about the norms we should get philosophically serious. Fact and value are distinct only at a high and mostly useless level. Yes, there are facts of the world, sitting there like stones. Yet what stones to pick up is a normative issue, qualitative, a matter of humanistic theorizing: as Einstein remarked during a lecture in Berlin in 1926, "Whether you can observe a thing or not depends on the theory which you use. It is theory which decides what can be observed." And, yes, there are values that people have, distinct from the stones (although, as Bart Wilson has argued, many of our values are located out in the language, not in our heads[5]). But most of our lives take place in picking up a stone and, say, hurling it at a leader we do not like or examining it in some scientific program for its iron content or placing it pleasantly along the garden path. The Danish physicist Niels Bohr said in 1927 that "it is wrong to think that the task of physics is to find out how nature is. Physics concerns what we can *say* about nature."[6] We. Say. With words. About categories involving philosophical and ethical analysis and ethical purpose. The German poet Rose Äuslander wrote, "In the beginning / was the word / and the word was with God / And God gave us the word / and we lived in the word. / And the word is our dream / and the dream is our life."[7] We dream of categories in our metaphors and stories, our models and histories, and with them make our lives, especially our scientific lives. It's ethical acting.

Consider for example the assertion, believed by economists and by almost no one else, that free trade is good. Erhard, I suppose, and certainly Jensen and I, for example, believe it. At a high level of Pareto optimality, we can note on a blackboard its efficiency, achieving the contract curve. At a high level of fact gathering, we can note in the newspaper different prices facing people for the same item, in or out of Pareto equilibrium ("out" on some scale we say and dream). At a high level of ethical philosophy in the style of Harsanyi, Buchanan, Tullock, and Rawls, we can deny the relevance of actual hurt to losers in trade, or else revert to a Kaldor-Hicks criterion undefended ("losers" again on some criterion we say and dream). But to arrive at the confident assertion that free trade is good, which in practice defines economists as professionals, we need to mix such facts and values at a lower and less pure level. Of course.

Of course "the prevailing financial economics paradigm requires a transformation." In particular it requires a dropping of an anti-ethical agency theory—for the adoption of which Michael Jensen personally gets a measure of credit and blame—not a reenactment of it, as in the paper. The paper does not refer to Rakesh Khurana's (2007) careful history of how business schools lost their ethical way under the fashion for Jensenist "positive" economics. It is distressing to see that Jensen has learned nothing over the decades about what to read and think after the ethical and economic disasters of "greed is good" derived from his earlier advocacy of agency theory.

Of course integrity is a factor of production. It is certainly so in our own science, as shown at length by example and counterexample in the recent *Oxford Handbook on Professional Economic Ethics*, edited by George DeMartino and me (DeMartino and McCloskey 2016). The assumption of scientific and commercial honesty, imperfect though each will be, is essential to any society, complex or simple, as, for example, to a society of scientists. It is not "heretofore hidden," as Erhard and Jensen say—though hidden it appears from Erhard and Jensen. Anyone slightly acquainted with history or society or the economy knows that integrity is central. For that matter, anyone who reads novels or plays knows it. Anyone who has lived with a little awareness inside an economy knows that ethics and professionalism, bundled into integrity, are central.

Erhard and Jensen say that they "draw on insights from other disciplines." It's a good idea, implied in fact by the economist's doctrine of free trade. Doing so, however, would have required them to actually read in other disciplines. Actually trade. There is little evidence that they have done so. To take a discipline highly relevant for thinking about the good, they have no idea of ethical philosophy because they have not troubled to read any, at any rate with the humility of students seeking actual learning. Their dependence on the first sentence of a dictionary definition of "integrity" as wholeness, for example, is in fact, and despite their naive claim that it is a value-free datum, a little piece of ethical philosophy (though incompetent as philosophy, and their use of it is the junior high school rhetorical ornament of quoting the first dictionary definition at hand). To understand the actual philosophy of the matter, Erhard and Jensen would need to have read Aristotle's *Nichomachean Ethics*, say, and to have entered as mature students into the gigantic library it generated on *telos*—"end," "purpose," that is, their "wholeness in performance." They haven't. And anyway, even without bothering with tiresome reading assignments, one can see that "good for one's word," the phrase they use, involves the word "good," and therefore, of course, has ethical valence.

I do not know why anyone would think they can talk confidently about ethics without having read any ethical philosophy, or for that matter without having thought through life or fiction. Yet many people do.

*　*　*

Then the two scientific mistakes.

For one thing, the paper supposes that *qualitative* existence theorems are scientific. Though universally taught and practiced in economics, I have observed, the supposition is mistaken, because existence theorems are unbounded in number and character and cannot be tested precisely because they have no quantitative expression. Unlike the quantitative propositions that characterize physics and geology, there is no way to test whether an effect "exists." Zero is zero. Unless one has a criterion rooted in the science or policy at stake of how far something is from zero to "exist," mere existence is scientifically useless. I have said this above.

For another, the paper depends on a supposition—again universally taught and practiced in economics—that null hypothesis "significance" tests are a meaningful way to do just such testing of existence, zero or not. I have said this too. Since the beginning of modern statistics around 1900, many of the leading voices have explained that "significance" is not inherent in a number itself any more than a word comes with its own interpretation, and can only be judged in substantive form within a scientific discussion of magnitudes. Thus spake Edgeworth, Gosset, Egon Pearson, Jeffreys, Borel, Neyman, Wald, Wolfowitz, Yule, Deming, Yates, Savage, de Finetti, Good, Lindley, Feynman, Lehmann, DeGroot, Chernoff, Raiffa, Kenneth Arrow, Blackwell, Milton Friedman, Mosteller, Kruskal, Mandelbrot, Wallis, Roberts, Clive Granger, Press, Berger, and Arnold Zellner, not to speak of Ziliak and McCloskey. How big is big is a scientific question, but it cannot be answered merely by staring at the numbers. If I ask, "Is it a good day?" and you answer, "Six, which is statistically significant," we have not gotten anywhere. We need to decide on a humanly devised scale (Celsius temperature, say, or a noninterval scale of 1 to 10 in human opinion, or whatever) and decide further whether "six" is sufficient to judge the day good or bad. It is a substantive scientific decision among humans and cannot be turned over to a table of t. By the standard of the surface of the sun, a normal day in Indiana is very cold; by the standard of interstellar space it is very hot.

The inventor of the table of t, William Sealy Gosset (his pseudonym was the "Student" of Student's t) said so, early among the others.[8]

Economists (and a few other scientists, such as, most alarmingly, medical scientists) have ignored such leading voices in statistics, as Erhard and Jensen do. Most other scientists, such as physicists, astronomers, chemists, and historians, do not. They judge daily how big is big, and do not think $p < .05$ is any sort of answer. (If you don't understand what I am saying here, or think you disagree with it, or are indignant that anyone would say such things, you need to read the declaration in April 2016 of a committee of the American Statistical Association, which said that tests of significance are silly; and then you need to betake your worried self to reading Ziliak and McCloskey, *The Cult of Statistical Significance* [2008], or the leading voices in statistics long before we spoke.)

Erhard and Jensen put their faith in "formal measurement of the statistically significant increase in performance created by integrity." The faith does not acknowledge the absurdity of such gratifyingly "formal" tests of significance in the absence of a substantive loss function. They say, "We look forward to the completion of additional formal statistical tests"—when, after all, the business world we are all studying has a straightforward loss function, called "profit" or "market valuation," which is plenty "formal" enough. When I used to eat lunch daily in the 1970s at the Quadrangle Club of the University of Chicago with Merton Miller, Gene Fama, Myron Scholes, and Fischer Black, I would hear—without quite grasping its import—that the *Journal of Business* did not accept tests of statistical significance of an alleged irrationality in the stock market but would instead demand to see the author's bank account. It's a good test, with a loss function surely relevant to a business discipline. (Later, when I finally got it, I wrote a book on the theme, called *If You're So Smart: The Narrative of Economic Expertise* [1990], and had meanwhile started to criticize tests of statistical "significance." Still no result, alas.)

The program of The Two Mistakes that Erhard and Jensen are innocently following was announced, I have said, in Samuelson's PhD thesis (1941) and in Friedman's "The Methodology of Positive Economics" (1953)—a paper, Friedman told me, that he later regretted. The program was set out most clearly in 1957, I have noted, by Koopmans. Devise *qualitative* theorems (such as Erhard and Jensen's statement that perfect performance requires perfections). Then "test" the "hypothesis" (as Erhard and Jensen then propose) with null hypothesis significance inherent in the numbers, without a standard of how big is big.

Most economists, including here Jensen, therefore stopped thinking in 1957 about what they were doing. My attempts during the late 1980s and later to get them restarted in thinking had essentially no result. A pity. Some years ago I was alarmed to hear that Economics at Indiana University assigns its graduate students Friedman's article as a *complete* guide to economic research. And all the best graduate programs require the theorem-proving *Microeconomic Theory* by Mas-Colell, Whinston, and Green (1995), which as I have noted is the sole reason that graduate students need real analysis in proofs of existence otherwise useless for actual economic science. And then the students do three terms of econometrics with no training in the numerous other ways to achieve quantitative knowledge and with no mention that how big is big is the chief scientific question and that its answer depends on judgment in light of the numbers, not on the numbers stripped of judgment ("no normative aspect whatever"), such as the "significance" tests buried in canned regression programs.

*   *   *

What would be the point of a "purely positive approach . . . with no normative aspect whatsoever"? Positivism has been shown decisively and repeatedly since the 1920s to be lacking in point. Erhard and Jensen quote Thomas Kuhn but do not appear to have understood what he was doing, namely, destroying positivism by actually studying science. They refer to *The Structure of Scientific Revolutions* (1962), not to his more unsettling *The Essential Tension* (1977), which showed how physics actually operates. In the philosophy, history, and sociology of science, the positivism that Erhard and Jensen admire was aborted as early as Duhem's Dilemma of 1914: "if the predicted phenomenon is not produced, not only is the questioned proposition put into doubt, but also the whole theoretical scaffolding used by the physicist."[9] The dilemma is that the scaffolding—the other hypotheses (such as proper identification in a regression study of causes)—is put in doubt *at the same time* as the particular questioned proposition (such as that an execution deters seven murders). No science ever, it has been shown again and again since 1914 and especially since Kuhn, actually follows the one test at a time of a naive positivism, or should. And no one could live her personal or scientific life on the positivist ukases against ethics that economists carry about with them on 3″ × 5″ cards.

Erhard and Jensen write, for example, "the state of being whole . . . is a necessary (and sufficient) condition for maximum workability." What would be the scientific point of such a tautology? They think they are articulating a theorem, with suitably fancy definitions. But qualitative theorems, I say yet again, contrary to the Samuelson-Arrow-Koopmans orthodoxy, are not how science works. In an early chapter of his notoriously difficult freshman physics course at Cal Tech, the Nobel physicist Richard Feynman told the kids that they needed to learn some matrix algebra and might as well see the simple proofs involved. Then he wrote, defensively, "What is [proof-oriented] mathematics doing in a physics lecture?" His rhetorical question—why proof? (he said "how various mathematical facts are demonstrated")—would startle an economist who has learned her math outside the departments of physical science.[10] Science (by the English definition since the 1860s) works with magnitudes. Math department mathematics, as against the application of some of its results (say, the first few terms of a *divergent* infinite series) to quantitative science such as physics and economics, does not.

The Math Department, I say again, wants to know whether there *exists* an even number that is not the sum of two primes and doesn't care at all that calculation up to high powers of 10 has not found a single instance. Nor does it allow divergent infinite series as an approximation of anything. The students of Hilbert brought into German physics departments in the 1920s because it turned out that Hilbert spaces had physical applications, were appalled when a physicist would show them the first few terms of a series without checking its convergence as N went to infinity.[11] Math department mathematics is, like theology and philosophy and the other humanities, interested in yes/no, exist/not, infinity/nothing. I greatly admire pure math, economic theory, theology, literary criticism, and philosophy. But they need to be recognized as humanities, necessary categorizing *first* steps in a descriptive science like economics or engineering, as I have said, yet first steps only. They are mere fancies if they lack the further step of quantitative testing.

Erhard and Jensen are practicing cargo-cult science. It has some supposedly hard math that they think evokes science. It claims to deal in numbers, like science. It proposes hypotheses, like science according to a positivism ignoring Duhem's Dilemma. But in truth their paper is like the coconut-and-candle "landing strips" of the New Guineans.

*   *   *

The paper, then, is an example of how unscholarly and unscientific economists and their fellow travelers can be if they work at it. Another feature of their unscholarliness and lack of science is worth a little further comment. Erhard and Jensen, with most students of the economy—but in their case with an illuminating simplemindedness worthy of the website Economics Job Rumors run by children—ignore and disdain the humanities.

I have noted repeatedly that the humanities deal with the categories of meaning that we humans regard as important, such as business ethics versus political ethics, corporation versus partnership, red giants versus white dwarfs, viruses versus bacteria, citizens versus illegals, ugly versus beautiful, dignity versus pleasure, good versus bad. Clearly, I say yet again (I bore you, I fear; but are you really getting the point and its importance?), you need to know the meaning of a category before you can count its members, which is why the humanistic sciences—the Germans call them *die Geisteswissenschaften*, a spooky-sounding "spirit sciences"—must always precede the quantitative sciences, whether social or physical. Meaning is scientific, and science cannot be done without human meaning. Piling up "existence" theorems and "significant" results is meaningless.

It is not therefore only technical philosophy among the humanities that can illuminate the business of ordinary life. You can learn from the plays of Henrik Ibsen or Arthur Miller about the meaningful categories in a bourgeois life—such as that a Master Builder fears entry by the young; or that attention must be paid ethically even to the unsuccessful salesman. You can learn from Milton—John, not Friedman—that "evil be thee my good" is a clever fool's plan for a life, even for an angelic life, as is also an aristocratic or peasant or bourgeois plan such as "he who dies with the most toys wins," or "greed is good." You can learn from linguistics, or from the Dilbert cartoon, that the surface rhetoric of a manager's declaration can have the opposite pragmatic or illocutionary force. You can learn from the existence theorems in the sort of mathematics beloved in highbrow economic theory—itself part of the humanities, not of the quantitative sciences—that there *might* exist a category of spillovers in free markets that *might* justify massive intervention by a hypothetically perfect government of benevolent philosopher monarchs. The categories themselves of spillover (any effect however small?), justified intervention (shooting polluters?), government (carelessly exercising the monopoly of violence?), benevolent (toward whom?), and philosopher (not rhetoricians?) are themselves appropriate subjects for a humanistic inquiry.

Bart Wilson has used the philosopher Ludwig Wittgenstein to locate the sense of justice not merely in the utility functions of individuals but in the language game they play.[12] He is the only economist to use Wittgenstein deeply. I myself have begun to use the philosopher John Searle

(1932–) to bring the study of economic institutions up to philosophical and literary speed in the matter of categories to count, as I'll show in chapter 7. Such a tactic pays off scientifically. That is, you can learn the categories of human meaning, the first step in a science, by getting to know, on all the matters that most concern us, the best which has been thought and said in the world by a variety of philosophers, from Confucius (Kongzi, Kung the Teacher) to Amartya Sen.

It is therefore a childish error to suppose that the central question in the humanities—What *kind* is this or that?—is *un*scientific. The avoiding by Erhard and Jensen of serious engagement with the humanism of ethical philosophy participates enthusiastically in the error. The what-kind question occurs prominently in biology, for example, and is central to art history and mathematics and systematic theology. The systematic, scientific humanities are an exploration of kinds. The disdain that most economists have for humanistic thought is without scientific or philosophical justification.

The ornamental gestures by Erhard and Jensen toward a claim of philosophical literacy merely confirm how little they have thought through the humanistic step of a science. Their footnote 8, for example, is supposed to illuminate their so-called veil of invisibility (which says merely that people often don't notice when they are being unethical; all right: lacking integrity, "not whole"). One is startled to find references there to Harsanyi and Rawls on the veil of *ignorance*, which Erhard and Jensen proudly declare they are "playing on" (they could have mentioned Buchanan and Tullock and Rawls in the same connection). But their veil has nothing whatever to do with a veil worn in imagination precisely for the establishment of ethical principles. Ethical principles are not on the agenda of Erhard and Jensen.

* * *

Why not pass over in silence the ethical and scientific offenses of Erhard and Jensen? This: I live in hope that my grumpy plainspokenness will lead even a handful of the younger readers to question the Received Paradigm, 1957 to the present. I hope they will venture to learn something serious about philosophy, say, or literature, or sociology of science, or economic and business history, or for that matter statistical theory. It would save their intellectual lives from cargo-cult science, such as the essay by Erhard and Jensen.

We've got to do better.

PART II

Neoinstitutionalism Shares in the Troubles

CHAPTER SIX

Even the Best of Neoinstitutionalism Lacks Measurement

Is the neoinstitutionalism of North and Acemoglu and followers the way out of the dead end that economics has wandered into? I would like to think so, considering that so many of my friends in economic history and Austrian economics and the economics of property rights think so. I do not like to contradict my friends.

In a deeply researched and elegantly written book of 2012 the historical economist Douglas W. Allen proposes explanations of many interesting puzzles about how the British government worked in olden times. It is a brilliant book, from which I learned much. Yet I don't believe its main argument. Why? Because even a superb piece of historical economics in a neoinstitutionalist vein shows the lack of quantitative oomph characteristic of economics more broadly. If such a fine piece of Northian economic history lacks oomph, so much the worse for the normal run of neoinstitutionalism and still worse for other versions of conventional economics.

Allen's main argument goes like this. Before 1800 even the *British* government, that envied instrument of imperial aggression, could not measure excellence in its servants very well. Therefore, in the same way the criminal code of the time would hang people for stealing even a little — because the nonexistent police could not actually do much to increase the probability of apprehension — the government made foul-ups in its servants very, very expensive. The classic example of making foul-ups expensive in an environment of low information (the fog of war, one might say) is the execution by firing squad of Admiral John Byng for failure to do his utmost in 1756 at the Battle of Minorca. Voltaire had his idiotic hero Candide remark famously that "in that country [Voltaire was a great admirer of Britain, though no one, including Voltaire or at length even the British public howling against the loss of Minorca to the French, thought justice had actually been served in this case] it is good to kill an admiral from time to time, to encourage the others." *Pour encourager les autres*. Ha, ha. Transportation to Australia for poaching even one of the landlord's rabbits served to *dis*courage some other of the others. In parallel fashion, and for the same reasons of uncertainty, Allen argues persuasively, to get things done the British government had to rely on honor—"trust and hostage capital" he calls it—because, he claims, Britain lived in "a world dominated by the large role of nature [e.g., the vagaries of getting and holding the weather gage in a sea battle in the age of sail], which in many contexts precluded the measurement of merit."[1] It was hard to measure the influence of nature. When measurement became better, we got a modern world, which according to Allen does *not* depend on honor and trust and hostage capital.

My basic problem is that Allen, in offering measurement as the explanation, does not measure the measurement, either as a cause or in its effects. He does not so much as offer an adumbration of potential measurements. The procedure is typical of neoinstitutionalism, as of many other parts of economics (setting aside meaningless "measurements" depending on one-by-one null hypothesis testing on nonsamples without a substantive loss function). Allen models possible explanations in a style called "analytic narratives," in which typically, and also in Allen's case, the modeling far outruns the empirical evidence that the parameters in the model are in fact of the magnitude required to have the effects claimed for them.

I repeat my charge that the admirable Paul Samuelson and his equally admirable brother-in-law Kenneth Arrow are to be blamed for setting modern economics off in pursuit of "qualitative theorems"—though in truth, from Ricardo onwards, with or without mathematics, economists have been inclined to rest easy with analytical narratives, those amusing just-so stories of modeling without measurement. Or indeed from Aristotle on. The trouble with *just* modeling is that an infinitude of models can explain any given effect, a point which I called above the *A*-prime–*C*-prime theorem. Because modeling without measurement is what is scientifically disappointing about most of the work in neoinstitutional economics, from Avner Greif on down, it is worth taking Allen's excellent work as a hard case in point. If there is a serious problem with such fine work as his, I repeat, perhaps we should worry about less fine work, such as Douglass North, *Understanding the Process of Economic Change* (2005) or Daron Acemoglu and James A. Robinson, *Why Nations Fail* (2012).

A proper humanomics, that is, includes measurement, though well beyond the narrow writ of official econometrics—all the way to simulation and charting and reading and mapping and experimenting and issuing questionnaires, and then listening, really listening. When magnitudes are an important part of the scientific issue, as they are in explaining the Great Enrichment, they must be attended to. Allen doesn't attend to magnitudes. I do not mean that he does not offer up irrelevant tables and worse-than-irrelevant t-tests. Thankfully, he does not, showing in this, as in many other matters, his excellent scientific taste. I mean that there is no sense given anywhere in the book of how big this or that cause or effect might be.

(Lest the evil thought is by now forming in your head, dear reader, that the very literary Deirdre is a pot calling the kettle black, consider my long career of measuring in British economic history, which I have continued to pursue, quantitatively.[2] And consider, about my recent work, the following anecdote. An otherwise insightful friend said of *Bourgeois Dignity* (2010), without thinking the matter through very carefully, that it "was not quantitative." But he was being fooled by the absence of very many tables in the book or any t-tests at all—not a standard error in sight. Yet on every page, and often several times per page, the book *is* asking how big and suggesting ways to answer it, and sometimes coming up with relevant orders of magnitude, engineer style. When I pointed this out to him, my friend agreed, and apologized. You can see that he is a most learned gentleman economist. He was trained, actually, in a famous engineering school.)

* * *

One problem created by the absence of how big is that Allen's ingenious examples of *governmental* systems of incentives have no scientifically plausible connection to *private* prosperity. It is private prosperity he claims to account for, as North and Acemoglu and others also claim to do. But the state's systems were small in those days relative to voluntary activity. They bulked large—surprisingly large, actually—only during the frequent outbreaks of Anglo-French wars, in which the state was busy throwing away economic output to no gain.

My city of Chicago was from 1870 to 1900 something like the fastest growing city in the world and was in its large voluntary sector a wonder of innovation (steel-frame skyscrapers, reinforced concrete skyscrapers, mass processing of meat). But it was also in nonvoluntary matters fantastically corrupt (I can give you the relevant magnitudes), depending on a patronage system like the one Allen thinks was such a drag on modern-ization in Britain (for all its optimality in the conditions of the time, as he wisely insists). As late as 1948 in Chicago, when an idealistic young law student, Abner Mikva, wanted to volunteer for the Democrats, the ward committeeman asked him, "Who sent you?" "Nobody sent me." "We don't want nobody that nobody sent." Another corrupt politician later de-clared, "Chicago ain't ready for reform." Samuel Pepys and Robert Wal-pole couldn't have said it better. Yet Chicago did just fine economically, thank you very much. It had for decades the largest seaport in the world, handling grain and especially lumber. "Hog Butcher for the World, / Tool Maker, Stacker of Wheat / Player with Railroads." Such signs of economic growth didn't depend on City Hall. And likewise Britain's enrichment did not depend on crown patronage. Its armies and navies did, but not its iron-works and cotton mills. The governments in Britain and Chicago, unlike in the same places now, were too small to obstruct commercially tested betterment very much.

Allen's argument, admirable as are many of its details, is the opposite of the one I would favor. He believes—with North and Liah Greenfeld and Patrick O'Brien and recently Prasannan Parthasarathi and Marianna Mazzucato—that a powerful *government* is a precondition for economic growth.[3] I say that it has been mostly an obstacle, in the usual ways, divert-ing activity into rent seeking and military waste. "Trustworthy service to the Crown," which is Allen's touchstone, was no road to private economic growth. He says, "Britain, by becoming the most aristocratic of all societ-ies, also became the wealthiest and the most powerful."[4] "Most powerful," yes: a navy that practiced gunnery fanatically under the eyes of faux and actual aristocrats whose whole identity was tied up in naval warfare was for that purpose a very good thing. The aristocracy ran the *involuntary*, *public* sector in Britain for a long time. The last British cabinet still hav-ing a majority of literal aristocrats (a stringent measure, considering the tiny size of the British peerage) was surprisingly late: Gladstone's of 1892. Thirty years later, in Bonar Law's cabinet, there were still equal numbers of peers and commoners. Thatcher's cabinet of 1979 still contained nearly a quarter from the "landed establishment" (though some quite recently recruited to it).[5] But "wealthiest" had to do not with Britain's aristocracy or even its much larger gentry, but with its bourgeoisie. The *economy* of the "polite and commercial people" was in the hands of the bourgeoisie and its nonaristocratic values increasingly approved by the rest—and adopted indeed by much of the improving aristocracy from 1730 or so at the latest.

Allen does not compare internationally, and therefore he does not get much beyond the English Channel. Comparison is the humanist's version of counting, and it is often more conclusive scientifically than the counting. Historians or economists focused on a single case, such as Britain, no matter how much they count, are liable to overlook similar conditions elsewhere that belie their celebration of, say, English (but not Scottish) law or British (but also French) empire. Douglass North, John Wallis, and Barry Weingast, in their book modestly subtitled *A Conceptual Framework for Interpreting Recorded Human History*, overlook all recorded human history except that of England, France, and the United States, and they treat even the trinity partially and often enough erroneously.[6] (The reader is therefore gratified when reading the book to find mention of *Spain* on fully eight pages, with *Rome* on seven pages and *South Korea* on one, on a scale of attention given by France on at least 30. These are the few deviations from a "recorded human history" that consists otherwise of England, France, and the United States alone. Their index contains no entries for Africa, Arabia, China, Germany, Greece, Iran, Italy, Japan, Sweden, the Ottoman Empire, the Mughal Empire, the Netherlands, and Russia, except the USSR.)

To be fair, Allen has enough on his hands getting straight the array of British historical facts he has in fact gotten straight, a jolly good show. But to prove his point he needs to explain why other aristocracies and service classes—such as the Russian, Ottoman, Prussian, and especially Tokugawan Japanese—did not make their countries wealthy. "The purpose of the aristocracy was to provide a pool of trustworthy types," the better to do their utmost in naval or land warfare.[7] All right, suppose it was. Why not samurai riches, then? It won't do to reply that at the Meiji Restoration many of the samurai did in fact go into commerce and industry. They did so precisely by adopting a wholly new admiration for bourgeois versions of the classical virtues and, for example, casting aside aristocratic dueling (Allen's brilliant chapter on dueling, by the way, is worth the price of the book).

* * *

We economists have been trying ever since 1776 to explain the Great Enrichment. About the lower end of the Great Enrichment, the economic historian Cormac Ó Gráda documents the recent sharp decline in famines.[8] The world's highest end of productivity and consumption, enjoyed now by perhaps three-quarters of a billion people, and each year by more and more, supports a flourishing life of loft apartments, art museums, advanced education, adventure holidays, spiritual exercises, serious fiction, surviving the COVID-19 unemployment, and all the ennobling and not-so-ennobling goods and services of a modern bourgeois town. Visit the enormous, modern, and elite Zhejiang University in Hangchou, a place in China you've never heard of, and stand amazed.

In other words, when we lecture to undergraduates about economic history, our message of hope is that human welfare has shot up startlingly since 1800, giving it a pattern like the handle *and blade* of an ice-hockey stick (many economic historians are Canadian men, as Allen is, or Swedish men, and delight in such talk). History in 1800 reached the business end of the hockey stick.

How to explain it? One thing that does *not* explain it, contrary to what has become orthodoxy in neoinstitutionalism since Allen's masters Douglass North and Barry Weingast put it forward in 1989, is the alleged legal changes arising from the Glorious Revolution of 1688–1689.[9] For one thing, the laws did not change. For another, English contract and property law were well developed and enforced "before the reign of Edward the First," which is to say 1272, as Pollock and Maitland established as long ago as 1895, a fact confirmed repeatedly by later legal historians. In 1972 (exactly seven centuries, as it happens, after the beginning of the reign of Edward the First) I modeled the change in property law of eighteenth-century enclosure of open fields—in the way the neoinstitutional economists from North and Thomas in 1973 to Allen in 2011 and Acemoglu and Robinson in 2006 and 2012 and 2019 came to model institutional change more generally. The idea was that in the bad old days of bad law (I repeat: it never happened), the supply-and-demand equilibrium for land or labor or whatever was obstructed by a transaction-cost wedge. The alleged bad property law in English open fields, I supposed in 1972, prevented land from being used efficiently. Then a betterment in law, such as the English enclosure movement, would allow marginal product to be equalized to marginal opportunity cost, reducing the wedge, and would lead, voilà, to higher income. It is the blackboard argument that North and others have in mind when imagining that, say, the introduction of patents in England in 1618 made invention into private property, increased efficiency, and therefore caused the Industrial Revolution (Joel Mokyr has demolished such a view[10]).

The decisive economic point against the neoinstitutional story of how we got rich can be made with any of the numerous supply-and-demand

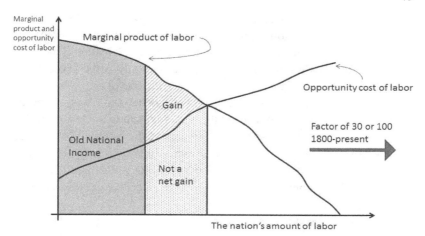

Gains of efficiency are dwarfed by the Great Enrichment 1800-present

FIGURE 1. Institutional change of a static sort cannot explain modern economic growth.

diagrams that fill elementary texts in economics.[11] Take, for example, a nation's supply of and demand for labor. Suppose that the opportunity cost of labor is upward sloping, measuring the value of the next hour of labor in activities alternative to working in, say, Britain, such as working abroad or taking one's ease. Now add into the diagram the demand curve for British labor, which of course is downward sloping because any extra labor gets employed in less urgent employments. Such a marginal-product-of-labor curve, as labeled in figure 1, is the market value of the product of the last hour demanded.

If there is no misallocation of labor, the nation will be led by market forces to employ labor up to the point at which the two curves cross. At that point, national income will be as large as it can be, considering the existing marginal product and opportunity cost of labor. (To speak more technically, total product obviously is, up to a constant of integration, the integral under the marginal product curve—that is to say, the area under the partial derivative curve known to economists, who would have to have invented calculus if it had not already been invented, as the marginal product of labor.)

And it will be good for the society as a whole to be at such a point of efficiency. Efficiency, after all, is that the last hour of work gets in goods what it sacrifices in, say, taking one's ease. Don't go further, as the market or the all-wise central planner say, at which the gain is smaller than the cost. It's what you individually want to do in allocating your own hours between labor and leisure. So, too, the nation. If by misallocation it happens that too little labor is employed, putting the economy at the vertical line to the left of the crossing point of the curves—the line of too little labor—there would be a gain foregone of national income, the triangle labeled Gain. (Technical remark: Why does the gain not include the trapezoid *below* Gain? Because the trapezoid is the value of the opportunity costs of labor—taking one's ease or working abroad—of the work not employed at home and is not a gain to the workers enjoying it. The inefficiency of foregone Gain, by contrast, is a gain to no one, a deadweight loss, as economists say.)

A government can impose policies that make quite large the foregone Gain compared to the income at the efficient point. North Korea, for example, is good at such a task. But in the other direction, on any reasonable view of how economies work, a government can't, by laws hampering free exchange, make the marginal product of labor *rise*, at any event not by a factor 20 or 30.

The crucial point is that even laws that reduced the misallocation leading to a Loss in the first place would yield gains which are small even by comparison with pre–good-law income. And it is utterly trivial by comparison with the gigantic outward movement of the marginal product in the Great Enrichment. Look at the diagram again, and note the big arrow labeled "Factor of 30 or 100 1800–present." It's the big arrow, not the little gains from efficiency, that explains the order of magnitude of the Great Enrichment. That is, the great bulk of the enrichment of the modern world has not come (as some of the right argue) from repairing technically inefficient institutions, and in any case it could hardly come (as some on the left argue) from laws further *hampering* free exchange.

The point is to show that the static assumptions of neoinstitutional economics cannot have the quantitative oomph they claim in explaining the elephant in the room of modern social science: massive modern economic growth in the past two centuries. It will not do to reply that a small change, 2 percent per year, say, adds up to 6,000 percent (or so) in two centuries. "Compound interest" is not an economically competent reply. It does not tell why the compounding only started in 1689 or 1776 or whenever. And more to the point, a static gain is *not* compounded. If railways increased national income by about 2 or 3 percent, as in 1964 Robert Fogel determined for 1890 for the United States, then they did it once, not every year by another 2 percent in addition to the new, higher-by-2-percent US income. We need to find out why the economies of northwestern Europe and then the rest changed to give a dynamic betterment of 2 percent every single year—that is, fresh betterments as important as the railways every year for two centuries. Something very widespread was happening, a million mutinies, a British navvy willing to move to Sweden to dig a canal, a Scottish woman willing to open a shop in Kirkaldy, an engineer inspired to make a great iron ship. Widespread liberal permission and approval was the key, not a little bit of legal improvement.

Misallocation has limits, in other words, and therefore repairing it has limits far below the order of magnitude of the Great Enrichment. It is possible to reduce even a very high income to $1 a day or less if the government goes insane, as governments have with some regularity been doing since they first came into existence. Witness Assad's Syria, or Nero's Rome, or the conquering Mongols' original plan (they soon came to their senses) to turn the rich agricultural fields of south China into depopulated grazing grounds for their horses.

But suppose bad government and market failure and wretched property rights reduced income originally by as much as 80 percent of its potential. In that case a perfect government correcting all market failures and establishing ideal property rights would increase income by a factor calculated by dividing the gain of eighty by the original, miserably inefficient twenty, a factor of four. Splendid. Highly recommended. But the Great Enrichment was a factor not of four but of twenty or thirty or one hundred.

The repair can have, to be sure, secondary effects of encouraging betterment—permission and approval of the Bourgeois Revaluation—that does in turn produce enrichment at the astonishing order of magnitude of 1800 to the present. But the neoinstitutionalists have no theory for this crucial step, the step of the creative production of novelties, except an illogical theory proposed long ago by John Habakkuk and revived by *Robert* Allen (no relation) that scarcity of labor makes for betterment (even though a shilling saved on any margin is a shilling), or a more promising theory (exploded by Mokyr's and Boldrin and Levine's recent work) that patents make novelties into routine property, and innovation is therefore remade into the routine investment beloved of neoinstitutionalist and Samuelsonian and Marxist economists.[12]

So what? (Always the best question to ask in science.) This: little Harberger Triangles of betterment are not going to explain a factor of thirty or (if quality is allowed for) one hundred. *And if they do, the model is instable*, which is not a good way to model, since instable models can prove anything, explosively, all over the place. That is, if you want to claim that (literally) marginally better ways of measuring inputs and outputs resulted in an industrial revolution, which is Douglas Allen's claim (and which is, by the way, similar to *Robert* Allen's; something about those Allens), then you are going to have to explain why small causes have grotesquely large effects and then why they *didn't* have such large effects earlier or in other places, in Roman times or in China.[13] You can't merely, in the style of New Growth Theory, introduce economies of scale when convenient, say in 1750, and where convenient, say Britain, to get a nonlinear, non-Harberger effect. We economists have recently saved our models in the face of a new realization of how radical the Great Enrichment was, in other words, by going on with the same supply-and-demand models but adding in those empty economic boxes of "nonlinearities" or "economies of scale" or "multiple equilibria."

I claim that on the contrary, in the eighteenth and especially the nineteenth century, the economy grew far beyond all previous expectations and far beyond what static economics can explain, or even a mechanically jazzed-up "dynamic" economics, because the forms of speech about enterprise and invention suddenly changed. In a phrase, Adam Smith's "liberal plan of equality, liberty, and justice" started to become the ruling ideology of the age, inspiring ordinary people.[14] Technically speaking, the new conversation caused the dimensions of the Edgeworth box to explode. Reallocation by exchange within a fixed box, which is Douglas Allen's story, or reallocations by aggression along the contract curve, which is Douglass North Mark II's (and Marx's) story, was not what happened. If it did happen, it didn't matter much. Instead, the production possibility curve leapt out. The English habits of the lip changed in the late seventeenth and especially in the eighteenth century for various good and interesting reasons—some in turn material, but some rhetorical. Speech, not material changes in foreign trade or domestic investment or methods of measurement, caused the nonlinearities or (in more conventional theorizing) the leaping out of the production possibility curve. We know this historically, too, technical economics aside, because trade and investment were ancient routines, yet the new dignity and liberty and massive enrichment for ordinary people were unique to the age.

The greatness of the Great Enrichment, in short, is the main intellectual puzzle in explaining the wealth of nations. Its greatness creates terrible problems of how much for the usual allocative economics. Shuffling stuff around a little better is not the sort of stunning innovation that made the modern world. As the economist and rabbi Israel Kirzner expressed it, "for [the British economist flourishing in the 1930s Lionel] Robbins [and the Samuelsonians], economizing simply means shuffling around available resources in order to secure the most efficient utilization of *known* inputs in terms of a *given* hierarchy of ends."[15] Yet the path to the modern was not through shuffling and reshuffling. It was not by the growth of foreign trade or of this or that industry, here or there, or by shifting weights of one or another social class. Nor indeed was it by reshufflings of property rights or their more exact measurement. Nor, to speak of another sort of reshuffling, was it by rich people piling up more riches. They had always done that. Nor was it by bosses being nasty to workers, or through strong countries being nasty to weak countries, and forcibly shuffling stuff toward the nasty and strong. They had always done that too. Piling up bricks and money and colonies had always been routine. It resulted in no big enrichment: look at Spain from the sixteenth century on.

The new path was not about accumulation or theft or commercialization or reallocation or any other reshuffling. It was instead about discovery, I have said, a creativity supported by novel words of permission and approval. Douglas Allen notes that nowadays we expect to have equal social status. Yup. A newly dignified bourgeois commoner was suddenly invited to innovate, radically. As Kirzner put it, such entrepreneurship is not about optimal shuffling—since, as Frank Knight noted, a hired manager can carry out such a routine. "The incentive is to try to get something for nothing, if only one can see what it is that can be done."[16] A new rhetorical environment in the eighteenth century encouraged (literally: gave courage to the hope of) entrepreneurs. "Ours is a society," Allen notes, "based on a concept [if not always a reality] of merit. . . . Not so long ago . . . personal connections, conduct, and birth mattered much more."[17] Bingo. As a result, over the next two centuries the production possibility curve leapt out by a factor of ten or thirty or more.

Allen solves the problem of the Great Enrichment by stopping his analysis with the classic period of the Industrial Revolution, 1750–1850 or so. Robert Thomas and Douglass North had similarly declared in 1973 that "the industrial revolution was *not* the source of economic growth."[18] You *must*, they were claiming, start much earlier. Well, who says? Who says that all causes must be deep in history? Only if you stop the story of Europe in 1800 CE or even at a stretch in 1880 CE can you persuade yourself that the run-up to the Great Enrichment is best viewed as being a thousand years, or five hundred — which saw, as Thomas and North put it, a "sustained economic growth" of . . . about a tenth of 1 percent per year. Bravo for the early modern British. That way real income per head will double at the blistering pace of . . . once every seven centuries. If instead you end the story at the present you realize that the Industrial Revolution and its much more important follow-on of the Great Enrichment was not, I tell you once again, a mere factor of two (as in 1750–1850) but, depending on exactly what you are measuring, of ten or thirty or one hundred in a couple of centuries for the first industrial nation and in a couple of long generations for the recent followers, such as Sweden or Japan or Hong Kong or Ireland, and now China and India.

Some of my fellow economic historians, such as Stephen Broadberry and Gupta Bishnupriya and Robert Allen and Jan Luiten van Zanden, make much of that doubling of incomes in Europe over the hundreds of years before the Industrial Revolution.[19] That way they don't have to face up to the largest material anomaly in world history of thousands of years at $2 or $3 a day or so and then a leap in a couple of centuries to well over $100 a day. They don't have to face up to the problem that if little changes in law and "institutions" could have such astounding effects, then surely the experiments in good property rights and budget lines all in order such as Hannibal's Carthage or Kublai's China would have had the same outcome.

Eric Jones attacks the view I favor that nothing much happened until 1800, instancing as he did in his *Growth Recurring* (1988) such "major growth phases" as early Song China and early Tokugawa Japan.[20] Jones opines that "what kept growth episodes so few was mainly excessive rent-seeking on the part of the holders of political power."[21] Probably, such as the Ming and then Tokugawa closing of international trade down to the Tokugawa outlawing of mica in prints and (get this) wheeled vehicles, now revived in statist "protection" and "industrial policy" directed by the interests. But I say again the "major growth phases" were factors of two in rising income per head in seven centuries, not factors of thirty or one hundred in two centuries. On a scale of human events, two is very, very far from thirty or one hundred, and Jones's eloquence against the nothing-new-until-1800 folk (such as myself and Ken Pomeranz [2000] and Joel Mokyr and Jack Goldstone [2002]) is here misplaced.

We need to distinguish quite sharply, as Eric Jones sometimes does not, in deference to gradualists such as the admirable demographic and economic historian Anthony Wrigley, the manufacturing cum regional specialization that we call "industrialization"—which happened in other places, such as Japan and China, and leads to a factor of two—from "modern economic growth," in Kuznets' phrase, which leads to a factor of one hundred. Jones himself in the same book put the point well: "Had the Enlightenment idea of progress not influenced practical affairs, England might have become a normal country, in the terms of the period, content with a quietly prosperous but not forcefully progressive economy—like the United Provinces or Tokugawa Japan or Venice. Living standards would have been well ahead of Stone Age affluence but stalled on a plateau of bucolic prosperity, the potential for growth meandering away in a Venetian twilight."[22] Precisely. The problem, as Mokyr has noted, is to explain why the meandering did not occur, as it so often had in earlier "efflorescences," as Goldstone put it. The Enlightenment conceived as French cannot be the explanation, because the French, absent a British irritation, would have gone on chattering in their salons and inventing military devices of doubtful practicality, just as the English, absent a Dutch irritation, would have stayed nonnaval and nonfinancial and nonbourgeois.

* * *

Douglas Allen provides, too, a test case for what I would call the Max U Fallacy of Neoinstitutionalism. Ever since North spoke out loud and bold, most economists have itched to go on with their Samuelsonian tale to reduce all human interactions to maximization within the rules of the game. Love, loyalty, honor, courage, professionalism, identity are to be so reduced to prudence. The trouble is that Samuelsonian economists cannot hear the word *rules* without thinking "budget constraints on Max U." When listing "institutions that get the job done," for example, Allen names every human interaction, from rule of law understood as Keep Off the Grass to families and customs. But then he characterizes them, revealingly, as "economic property rights that . . . work together to make people behave a certain way," and later "an institution is essentially a system, or collection, of economic property rights."[23] Allen quotes Avner Greif's elastic definition in 2006 of an institution as "a system of social factors that conjointly generate a regularity of behavior."[24] Every social thing is gathered under the I-word—markets, cities, families, languages, symbolic systems, habits, beliefs, laws, passions, rhetoric, philosophies, ethics, ideology, religions, whatever. So society causes society, which is hard to dispute. But Greif and Allen then reduce the social thing to incentives—the word *generate* in Greif's definition becomes "results from self-interested, Max-U, behavior." In particular, noncooperative game theory.

Allen argues in an aside, for example, that the uncertainties of human procreation implied, according to his model of institutions adjusting when nature becomes more controllable, that marriage changed only in "the middle of the 20th century, when technical innovations allowed some control over pregnancy and disease prevention."[25] But the claim is doubtful. It has long been known that family limitation is ancient, even if not having The Pill, and that the ideology of the Feminine Mystique had as much impact as did any pill.[26] On the same page he offers the changing master-servant relationship 1750 to 1850 as caused by the cheapening of time pieces, which seems even less plausible, and is, if you will, timed incorrectly by some five centuries: Europe had ringing church clocks from the thirteenth century on, and in any case other societies such as the Chinese had public clocks hundreds of years earlier with no alteration of the relation of master to servant. The emerging ideology of liberalism seems a much more plausible cause. Allen and the other neoinstitutionalists, you see, want to reduce society to incentives. I am an economist, too, and yield to no one in my admiration for well-aligned incentives. I've written whole books in their praise. But the world, including the modern world of clocks and other instruments of measurement, works as much through professionalism and ideology as through incentive—as much through faithful identity as through profitable prudence. You can show it quantitatively.

Let's, then, do the numbers. Allen explains very plausibly the role of prize capture and other strange business in the Royal Navy as designed, or at any rate evolved, "to encourage others to fight in an age in which measurement of performance at sea was so difficult."[27] But aren't we *still* in such an age, exacerbated by the gigantic size of modern organizations? In a merchant's warehouse in 1700 London or even on the quarter deck of the *Victory* at Trafalgar 1805, the head merchant or Lord Nelson could watch with a little effort virtually everyone, in the commercial emergency or in the desperate engagement (at any rate if it involved only the *Victory* itself). How does a high-ranking executive for Macy's watch its 166,000 employees, or how does the captain of the USS *George H. W. Bush* watch its six thousand sailors?

And why would one believe that measuring the output is *easier* now in actual, relevant practice than then? Look at Major League Baseball, for example, and its shocking mismanagement on the field despite living in a paradise of measurability. We've known since Earnshaw Cook's

Percentage Baseball in 1964 that the sacrifice bunt is a mistake. We can measure the marginal product of players highly skilled at such beloved idiocies. Or what is the marginal product of an extra ticket agent with grace and common sense at United Airlines at O'Hare Airport in the middle of a weather delay? Allen argues that "the major problem of the premodern world was the enormous role nature played in the ordinary business of life."[28] Yes (and thunderstorms at O'Hare Airport are not about "nature"?). But the major problem of the modern world is the enormous role that human spontaneous orders and directed organizations play. If it were now easy to monitor professors or doctors, there would be no need for professionalism at all, since the customers or the bosses could reward and punish them to maximize wealth. It is the point that Ronald Coase made long ago, that a firm and its professionalism and management and solidarity is a substitute for a market.

Allen's central assumption in support of incentives as all we need in a social science is unbelievable, in short, and needs to be established in its magnitude by quantitative evidence, which he does not offer. It's the problem with analytical narratives—some I have noted call them just-so stories, as for example in evolutionary psychology—without evidence testing them, or indeed with evidence contradicting them. Allen says that it's easier to measure performance now than it was in 1700. I doubt it. And if he thinks so he needs to measure the rise of *efficacious* measurement. I have no doubt that moderns *like* measurement, and *honor* it. But that does not mean they do it correctly or even use it for many practical purposes. Body counts in Vietnam were phony baloney. Accounting, note, is necessarily about the past. Yet economic decisions are necessarily about the future. Remember Yogi Berra.

Most moderns, such as Allen and I, are employed in massive bureaucracies, in our cases massive educational bureaucracies. For all the research assessment exercises and student evaluations of teachers and the other mindless attempts by our masters to reduce education to an assembly line, we cannot measure the contribution of Allen or me to the output of our universities. It's hard enough on an assembly line. The measurement is much more difficult in the steadily enlarging part of the economy—a quarter of labor income right now—that consists as in education of changing people's minds, "sweet talk." You can make up many numbers, rather the way some economists and psychologists nowadays make up numbers about "happiness." But possessing a number does not mean you have the phenomenon by the tail except for a scientific question that is naturally quantitative, and when you have in fact chosen by humanistic analysis the relevant measure.

Management in a liberated society does not mainly spy on people ("monitor the workers to make sure they do not shirk"[29]). Mainly it *persuades* them to do their duty, which they do out of a professional sense of self-worth or out of affection for their boss and their fellow workers as much as in fear of a stopped paycheck. The British had a large and successful navy, says Allen, and he asks how it was accomplished. He replies, by a clever indirect monitoring system that was only slowly copied by opponents—slowly for unexplained reasons, if it was so very clever.[30] (Allen does not note the more usual explanation for the Royal Navy's success: "Rum, buggery, and the lash.")

To which I would reply, yes, "incentives do matter," but so do identity and justice and love and other matters not reducible in a serious empirical study to Prudence Only. Thus humanomics. Lord Nelson, Allen notes, was unusual for his personal courage and for the courage he evoked in others. "England expects that every man will do his duty" was his opening flag signal at Trafalgar. But the cheer that went up from the fleet in response to it, and the eagerness with which the tars and their officers followed his standing signal during the battle, "Engage the enemy more closely," were not achieved by offers of money or by the threat of courts martial or the lash. Incentives be damned. Come on, lads: board the Spanish vessel with flashing cutlasses, *con brio*.

*   *   *

So if we're going to say that "institutions matter," we are going to have to measure, to show that this or that institutional arrangement had oomph. I would rather say that "language matters," because one can show as quantitatively as one wishes the language of the economy changing, 1600–1848, in ways highly relevant to the functioning of markets and especially and crucially the functioning of innovation. Whatever explanation we give has to face up to the Great Enrichment and has to entail economic arguments capable of explaining its scale and its uniqueness. Liberty and dignity for ordinary people seems a good bet. Improving a few techniques of measurement does not.

CHAPTER SEVEN

And "Culture," or Mistaken History, Will Not Repair It

Let me again praise and yet criticize a little, perhaps less stringently than Allen, a brilliantly heterodox Austrian property-rights economist. He, too, is influenced as Allen is by Douglass North. I pick on this brilliant scholar again on the a fortiori figure that if he is lacking in some respects, all the more are the Samuelsonians and others of the orthodoxy. And so would the old institutionalists and the Marxists of the heterodoxy.

Virgil Henry Storr's elegant book *Understanding the Culture of Markets* needs to be read widely. Economists are fond of exporting economic ideas but notoriously reluctant to import anything from the humanities or even from the other social sciences. Such intellectual mercantilism violates the precepts of their own science. Storr, by contrast, is a free trader in ideas.

In particular, Storr brings back into economics the matter of meaning. It was banished for a long time, I have noted, by behaviorism, the doctrine that we must view people as though we had no idea what they meant and could only observe them from the outside, like rats in the psychologist's maze. Yet I have also noted that psychology, where behaviorism originated and found its most extreme scientific expression, got over meaninglessness in the 1950s. Seventy years on, it's about time economics did too. I remember how thrilled we economists were in the 1970s by the finding of the Texas A&M economists that rats and pigeons were rational Max U-ers.[1] Rats viewed cherry soda as a luxury good. It didn't occur to us that such confirmation of Prudence Only would apply to *all* forms of life. In its observable behavior, grass is rational. Only humans, so far as we know (though with some emerging exceptions in the brighter animals such as gorillas, elephants, and parrots, and even maybe octopuses), exhibit

meaning in their courage, temperance, justice, faith, hope, and love. Such
are the nonprudent virtues (yet prudence *is* one of the seven principal virtues), which Amartya Sen gathers under the label of "commitment."[2]

The antibehaviorist Alfred Schütz (1899–1959), whom I learned about
from Storr himself (exhibiting in my initial ignorance a failure in intellectual trade), argued that human action is "meaningless apart from the
project that defines it."[3] We. Say. With words. Raising my arm in a philosophical demonstration of a liberated will has meaning because it is part
of a little project of philosophical argument. Raising my arm "idly," we say,
with no project in view, is meaningless, motiveless. Motives, says Schütz (as
exposited lucidly by Storr), are imparting meaning by way of "in-order-to"
explanations during their planning or their exercise or their post facto accounts. "Why do you raise your arm?" "I mean to do it in order to persuade
you of free will." The meaning of a lion's attack on a wildebeest is in order
to eat, Prudence Only. Humans, by contrast, in their courage, temperance,
justice, faith, hope, and love, and their corresponding vices and derivative
virtues, shoot the wildebeest in order to serve other meanings too.

After all, human meanings are scientific observations and often no
harder to find out than the national income of Nigeria or the full price
of a smart phone with contract. As Hayek put it, somewhat too radically
(would it apply to a traffic jam?), "Unless we can understand . . . what people *mean* by their actions any attempt to explain them . . . is bound to fail."[4]
In urging us to take the meaning of markets seriously, Storr says early in
his book, "The market is a social space where meaningful conversations
occur."[5] Yes. And on the next to last page he notes that "market relationships [can] develop into social friendships. . . . Most of our experiences in
the market are not with strangers."[6] Yes again. The friendship could easily
be quantified, this strength of weak ties, and has been by economic sociologists.[7] But most economists are not listening. The same point was made
by a few in the earlier generation of economy watchers, such as the economists and social philosophers Knight and Mises and Hayek, as Storr wisely
notes.[8] Now it is made by the cultural economist Arjo Klamer, the economic sociologist Viviana Zelizer, the experimental economists Vernon
Smith and Bart Wilson, and the empirical Austrian economists inspired by
the saintly Don Lavoie, such as Emily Chamlee-Wright and Virgil Storr.[9]

*   *   *

From beginning to end, however, Storr treats the neoinstitutionalists such
as North and Greif gently. He should be a lot harder on them. North and

Greif and a host of followers, such as Daron Acemoglu and Douglas Allen, have a meaningless concept of institutions. Instead of the "patterns of meaning" that Clifford Geertz assigned to culture through its metaphors and stories, an "institution" is defined by the neoinstitutionalists merely as a budget constraint, the rules of the game, like the rules of chess. Even when Greif tries to acknowledge the role of culture, he sees it not as meaning but as constraint. It leads merely, as Storr quotes him, to "path dependence of institutional frameworks, . . . forestalling successful intersociety adoption of institutions."[10] It's more imperfections, unmeasured. As Storr says with characteristic generosity of spirit when summarizing North's *Understanding the Process of Economic Change* (2005), "beliefs [that is, culture, including meanings] . . . influence the institutions [people] select to constrain the choices they make."[11] "Beliefs" and "institutions" in the neoinstitutional orthodoxy are constraining chains only. They are not a mobile army of metaphors, the poetry and stories of the culture, human dances like Matisse's *La danse*, webs of significance in which humans are suspended and which they themselves have spun (as Storr paraphrases Geertz). Storr puts well the relevant criticism of the neoinstitutionalists when he remarks that the social-capital metaphor characterizing "beliefs," used repeatedly by North and others, "exaggerates . . . the degree to which actors are slaves to their culture," automatons rather than dancers or poets.[12]

So much Storr gets right, and without perhaps quite realizing it he leans against neoinstitutionalism. Still, I was alarmed that Storr swallowed whole Paul David's example of path dependence of institutional frameworks, the typewriter's arrangement of the keys known as QWERTY (wow: that was very easy to type!), which the neoinstitutionalists have swallowed too.[13] Path dependence undoubtedly occurs in human affairs. That English has become, in a phrase that must depress the French, the lingua franca of the modern world surely arose from the accidents of English-speaking dominance of first engineering and then warfare and then pop music and then computers. But the conventional organization of the typewriter keyboard is an exceptionally poor example, quantitatively speaking. The experiments alleged to prove the superiority of the Dvorak keyboard were organized by the professor of psychology Dr. August . . . Dvorak.[14] And in the age of computers, a typing-intensive industry such as insurance could shift to another keyboard as easily as a clarinetist can shift to a saxophone. Not one such industry has. The history of jazz after World War II shows how easy is the shift from clarinet to saxophone.

Though it is comforting to neoinstitutionalists and their siblings in arms, the Beckerian Samuelsonians, to think so, it is not obviously true, as Storr puts it with apparent approval, that "*informal* institutions [e.g., beliefs, habits, practices, such as QWERTY] tend to be more stable [than *formal* institutions, the budget constraints] and, when they do change, it tends to be slow and incremental."[15] The *formal* institution of the American constitution has lasted well over two centuries. The *informal* institution of judicial activism in the Supreme Court has waxed and waned. The formal institution of the holy, catholic, and apostolic Church has lasted almost two millennia. Its informal institutions can change on what is, compared to such stretches, a dime, as they did for example in the Second Vatican Council 1962–1965. One would like to see the evidence for North's or Greif's confidently asserted hypothesis that *beliefs* move sluggishly: they didn't in China after 1978 or India after 1991, or for that matter in British North America in 1775. The recent change in attitudes toward homosexuality in northern Europe and its offshoots, after a century-long reign of terror, has happened with lightning speed. The churches in Europe emptied out in a period of twenty years—in a once-devout Netherlands during the 1960s, more like ten years. Beliefs about Germans changed in the United States within a few months around the country's entry into the War to End All Wars. Beliefs about Uncle Joe Stalin turned around twice within half a decade. The nasty habit, to take a bizarre example, of letting one's dog foul the pavement flipped in the United States in about ten years. The belief in the purity of Coca-Cola, bond-assured by massive advertising, would flip overnight if a plausible case arose of even one dead mouse in a can.

* * *

Let me tell you more about why Storr should be harder on the neoinstitutionalists. Storr quotes Hayek in 1943 writing that "in the social sciences the things are what people think they are," and Storr himself writes that "reference to what people think and believe is necessary in order to explain why people accept certain metal disks as money and not others."[16] Again, yes. As Storr argues, even so fundamental an economic activity as picking up a $100 bill from the floor—the model for arbitrage and the model for Kirznerian alertness that precedes the arbitrage—requires hermeneutic interpretation, that is, the assignment of cultural meaning.[17] What is a $100 bill? To a Trobriand Islander in 1915 it would be a funny-looking piece of paper, hardly worth a second glance. To Tom Sargent in the economic joke, walking with Bob Lucas, it would be by rational expectations an illusion: "It can't be there, Bob. If it were, someone would already have picked it up."

It's interpretation all the way down. The rules of the game are breakable, as in the B' Rabby and B' Bouki stories in Barbados that Storr deploys so effectually (similar to the Coyote tales among Plains Indians or tales of Loki the trickster in Norse mythology[18]). Every rule of the game comes with an invitation to reinterpret it in the light of new ideas. B' Rabby does, though his "ideas" are better called "schemes."

The "capital" or "tool" or "rule" concept as an explanation of how well we do—for example, as an explanation of the factor of thirty or one hundred by which real incomes per head exceed those of 1800—is much beloved by the latter-day children of Adam Smith. William Easterly calls it "capital fundamentalism," and I have shown its lack of quantitative oomph in explaining modern economic growth.[19] In the present context the problem is that capital or tool or rule can evaporate in the instant of a new idea or scheme. Laboriously acquired proficiency in Latin was an essential tool for diplomacy and science in the seventeenth century. Well into the twentieth century it was an essential ornament of the educated gentleman. And then the society said, in effect, Valley girl style, "Whatever" (that is to say, *Quicquid*). And Latin died. London black-cab drivers had to spend a full year driving around on motorbikes to acquire The Knowledge of every street and route. The smart phone and GPS made their human capital useless—instantly, though the black cabs are still arranging for governmental protection, such as recently from the Mayor of London, Sadiq Khan.

As Storr puts it, "culture influences how individuals and societies identify and conceive of the tools they have at their disposal."[20] A McDonald's restaurant is used differently by Dutch teenagers (it stays open later than native Dutch restaurants and welcomes *pubers*) than by American families looking for a break today. A tool or a rule is not interpreted the same in different cultures. The South African film comedy in 1980, *The Gods Must Be Crazy*, shows how Khoisan tribesmen reinterpret a Coke bottle thrown out of an airplane too high to be noticed as the source. A friend of mine in her youth was a nun in Mother Teresa's Missionaries of Charity. She and Mother Teresa traded rosaries. In the toilet of a big passenger airplane, struggling with her habit, she accidentally dropped the rosary irretrievably down the toilet. If (as in the very old days) the plane emptied its toilets at thirty thousand feet, imagine the interpretation a stoutly Protestant farmer would give to an inexplicable rosary landing on his front porch. Interpretation's the human thing.

The same point was made about "resources" ("natural capital") in 1981 by Julian Simon: "resources" are creations of human ideas, the idea that petroleum might be refined into kerosene for lighting, or an idea that rare earths might be used in electronics and batteries.[21] Culture, as Don Lavoie and Emily Chamlee-Wright said, "is not a static thing but an ongoing process."[22] Indeed. The usually empty word "process" here stands in for the changes that, say, a shift in the comparative advantage of a cultural practice causes. Japan's excellence in quality control in manufacturing, the result in part of the adoption of the statistical ideas of the American W. Edwards Deming (which by the way were hostile to mechanical tests of statistical significance) and in part the result of the team play valued so highly in Japan, was just the ticket in the 1970s and 1980s. By the 1990s it did not look all conquering. The Japanese practice of hands-off greetings, with bows, looked silly to Westerners, with their kissing and hand shaking and then even male hugging, until in the coronavirus crisis it looked brilliant. The idea's the thing. The Maginot Line, a miracle of French military engineering, was defeated in six weeks by the idea the Germans had in 1940 (and had also used twenty-six years earlier) of a right flanking movement through Belgium and the Ardennes. (Fool the French once, shame on the Germans; fool them twice, shame on the French.) Resources, management, capital rise or fall when ideas change.

The Great Enrichment is of course the big instance. It was not, I say again in case you missed it, thriftiness leading to more and more capital that mattered (contrary to Smith, Marx, modern growth theory, and Max Weber) but the new admiration for a bourgeois life of creating economic value, a Bourgeois Revaluation arising from liberalism leading to an ideology of innovism. One "creates" economic value by buying low and selling high, that is, by moving coal and ideas from a place they are not much valued to a place where they are. That's where Weber was mistaken. It was the *rhetoric* toward business, not the behavior of accumulate, accumulate (as Marx put it), that enriched the modern world. "Worldly asceticism," as Weber put it, which he then imagined in conventional Smithian-Marxist logic led to high rates of capital accumulation, was not what made for the Great Enrichment. Ideas and innovation did. As the sociologists Victor Nee and Richard Swedberg wisely put it, "The enduring legacy of Weber's scholarship is perhaps not so much the Protestant-ethic thesis, but the view that the mechanisms motivating and facilitating today's [and the seventeenth century's] capitalism are rooted not in the materialist domain of incremental capital accumulation, but in the realm of ideas and institutional structures."[23]

Storr admires Weber's *The Protestant Ethic and the Spirit of Capitalism*.[24] I do, too. The book is surely one of the hundred greatest books of social science. Maybe one of the twenty greatest. Storr correctly attributes five themes to it. The news is that since 1905 only one of them, though—that "capitalism" can take on a variety of forms—has stood up to historical and economic criticism.[25] The criticism contradicts Storr's enthusiastic defense.[26] Storr concludes each of his fair-minded reviews of the criticisms of Weber's ruminations on Calvinism by saying that after all *The Protestant Ethic* was merely a preliminary sketch. Well, yes. Studies of entrepreneurship such as Weber's have the crucial flaw that they think of it as capital, a pile of enterprising folk, instead of a culturally embedded practice. The embedding tells whether the plant will grow. A society that scorns or fears commercially tested betterment will not do it, whatever the percentage of hopeful or courageous or prudent people might be.

It's quite true that different market societies—from the Middle Paleolithic trade in ornamental shells through the Russian brand of "state capitalism" (as the leftists call it to deflect the blame for Stalinism)—have been supported by different "spirits." Marxists call it ideology. But the real spirit or ideology of modern "capitalism" is not an alleged Protestant ethic or a rise of greed or "commercialization" but the admiring and accepting of commercially tested betterment. That new attitude ("spirit," *Geist*) had stupendous economic consequences. Weber's words if not his actual meaning can be appropriated: "capitalism appeared in China, India, Babylon, the ancient world, and Middle Ages ... [but] just that particular [modern] ethic was missing in all these cases."[27] Weber thought the ethic was of "endless" accumulation "as an end in itself" (a calumny against merchants that goes back to Aristotle). He was mistaken. The ethic was of an entirely new admiration for betterment, novelty, risk-taking, creativity. In a word, innovism—the spirit, as Storr puts it, of the Junkanoo parade on New Year's Day on Bay Street in Nassau Town. In any case, a change in the superstructure (and in this Weber and Storr are spot on) caused a change in the base. Not the other way around.

* * *

Consider wider reasons, with which Storr may well agree, to be suspicious of neoinstitutionalism.

North urged us earnestly (as in North 2005) to attend to the new phrenology of "brain scientists" accumulating in the past couple of decades. Yet he ignored, as most people do when they are talking this way, the three-thousand-year old conversation of poetry, epics, novels, philology, rhetoric, philosophy, folk tales, and most of history. What is deeply superficial, so to speak, about the neoinstitutional notion of rules of the game is that the rules are always under discussion, for those three thousand years and now too. People in the Hood, for example, contend that you should not talk to cops. The cops devote effort to changing the rhetoric of not being a snitch, not cooperating with The Man, not getting involved in someone else's business. Watch *The Wire* for instruction in such matters. The broken-windows tactic recommended by Kelling and Wilson is often held up as an example in neoinstitutional, Samuelsonian fashion changing incentives and constraints. Not entirely. It's also an example of trying to change the conversation, change what people say to themselves when contemplating mugging the woman walking down the street: "Hmm. This place is pretty fancy. Must be heavily patrolled" or "Gosh. Things are so nice around here. I better do what my mother said and be nice." Yet its long-term effect, I have noted, was to overpolice the Hood, with disastrous results in brutality by the police and in resistance to the rule of the government's law.

In this connection you need to know about the work over the past few decades by the philosopher John Searle, summarized in his book of 2010, *Making the Social World: The Structure of Human Civilization*. He writes, "God can create light by saying, 'Let there be light!' Well, we cannot create light but we have a similar remarkable capacity." The magic among humans is performed by a "status function," as Searle infelicitously calls it, that is, a meaningful purpose (and here Storr, Searle, and I join against behavioral social science) performed by a person (such as a president) or a thing (such as a $20 bill) or an entity (such as a limited liability corporation) by virtue of a social agreement. The crucial formula is: X is treated as Y in the context C. The crossing of the goal line by the soccer ball (X) is treated as a goal in the context (C) of playing soccer (the example is an old one in Searle's thought).

Searle insists that any status function requires language. "Without a language," he writes, "you have only pre-linguistic intentional states such as desires and beliefs together with dispositions."[28] These are, you will note, what economists call utility functions and constraints. Economics (in this contrary to the Master Smith, I have noted) has been determinedly prelinguistic. Language doesn't matter in Marx or in Samuelson. What matters are desires and dispositions combined with powers expressed as budget lines. Yet Searle observes that the very powers come from speech.

"To get to the point that you can *recognize* an obligation as an obligation [e.g., to pay your bills along your budget line, or not to steal the stuff], you have to have the *concept* of an obligation, because you have to be able to *represent* something as an obligation, that is, something that gives you a reason for action [compare Schütz as exposited by Storr] independent of your inclinations and desires."[29] Notice the words *recognize, concept, represent.* They play no part in an economics understood as not needing language. Game theory in economics amounts to the claim that we can do without language and language-created meanings and persuasions. Just shut up and play the game, consulting your budget constraints and your preferences. Searle and Storr and I disagree with the game theorists: "games and other nonlinguistic institutional phenomena," says Searle, "can be explained only in terms of language. You can't use the analogy with games to explain language because you understand games only if you already understand language."[30]

Treating X as Y in the context C looks trivial, "merely" a figure of speech, "just" talk. So it is, Searle argues. It is merely a "linguistic institutional fact," such as "all unmarried men are bachelors." Treat a man as something called a bachelor under the circumstances that he is unmarried, by whatever the society means by "marriage," and you are speaking English. But treating X as Y under circumstances C becomes a "nonlinguistic institutional fact" with consequences ("powers") beyond mere language when the circumstances and the person doing the treating have extralinguistic powers arising from agreed conventions (themselves arising from language).[31] Language establishes the meaning of the word *bachelor*, but the extralinguistic context creates the powerful consequences: that Bachelor X can marry a woman (and nowadays a man).

Meaning is the only power inside language itself. This is what Storr is arguing too. If I promise to write a reaction to a book by Virgil Storr, the speech act of promising means . . . well . . . I hereby promise to review the book. But if the extralinguistic context obtains that the editor is a dear friend of mine, and Virgil is, too, then the promise plus the context, C, which is the story of my life and loves, creates a power beyond meaning. It gives me a reason for action independent of my lazy inclinations and desires. Commitment. Virtues.

"Once you have a common language, you already have a society," declares Searle.[32] True. And therefore as the language changes, so also changes the sort of society one can have. The language game, as Wittgenstein put it, determines a form of life. As "honest" shifts from aristocratic to bourgeois honor, the sort of deals we can make, the sort of action we can countenance, change.[33] To call a man "dishonest" in an aristocratic society requires a duel with swords next morning. To call a man "dishonest" in a bourgeois society requires a suit for libel.

Economic innovation "counts as" (to use Searle's vocabulary) honorable only in the Bourgeois Era. Or to be exact, what was honorable in the Aristocratic Era was military innovation without a market test. No one asked whether a new machine of war was profitable in money. Likewise the modern clerisy, those pseudoneoaristocrats of "merit," judge their merit in nonmoney terms. The well-named honorary degrees count for more than high pay. I witnessed a discussion of a candidate for an academic job once in which his success with a popular book *in addition* to his large and fine scholarly output was offered as a reason not to hire him. Profit makes a pseudoaristocrat dirty, at any rate if she cannot well conceal the dirt.

Searle needs a word I coined, *conjective*, which is neither objective nor subjective. "Institutional facts are typically objective facts," he writes, by which he means that they bite.[34] That a $20 bill, to take his favorite example, buys $20 worth of stuff will bite as deeply in our lives as does the physical fact that the bill falls to the ground if you let go of it. (And *after* it falls what does mere physics—"brute facts" in Searle's way of talking— imply about its future location? A mistaken prediction. Economics, as Steven Cheung pointed out to me long ago, predicts that someone will pick it up, which is not something one could learn from its brute-fact, physical equilibrium on the floor.) He continues: "oddly enough, [the institutional facts] are only facts by human agreement or acceptance." Human agreement or acceptance is precisely what I call the "conjective," as against merely subjective, what Searle calls "*I*-intentionality" or "taking the first-person singular" or objective in God's eyes ("brute facts" or "observer independent").[35] The conjective is what we know together as a result of human agreement or acceptance. The Latin is *cum* + *iactus*, that is, "thrown together," as we humans are in our mammalian cuddling and especially in our conversation. It is all we know, and what Storr is reaching for, and all Searle needs to know.

Searle argues persuasively that a society is glued together by conjective facts of the sort X counts as Y in context C. The German captain at the end of *The African Queen* says, "I pronounce you man and wife; proceed with the execution," which counts as marrying Humphrey Bogart and Katherine Hepburn in the context of a properly constituted marriage ceremony. A $20 bill counts as legal tender in the context of the territories of the United States. A ball going over the goal line counts as a goal in the context of a soccer game.

As the literary critic and public intellectual Stanley Fish so often notes, of course, such conjective facts are always contestable.[36] Objective facts ("water is two molecules of hydrogen and one of oxygen") or subjective facts ("Beckham intends to score a goal") are not. The physical facts of the world and the psychological states of human minds are "brute," to extend Searle's word, in the sense of being incontestable in their very nature, their "ontology" as the philosophers say.[37] Physical constraints such as gravity and utility functions such as my great love for vanilla ice cream are not the sort of facts we can quarrel about once we have grasped their nature. All we can do is measure them or their effects, if we can.

The conjective by contrast is always contestable and always in a sense *ethical*, that is, about "deontic status," as Searle puts it, what we *ought* to do. The priest or captain might be argued to be not properly authorized to perform a marriage (look at the controversy about gay marriage), the definition of "US territory" might be ambiguous (embassies abroad?). And the goal in soccer might be disputed. If *any part* of the ball breaks the plane of the goal line is it a goal? Was the linesman in a position to judge? Admittedly, the objective and psychological facts are at the level of human talk disputable, and subject therefore, as the philosophers Michael Oakeshott and Hilary Putnam, among others, argue, to ethical precepts about what we *ought* to believe.[38] Storr, again, is far ahead of most economists in getting such points. But the facts themselves, we all agree, exist independent of any observer. Rules of scientific persuasion by contrast do not: they are conjective, matters under discussion by their very ontology, their very natures.

So what?

Searle says that "creating institutional facts"—such as that the professor, not the students, leads the class or that a walker stays to the right on a crowded sidewalk or that Elizabeth is the queen of England—depends on "one formal linguistic mechanism."[39] That institutional facts carry deontic powers "provide us with reasons for acting that are independent of our inclinations and desires," such as the (recognized) responsibility of the professor to lead the class or the (acknowledged) right not to be bumped into on a crowded sidewalk or the (accepted) power of Elizabeth to exercise her advisory role.[40]

The institutionalist economists call them "constraints," or the rules of the game. But Searle notes, citing his understanding of one of the founders of sociology, Émile Durkheim, that "Some social theorists have seen institutional facts as essentially constraining. That is a very big mistake."[41] Whether Durkheim committed the mistake is not so clear. But Douglass North and associates certainly do. Institutions, Searle is arguing, are not only about regulating relations between preexisting people and objects. They are, with great consequences, such as those from the Bourgeois Revaluation, about creating entirely new power relationships between people.[42] That is what is magical about status functions. Americans *declared* our independence on July 4, 1776, and thus fashioned a new relationship of power between King George and his former subjects.

In other words, institutions are much, much more human and humanistic than mere budget constraints between buying ice cream and paying the rent. Searle points out that there are two kinds of rules, regulative ("Don't steal"; "Drive on the right"), which apply to *already existing activities*, and constitutive, which *create the very activity* ("Follow these rules and you are 'playing chess' "; "Act in this way and you are 'being a proper bourgeois' "; "Reduce everything to a meaningless Max U and you are being a proper Samuelsonian"). It is language, in particular the combined metaphors and stories we use to create the allegories called institutions.

If the science of economics, as Storr argues, needs meaning, in short, it needs not rules of the game or brain science but the humanities all the way down.

*   *   *

The leader of the new empirical Austrian school centered at George Mason University and a teacher of Storr, Peter Boettke, argues that price theory was, "especially in the hands of Mises and Hayek, *institutional* in nature: they placed a priority on the framework within which economic life takes place."[43] But they also placed a priority on the framework of ethics, which neoinstitutionalism (of which Boettke approves) strides by. "An institutional framework of property, contract and consent," writes Boettke, "is a fundamental pre-requisite for the operation of prices and profit-and-loss. Prices guide, profits lure, and losses discipline within the competitive entrepreneurial market process." True. But such a neoinstitutional framework à la North leaves unanswered the central question of the *causes* of the wealth of nations. The old wealth was indeed caused by property, contract, and consent, but the triad was ancient and universal. The startling *new* wealth was caused by an ethical change in the eighteenth century, from mercantilism and poverty to liberalism and innovism. Long may they reign.

What economists need to understand from historians but do not is in fact available to an empirical Austrian economics in the battle, as Boettke wisely puts it elsewhere, among "Smith, Schumpeter, and Stupidity."[44] He is referring to the liberalism of Smith yielding efficiency, the liberalism of the young Schumpeter yielding (a much more enriching) innovation, and the antiliberal mercantilism we still are tempted to adopt in protectionism and industrial policy, which yields neither. The correct, evidence-based history can be our guide. But an incorrect, just-so story history such as North retailed leads us astray in policy and in understanding the economy.

The central historical error in the North-Weingast argument of 1989 underlying the neoinstitutionalist explanation of the Great Enrichment (an argument which unhappily, I have said, Storr admires and Boettke swallows whole) is to think that it started in 1689.[45] The evidence is powerful, as I and others have shown, that it did not.[46] Yet people influenced by North who do not look seriously into the history themselves (as indeed the good North himself did not), such as Daron Acemoglu, go on and on saying "property, rules of the game, 1689, hey presto!"

The Northian story passed rapidly into conventional thinking in economics, as, for example, in an alarming article by Acemoglu in 2008 titled "Growth and Institutions" for *The New Palgrave Dictionary of Economics*:[47]

> Consider the development of property rights in Europe during the Middle Ages. Lack of property rights for landowners, merchants and proto-industrialists

No, as has been known by historians of medieval Europe for a hundred years. Property was very fully developed, especially in land and in personal possessions, even in backward England. For northern Italy, of course, the fact is obvious, and the evidence there of fully developed rights in all sorts of property including labor and capital is overwhelming. But a market even in land even in remote England functioned vigorously in large and small parcels. Exchange on secure terms took place there in all commodities and factors of production at the latest from the Normans and their lawyers—or, outside the king's court, in leet courts registering peasant deals in the thirteenth century—and in most respects hundreds of years earlier, as has been a commonplace among English medievalists since the 1950s at the latest. Edward Miller wrote in 1951 that "there was a very flourishing land market amongst the [southern English] peasantry ...

in the early 13th century."[48] One of the leading recent students of medieval English agriculture, Bruce Campbell, notes that "tenants of all
sorts were active participants in the market, trading in commodities,
buying and selling labor and land, and exchanging credit," citing some
of the numerous medievalists who agree.[49] That does not mean that everything worked smoothly. Campbell argues that the fourteenth century
before the Black Death was characterized in England by "rural conges-
tion engendered by the lax tenurial control exercised by most landlords."[50]
Overfishing. But anyway, Campbell's picture, based on the best scholarship
over many decades, is the opposite of the exploitation and the absence of
markets posited by Acemoglu. It is almost the case that the serfs owned
the lords, not the other way around. Such a conclusion is found in most
of the modern evidence-based literature on the peasantry in England, as
for example in the pioneering work on peasant records by Fr. Ambrose
Raftis.[51]

To continue with Acemoglu's just-so story,

> was detrimental to economic growth during this epoch.

No. Lack of property rights had little to do with poor medieval productivity.[52]
Listen to Raftis: in the medieval historiography developing since the 1940s
"customary tenure [that is, serfdom] becomes no longer a block to [English]
economic development but an instrument for such development.... Peasant
progress occurred despite the limitations of the manorial system."[53]

Yet Acemoglu says,

> Consequently, economic institutions during the Middle Ages provided little in-
> centive to invest in land, physical or human capital, or technology

No. Incentives of a strictly economic sort did not change between 1000 and
1800, not much. See Berman (2003) and again Raftis (1996): "The major
customary tenants [were] the most active economic agents" even in the
"purest type of manor."[54] (A good, rough test, indeed, of whether a student of the medieval English economy actually knows the terrain is to ask
whether or not she is familiar with the findings of Raftis. On this account see
Raftis's strictures on Robert Brenner.[55] Acemoglu and before him North do
not pass the test.)

Again,

> and failed to foster economic growth.

Economic growth did not occur. But—outside of Russia, and even there late—the absence was not because of a lack of property rights but because of a lack of massive innovation because of a lack of bourgeois dignity and liberty.
Yet again,

> These economic institutions also ensured that the monarchs controlled a large fraction of the economic resources in society,

No. Even in early modern times the percentage "controlled" by monarchs was small by modern or some ancient standards: think 5 percent of national income (again except in thoroughgoing tyrannies such as Romanov Russia or the Mughal Empire). Rents from royal estates, until sold off, would make the figure higher. But the estates yielded *rental* income, which is an affirmation rather than a violation (which any taxation represents) of the rights of private property. The *aristocracy* did "control" a large share of the land, though freeholders in Western Europe owned a great deal, too, and the serfs that Acemoglu thinks were part of the economic resources "controlled" by the "monarchs" were in fact largely independent—massively in England from 1348 on—and in their ability to sell their labor and buy their long-leased land, earlier. But again there was ordinary property and ordinary labor markets, contrary to the cargo cults initiated by Karl Polanyi (1944) and lately by North and followers.
Further,

> solidifying their political power and ensuring the continuation of the political regime. The seventeenth century, however, witnessed major changes in the economic institutions

No. The *economic* institutions, if by that one means property rights, or even taxation, did not change much in the seventeenth century in England by comparison with changes in other centuries. The great changes in property and especially contract law happened in the nineteenth century, not in 1689.
More:

> and political institutions

Finally a partial truth, but only in England and Scotland and a few other places such as Poland: not in "Europe" as he claims.

> that paved the way for the development of property rights

No. Property rights, I repeat (are you really listening?), were already developed, many centuries, or indeed millennia, earlier. Read the Bible, Hebrew or Christian, or the Holy Koran. Or consult with students of the ancient Near East on business practices as they can be discerned in cuneiform tablets in 2000 BCE.

And finally,

> and limits on monarchs' power.

A truth, but a Dutch and later a British and still later a Polish and a Swedish truth and having nothing to do with an allegedly novel security of property—for all the self-interested talk by the taxpaying gentry at the time, from John Hampden to Thomas Jefferson, against the modest taxation by the Stuarts and their heirs. The share of British government taxes in national income did not fall in the eighteenth century after the transcendent power of Parliament (in Maitland's phrase) had been established: it strikingly rose, to fight the French.[56]

Acemoglu in short has gotten the history embarrassingly wrong in every important detail, and his larger theme is wholly mistaken. In one paragraph he manages to retail ten or so childishly unscholarly just-so stories about the past. The stories dominate his thinking.

It is not his fault, however. The few economic historians he has consulted, especially North, told the history to him mistakenly since they, especially North, had not consulted the work of historians using primary sources and had not sufficiently doubted the tales told by nineteenth-century German Romantic historians and sociologists about ye olde tymes of the Middle Ages and about the allegedly modern rise of rationality.

The problem is, to say it yet again, that much of Europe—or for that matter much of China or India, not to speak of the Iroquois or the Khoisan, when it mattered—had credible commitments to secure property rights in the thirteenth century CE, and indeed in the thirteenth century BCE.[57] China, for example, has had secure property in land and in commercial goods for millennia. And in the centuries in which the neoinstitutionalists claim that Europe surged ahead in legal guarantees for property, the evidence is overwhelming that China and Japan had equally secure property. True, early in the short century of their rule, the Mongols (Yuan dynasty, 1279–1368), I have noted, were tempted to put in place such antieconomisms of bad property rights as prohibiting autumn planting—in order to give ample grazing for Mongol horses. But even the Mongols quickly realized that a prosperous and property-respecting China made for a more profitable cash cow. And under the Ming and Qing (1368–1911) property and contract laws were enforced on high and low, as they had been during most of recorded Chinese history. Merchants, for example, appear to have been more, not less, secure in recent centuries on the roads of the Chinese Empire, or the Tokugawa shogunate, than they were in a Western Christendom, plagued until the nineteenth century by pirates or by highwaymen riding up to the old inn door. Chaucer's merchant in 1387 "wished the sea were kept [free of pirates] for anything / Betwixt Middleburg [in Zeeland in the Netherlands] and Orwell [in Lincolnshire]," as the Chinese and the Japanese and the Arabs and Ottomans had already long kept their seas, though not without difficulty or indeed some government policies even more crazy than European mercantilism.[58] Instead of going after them with his superior ships, the Chinese emperor thwarted Japanese pirates by depopulating the seacoast. Thus the antieconomic policies of Ming emperors. The conservatism outside Europe at length contrasted their economies with the gradually liberalizing ones around the North Sea.

That Is, Neoinstitutionalism, Like the Rest of Behavioral Positivism, Fails as History and as Economics

Like the old Marxists, and the older Christians, the neoinstitutionalists among Samuelsonian economists want a theory that would have, if it were true, allowed them in 1700 to lay down the future. They want the story of the Great Enrichment—the utterly strange magnitude of which they of course acknowledge, being competent economists and economic historians—to be a story of institutions.

I've said this. By "institutions" the neoinstitutionalists do not mean what other social scientists mean by institutions, such as marriage or the market or for that matter language—which is to say the good or bad dance of human lives, full of human meanings and improvisations. As Mae West said, "I admire the institution of marriage. But I'm not ready for an institution." Norms are ethical persuasions, bendable, arguable, interpretable. Rules are, well, rules, such as that bribes are illegal in India, or that jaywalking is illegal in downtown Evanston. The rules of bribery in Sweden are probably the same as in India, and the jaywalking rules in Bremen, Lower Saxony, the same as in Evanston, Illinois. The difference is ethics.

The English novelist and essayist Tim Parks, who has taught at universities in Italy since 1981, notes that "it is extraordinary how regularly Italy creates . . . areas of uncertainty: How is the law [of, say, train travel with a valid ticket] to be applied?" The "culture of ambiguous rules" seems, "to serve the purpose of drawing you into a mindset of vendetta and resentment. . . . You become a member of [Italian] society insofar as you feel hard done by, . . . [playing in] a gaudy theatre of mimed tribal conflict." He gives the example of *il furbo*, the crafty one, who jumps the queue to buy a ticket at the train station in a way that would get him assaulted by grandmothers in Germany and by handgun licensees in the United States. The law-abiding Italians groan but do not act effectively to protect the public good of queues. They would rather be resentful, and therefore be justified in taking advantage at another time of their own acts of *furbismo*.[1]

Economists call ethics often by another name, *enforcement*. But the new word, with its whiff of third-party intervention somehow made legitimate, does not make it any less about the ethical convictions with which a group operates, Searle's "status functions," Storr's "meanings," Allen's "honor." "Norms" are one thing, "rules" are another. The neoinstitutionalists turn their arguments into mush by melding the two. They end up saying, I have noted, "Social change depends on society." One supposes so. "Informal constraints" are not informal if they are constraints, and if they are informal the theory has been reduced to a tautology, because any human action is now by definition brought under the label "institutions."

The neoinstitutionalists have nothing nontautological to say about ethics because they scorn the immense literature on ethics since 2000 BCE, including the literature of the humanities turning back to look at the rhetoric of language. Being economists, raised, as I have noted Michael Jensen was, for example, on the childish philosophy that separates positive and normative when most of our adult lives in social science are spent in their intersection, they are scornful of bringing ethics seriously into their history and their economics. As one of them said genially to me, "ethics, schmethics." He would reject the newest initiative in research on artificial intelligence, "value alignment," in which the machine reads human history and literature and politics to infer human values from behavior. (True, a quicker way might be to open up your copy of Shakespeare.)

The historian of the medieval English economy I have mentioned, James Davis, concludes on the contrary that "without a proper understanding of the morality and social conventions of the marketplace, the historian cannot understand the influence of formal institutions," such as the assize of bread or the rules of guilds. "In medieval England," Davis writes, a "pragmatic moral economy . . . was not a simple, efficient alignment of institutions and cultural beliefs, but rather a heady and complex mixture of vested interests, pragmatism and idealism that varied according to the prevailing circumstances," ranging from the pressures of the market to the preachments of the priest.[2] One reason that bankers in Florence financed the explosion of sacred art and architecture in the Quattrocento is that the priest was telling them they would go to hell for the sin of usury and that they had only this one chance to prevent it.

The political economists Guido Rossi and Salvatore Spagano have argued plausibly that evolved custom can work pretty well in contexts without the printing press but that black-letter law gives all parties public knowledge and leads to some efficiencies.[3] The argument is surely correct. And yet, as Rossi and Spagano would perhaps concede, it leaves a gigantic area in an economy for play or custom or ethics not capable of being written down. Yes, sometimes writing down the customs/ethics is a clarifying betterment in just the way Rossi and Spagano propose. A parallel point is an old and conservative one, arguing for the educational function of written law. But black letters, no more than black numbers, never come with their own interpretation.

The economists want to narrow the word *institution* to fit their conception that a dance can be reduced to formulaic steps, maximization under constraints, rigid rules of the game known to all, the constraints being the institutions. That is, economists want formulaic, public incentives to be the main story. One, two, three: ball change, brush, brush, side essence, riffle. True, parts of tap-dancing routines by Bill Robinson or Fred Astaire can be described after the fact by such a formula.[4] But without Robinson or Astaire it's rubbish. It don't mean a thing if it ain't got that swing.

I get the price theory: that people are moved by price and property, the variables of prudence, price, profit—or, as I have called Max U's motivations, the Profane.[5] But the point here is that people are also moved by the S variables of speech, stories, shame, the Sacred, and by the use of the monopoly of coercion by the state, the legal rules of the game and the dance in the courts of law, the L variables. Most behavior, B, is explained by P and S and L, together, metaphorically speaking:

$$B = \alpha + \beta P + \gamma S + \delta L + \varepsilon.$$

The equation is not wishy-washy or feminine or unprincipled or unscientific. The S and L variables are the conditions under which the P variables work, and the P variables modify the effects of the S and L variables. Of course.

For example, the conservative argument I just mentioned that laws serve as education would connect L causally to S by a separate equation. Or again, when the price the Hudson Bay Company offered First Nations in Canada for beaver pelts was high enough, the beaver population was depleted, in line with *P*-logic. But *S*-logic was crucial, too, making the *P*-logic relevant. As the economic historians Ann Carlos and Frank Lewis explain, "Indian custom regarding the right to hunt for food and other aspects of their 'Good Samaritan' principle mitigated against the emergence of strong trespass laws and property rights in fur-bearing animals; conflict in the areas around the Hudson Bay hinterland contributed to an environment that was not conducive to secure tenure, and attitudes towards generosity and even a belief in reincarnation may have played a role" in running against better *P*-logic rules that would have preserved the stock of beavers.[6] The institutionalist John Adams speaks of the market as an "instituted process," which is correct.[7] The institution is the *S*, the process of the *P*, the legal limits *L*. Or sometimes the other ways around. Anyway, often, all.

You can get as technical as you want about it. For example, econometrically speaking, if the *P* and *S* and *L* variables are not orthogonal, which is to say if they are not entirely independent—or alternatively if there is reason to believe that a combined variable such as *PS* has its own influence—then an estimate of the coefficients that ignore *S* (or *PS* or *PL*) will give biased results. The bias is important if the *S* variables are important. If laws adjust to markets, to give another example, then *L* is affected by *P*, and an attribution of an exogenous effect of *L* would be biased—as it has been, often. The example is important, considering the obvious endogeneity of many institutions. Consider the puzzle of lack of corporations in old Islamic law.

*   *   *

An economist's tale of increased efficiency, I have said, can't explain the Great Enrichment. For one thing, if the slight betterments of incentives that are imagined were so very efficacious, they would have been so on the many other occasions in which societies improved a bit, doubling per person real income, say, such as Song China or Imperial Rome. For another, if mere incentives were all that stood in the way of correct allocation, then a reallocation paying off one hundred to one, predictably, with given tastes and technologies, in Samuelsonian fashion—no Schumpeter or Hayek or Kirzner about it—would presumably have happened and even would have consciously occurred to someone in the previous millennia sometime, somewhere. Having a liberal revolution would have been a $100 bill lying on the floor of a $1- or $3- or $6-a-day society—as it does today, but it is ignored by elites clinging to power unless, as in India and China, they realize that economic liberty makes them rich too. The unique magnitude of the Great Enrichment tells against the economist's reliance on routine incentives. Surely what had to be the cause was something highly peculiar (for a while) to northwestern Europe, not a reallocation of the old things prevalent in most civilizations such as literacy, private property, rule of law, cheap exchange, and predictable investment.

Postulate in charity, though, the partial failure of incentives—as neoinstitutional theories based solely on a *P*-logic do. It is, I repeat, high charity to do so: virtues other than prudence matter too. Ideology, rhetoric, a public sphere, public opinion, all mattered greatly. The Scientific Revolution was largely a matter of such nonprudential forces, though it did not amount to much economically until much later. As the Catholic economist Stefano Zamagni puts it, "Modern economic development did not occur due to the adoption of stronger incentives or better institutional arrangements, but mainly because of the creation of a new culture."[8] Or as the Indian businessman and public intellectual Gurcharan Das puts it, "Social scientists [under the influence of Max U thinking among economists] think of governance failures as a problem of institutions, and the solution they say, lies in changing the structure of incentives to enhance accountability. True, but these failings also have a moral dimension."[9] It is no surprise that an Italian and an Indian make such an anti-institutional point from countries as corrupt as the United States was in the nineteenth century and as Illinois and Louisiana still are. They have seen the miserable failure of fresh institutions, such as the Italian insertion of a level of government between the national and the commune or the Indian regulation before 1991 of every detail of economic life.

Bettering institutions of government do not explain the bulk of modern levels of income even if they do explain the most depressing local failures to achieve them in Oahcha, Mexico, and in Zwa Zulu Natal, South Africa. New Zealand, for example, is honestly and efficiently governed. Italy is not. In ease of doing business, New Zealand ranked in 2010 and 2012 (among 183 and 185 countries) third from the top. Italy in 2010 ranked eightieth, slightly below Vietnam, and seventy-third in 2012, slightly below the Kyrgyz Republic. In 2012, according to the Corruption Perception Index of Transparency International, among 173 ranked countries New Zealand was tied for first, the most honestly governed. Italy was seventy-second.[10] In 2009 in the Economic Freedom Rankings, New Zealand ranked first in its legal system and fifth from the top in its freedom from regulation. Italy in its legal system ranked sixty-third, just above Iran, and ninety-fourth in its freedom from regulation, just above the Dominican Republic.[11] Italy, as any sentient Italian can tell you, has terrible public institutions.

Yet in real GDP per person, New Zealand and Italy in 2010 were nearly identical, at $88.20 and $86.80 a day, a little above what Hans Rosling called the Washing Line, the point at which people start buying washing machines. It is not efficiency as economists think of it that is the best of the good news of the Great Enrichment, but utterly novel betterments causing the marginal product of the labor curve to zoom out, such as zippers, asphalt-paved roads, cheap screws and bolts, cardboard boxes, sewer traps in plumbing, screens on open windows, widespread secondary schools, computers and the internet—the sort of betterments that can be adopted even by a terribly governed economy, such as Italy's, with satisfactory results.

* * *

Liberty and dignity are not easy to achieve. They require accepting commercial profit, rejecting tribal protectionism, resisting the temptations of a reasonable sounding "planning" or "regulation," and embracing an ideology of equality for women and the poor and low-status castes that traditional societies and even some modern societies fiercely resist. As French economists reported about slow growth in Madagascar, "although the Malagasy people lay claim to democratic principles, they remain torn between the demands of democratic and meritocratic nature and the traditional values that impose respect for the real and symbolic hierarchies they have inherited from the past."[12] The miracle is that France itself, or for that matter honors-drenched Britain, both heavily regulated, are not instances. Another case is the contrast between the governance of Russia and China, the one with a millennium-long history of an inherited aristocracy and the other with a millennium-long history of exam-selected bureaucracy. Little wonder that the hierarchy in Russia, whether the Communist Party or the Putin oligarchs, is inherited, and the Communist Party of China is a meritocracy, with corresponding economic results.

In any case it won't suffice to set up British-like courts of law, say, and even provide the barristers with wigs, if the judges are venal and the barristers have no professional pride and the public disdains the entire system of justice. The introduction of such an institution will of course fail to improve the rule of law. It may worsen it. Daron Acemoglu and James Robinson report on an attempt to curb absenteeism among hospital nurses in India by introducing the institution of time clocks.[13] The economists in charge of the experiment were sure that the bare incentives of the "right institutions" would work. They didn't. The nurses conspired with their bosses in the hospitals to continue not showing up for work. Acemoglu and Robinson draw the moral that "the institutional structure that creates market failures" is what went wrong. No. The continuing absenteeism was not about institutions or incentives or market failures. New institutions with the right, unfailing incentives had been confidently applied by the economists out of the tool kit of World Bank orthodoxy and went wrong. The wrongness was rather about a lack of an ethic of self-respecting professionalism among many of the nurses of a sort that, say, most Filipino nurses do have, which is why they are in demand worldwide. The time-clock experiment imagined P-only when humans are also motived by S.

Acemoglu and Robinson do not see that what failed was the P-only, Max U theory of add-institutions-and-stir. "The root cause of the problem," they conclude, was "extractive institutions." On the contrary, the root cause was ethical failure in the presence of which no set of instituted incentives will work well and under which extraction will persist and grow. The institutions—the time clocks and the management practices—and the incentives they are supposed to provide—as though to the rats in the maze—were not the problem. The problem was defects in the ethics and in the impartial spectator and in the professionalism of many of the nurses and their bosses.

The economist Douglas Coate shows in a paper on the swift recovery of San Francisco from the earthquake of 1906 that the existing (and corrupt) political institutions of the city were shoved aside. The army, stationed at the Presidio, and a committee of business and civic leaders took charge— which was, as was the army's seventy-three-day-long patrolling of the ruined city, Coate observes, "extralegal." Yet he quotes with approval in his conclusion a remark by the fine if orthodox economist Jack Hirshleifer (1925–2005): "Historical experience suggests that recovery [from a disaster] will hinge upon the ability of government to maintain or restore property rights together with a market system that will support the economic division of labor."[14] No again. It was the ethics, and the ethos, of the army and the committee and nothing like "the ability of [legitimate] government" that saved the city, just as in 2005 it was profit-making companies such as Walmart and Home Depot springing into action, not any level of government, that partially saved New Orleans during and after Katrina.[15]

In both cases, if existing formal institutions had been relied on the result would have been further malfeasance by the institutions—such as in the malfeasance of the police department and the office of Mayor Ray Nagin in New Orleans.

The ur-neoinstitutionalist Oliver Williamson, in his reflections on governmental bureaucracies—"public agency"—calls ethics "probity," that is, "the loyalty and rectitude with which the . . . transaction is discharged."[16] Like all proper Samuelsonian economists, Williamson wants to reduce ethics to incentives: "probity concerns will be relieved by governance structures to which reliable responsiveness can be ascribed." By this he means incentives that work to make it unnecessary for anyone actually to have probity. He claims that "probity concerns" only arise in "extreme instances." "Breach against probity is better described as inexcusable incompetence or even betrayal. In the limit, such breach is punishable as treason."[17] His is a common error in recent thinking about ethics in supposing that ethics is only about grand issues ("extreme") such as murder or abortion or outright fraudulence in accounting, *House of Cards* instances, one might say. But ethics is also about daily good will and professionalism, such as an accountant doing as well as she can, or a professor trying to tell the truth.

Williamson claims repeatedly, as economists do when adhering to the dogma of *de gustibus non est disputandum*, that ethical change happens only very slowly. I have noted how widespread such a lemma is in neoinstitutionalism. But there is no historical or experimental evidence for such a claim. Sometimes ethics—as I have said, a matter of S and parts of L—changes quickly. Sometimes it does not. You have to find out. The ethics of the Roman state in the late first century BCE did not change from republican to imperial slowly. The ethics of a good deal of western Christianity in the early sixteenth century did not change slowly from a relaxed regime of indulgences to a rigorous Protestantism of congregational shaming. It changed in many places in months.

And most to the point here, the British ethics about markets and innovation in the late eighteenth century did not change from contempt to admiration slowly. In fact ethics (understood not as individual ethics alone but also what is honored or dishonored by the society) is what changed in the eighteenth century rapidly, not the institutional environment. A time traveler from England in 1630 or Britain from 1730 would not have been astonished by the institutional arrangements of the United Kingdom in 1830 except for the shift to the transcendent power of a (thoroughly corrupt) Parliament and the weakening of the (thoroughly corrupt) king. The law courts worked as they had ("This is the Court of Chancery," Dickens intoned). Property rights had not changed. Criminal law in 1830 was still fiercely slanted against the poor. Institutions, such as corporate law, changed *after* the ethical change, not before.

Ideological change brings a new impartial spectator into the habits of the heart and lip. Institutions are frosting on the cake if they lack ethical backing, from the Chicago bus driver taking professional responsibility for the lives of the sixty people under his care to the Iowa politician resisting the well-placed bribe offered by the highway construction firm. New egalitarian ideas in Europe—according to which bus drivers and politicians, professors and housewives, felt themselves equally responsible—broke the cake of custom. Surprisingly, the idea of treating people as liberated and honorable made us all in Britain and Japan and the United States by historical standards immensely wealthy—that zooming out of the marginal product of labor.

CHAPTER NINE

As It Fails in Logic and in Philosophy

The neoinstitutionalist economists have not really taken on the idea that ideas can matter, independently (sometimes) of incentives. They say they have taken it on and become cross when some idiot claims they do not. But then they keep falling back into simplified arguments that say that Institutions (let us symbolize them by N, since the other term, *Ideas*, also starts with an I) suffice for growth (G)

$$N \rightarrow G$$

That is, (good) Institutions imply (positive) Growth. The neoinstitutionalists in their actual scientific practice are denying what can be shown to be true on the basis of masses of positivist, behaviorist, and Samuelsonian evidence but also on the basis of the humanistic evidence of plays, novels, philosophy, biography, and ordinary human experience, namely, that (remember: N is iNstitutions, I is Ideas)

$$N \text{ and } I \text{ and } f(N, I) \rightarrow G.$$

The ideas, I, are to be thought of as sound, pretty favorable ethical ideas about bourgeois and then working-class people acting in voluntary trades and trying out betterments such as the steam engine or, as Huck Finn put it, lighting out for the territories. Likewise, the Institutions, N, are to be thought of as not perfect but pretty good incentives, such as permission to invent mail-order retailing or to light out for the Oregon Territory. It includes as well the interests (also an n in its second letter) that drive rational-choice neoinstitutionalism such as that of Acemoglu and Robinson. The function $f(N, I)$ acknowledges that ideas and institutions (and interests) interact. For example, as Mark McAdam of the University of Siegen puts it, "Interests are thus not separate entities, but ideas shape the way we think about our interests."[1] Similarly, because of an embarrassment beyond material interest and anyway because of an interestless devotion to their truth, the opening lines of the Declaration of Independence placed a steady pressure on American institutions to fulfill the promise of actual equality of permissions. The institutions of Chinese censorship under Xi suppress the idea that Hong Kong might be a good model for the nation. And so it is all over the life of a speaking species. In the present case, what actually changed in the eighteenth century in Britain was I—ideas, not mainly N, institutions. Defective neoinstitutionalist histories to the contrary, such as North and Barry Weingast's classic article of 1989, N didn't change in Britain very much until late in the story, after the Reform Bill of 1832 and especially during Lloyd George's term of Chancellor of the Exchequer 1908–1915, well after the Great Enrichment, G, was under way.[2]

The neoinstitutionalists want human action to be reducible to material incentives stripped of ideas or ideology. "We emphasize," write Acemoglu and Robinson (2019), with a certain pride of method, "that the impact of various structural factors, such as economic conditions, demographic shocks, and war, on the development of the state and the economy depend on the prevailing balance between state and society"(30). And again, on page 31, they "identify the structural factors making this type of zero-sum competition more likely. . . . We emphasize several important structural factors." When they turn to causes, material "structure" and game theory rule. Not ideas. They see humans as rats in a structural maze or a narrow corridor. Students even of animal behavior are slowly extracting themselves from the Cartesian/behaviorist dogma that an animal is a machine. They have discovered that animals sometimes act without incentives, which is the distinctive character of the "human action" emphasized in Austrian economics. It is like you and me or any scientist of integrity, such as Acemoglu and Robinson.

If one believes the simple neoinstitutionalism of North and Acemoglu and others that, near enough, $N \rightarrow G$, then it follows in strict logic that not-$G \rightarrow$ not-N. The hunt is on for institutions N that failed and that kept nations failing, resulting in a sad not-G, as in Acemoglu and Robinson's book of 2012, *Why Nations Fail*. But if one believes that N and I and f(N, I)$\rightarrow G$, then it follows in equally strict logic that not-$G \rightarrow$ either not-N (bad institutions) or not-I (bad ideas) or bad consequences of f(N, I), or all of them.[3] (This elementary point in logic has been known in the philosophy of science since 1914, I note again, as Duhem's Dilemma; it disposes in a line of symbolic logic the Samuelsonian/Friedmanite falsificationism underlying econometrics and much of the other rhetoric of economic science.) If N and I and $f(N, I) \rightarrow G$, the hunt is on for *either* bad institutions *or* bad ideas *or* bad interactions between the two with no presumption that hunting for the bad-idea or the bad-interaction possibility is somehow less of a scientific priority.

I recognize the impulse to stick with the Max U version of institutions as the first on the agenda, since I used to say the same thing to conventional, nonecomonist historians such as David Landes: "First, David, let's use measures of total factor productivity. Then, if there's anything left over, we can look into the archives of the correspondence in the late nineteenth century of British ironmasters." I never intended to look at the archives and did not in fact do so, to my shame. Samuelsonian economics, I thought, sufficed. So here. (To the claim that Northian institutionalism steps *beyond* Samuelsonian economics, I say again, as I said to the good Douglass for thirty years without noticeable effect, no: neoinstitutionalism is Samuelsonian economics in drag.)

Consider, for example, an institution that undoubtedly did encourage growth, a large free-trade area, in which local vested interests could not block betterment. A typical product of early liberalism was to divest the local interests, for example the fiercely protectionist cities of medieval times, or the expansion to national protectionism in early modern times. The large free-trade area was expressed in black-letter law in the American Constitution, though requiring later ideational defenses (I interacting with another I) by Supreme Court justices (N). In practice in a Britain with a liberal I, it was prevalent as a *not-N* $= f(I)$ without a written constitution. Customs unions like the Zollverein or the Austro-Hungarian Empire were other examples. So was the Chinese Empire. In other places, by contrast, local monopolies unchallenged by wide competition surely did discourage growth, which is to say that not-$N \rightarrow$ not-G, from which one might want to deduce that $G \rightarrow N$, that is, that if there was growth there must have been the institution in place of a large free-trade area.

But the trouble is that even with a large free-trade area in black-letter law, the irritating competition from across the mountains or the seas might inspire people to petition the state for protection. Stop the unjust dominance from across the mountains or the seas. In fact, it does, and the larger the Leviathan the more private profit is to be gained by corrupting the state to get the protection. Look at K Street in Washington. In the individual states of the United States, for example, widespread state licensure laws for professions (tightening in recent decades) and the state prohibition of branch banking (though loosening in recent decades) have such a source. Without a strong ethical conviction in a liberal *I*, such as spread in the United Kingdom during the early nineteenth century, that such petitioning is shameful (Mill put it: "society admits no right"), though less so in the United States, the black letters will be dead letters. not-*I* → not-*G*. Ideas matter, ideology matters, ethics matter, in themselves and in their interactions with institutions.

*   *   *

The American columnist and political theorist George Will is good on this. He argues that "the Founders intended the Constitution to promote a way of life."[4] Will's term for the way government shapes the ethics of its citizens for good or ill is *soulcraft*. Soulcraft "is something government cannot help but do. It may not be done competently or even consciously, but it is not optional."[5] He is of course correct. By this route surely institutions "matter," and some of them are governmentally "crafted" (if that is the right word for what is done, Will concedes, often unconsciously and incompetently). The commercial values that the Constitution purposed did help create a new people in a new republic, if we can keep it.

In particular, from 1789 to 1865 some of the people acknowledged in the Constitution were slaves, and slavery among some other state-supported institutions mattered mightily as soulcraft, and not for good. Will quotes Tocqueville on the contrast in 1831 between the two banks of the Ohio River, slave Kentucky and free Ohio. On the Kentucky bank, Tocqueville wrote, "society is asleep; man seems idle," because the peculiar institution had made physical labor undignified for whites. On the Ohio bank, by contrast, "one would seek in vain for an idle man."[6] Will concludes that the two institutions, slave and free, "result in radically different kinds of people."[7] Hermann Gilomee comes to the same conclusion about the effect on the white Afrikaners of having Blacks enslaved. And even after emancipation the Blacks and Coloureds were anyway subordinated to an Afrikaner up on a horse. After the Boer War the Afrikaner leaders such as Jan Smuts took the Afrikaners in hand, giving them educations and jobs on the railways—and taking away the same from the Coloureds and Blacks.[8]

So of course "institutions matter." As an intermediate cause, the institutionalization of the idea of an entirely new liberalism in northwestern Europe and its offshoots after 1776, for example, mattered mightily for the explosion of creativity in the economy and polity and society after 1800. But observe in this example and Gilomee's example and Will's example the deep ideational causes of the very institutions (for instance in the US case, as the conflicted slave owner wrote of the idea that all men are created equal) and subsequently the ideational route of the mattering. An institution was in each case an intermediate cause inspired by ideas and having many of their effects by way of minds. It was largely not a physical matter but a mental matter, not chiefly the soil but the soul, not only the incentives but the ethics, *les moeurs, die Geiste*, the ideologies of elites and then of ordinary people. As Lincoln declared in the first Lincoln-Douglas debate in 1858, it came to the point where, for governing as for marketing, "With public sentiment, nothing can fail; without it nothing can succeed. Consequently he who molds public sentiment goes deeper than he who enacts statutes or pronounces decisions. He makes statutes and decisions possible or impossible to be executed."[9]

Thirty pages before the end of their 2019 book, by way of a *refutatio*, Acemoglu and Robinson quote Hayek at length, writing in 1956:

> The most important change which extensive government control produces is a psychological change, an alteration in the character of the people. This is necessarily a slow affair, a process which extends not over a few years but perhaps over one or two generations. The important point is that the political ideals of the people and its attitude toward authority are as much the effect as the cause of the political institutions under which it lives. This means, among other things, that even a strong tradition of political liberty is no safeguard if the danger is precisely that new institutions and policies will gradually undermine and destroy that spirit. (quoted in Acemoglu and Robinson 2019, 466)

Acemoglu and Robinson believe they are responding to Hayek's point by then claiming that anyway "society" can offset the Leviathan. But Hayek's point is that you make people into children if you treat them like the children of a feared or revered Papa or Mama Leviathan. Recent meanders in American politics are not reassuring that we can avoid the internal, psychological road to serfdom. The Leviathan, Acemoglu and Robinson hope, "is shackled by people who will complain, demonstrate, and even rise up if it oversteps its bounds" (27). But complaints, demonstrations, and uprisings are precisely about spirit and ethics and rhetoric. Consider January 6, 2021, in the halls of the US Congress, or January 23 in one hundred Russian cities. The rising up contradicts the structural materialism of Acemoglu and Robinson. When at one point they admit the insufficiency of a materialist account, they evoke "the *desire* to avoid the *fear*some face of the Leviathan" (53, emphasis added). But people fear it in their mind, not in their big toe. Then they desire to avoid it and are moved by ideas to move their mouths and toes with purpose. Unlike the Chinese woman I heard in December 2020 on the BBC, such revolutionaries are *not* persuaded by the idea that order trumps liberty every time. The woman *scorned* the silly Western stupid talk of so-called liberty. Individuals in her thinking *must* be subordinated to the *volonté generae*, and the general will is to be discerned by the Communist Party of China. Such institutions and policies, as Hayek said, will gradually undermine and destroy the spirit and idea of liberty, and turn people into dependent children, like the woman on the BBC. Another word for liberalism is *adultism*, and in this it contrasts with the infantile dependence on the state that Acemoglu and Robinson find themselves advocating.

To put it another way, what Acemoglu and Robinson and the other neoinstitutionalists ignore is the human mind and its liberated creations. The mind, I have noted, is more than a brain. The mind, quoth Andrew Marvell in the late seventeenth century, is "that ocean where each kind / Does straight its own resemblance find, / Yet it creates, transcending these, / Far other worlds, and other seas; / Annihilating all that's made / To a green thought in a green shade."[10] The onset of economic growth after 1800, I have argued, depended not on law and institutions, which were anciently routine and often obstructive, but on green thoughts about liberty surpassing these.[11] Creativity and the supports for it in liberty and liberal ethics explains why we are 3,000 percent better off materially, and not so very badly off spiritually, than our ancestors. Accumulation in all its mechanical forms, such as physical or human capital, and "structures" in all their mechanical forms, such as black-letter law and supreme courts, depend for their fruit on creativity supported by ideology and ethics.

You can see that ignoring the mind—as the neoinstitutionalists and for that matter most economists since Ricardo insist on doing (though not our blessed founder, Smith)—might be a fault in *une science humaine*. Admittedly, the tactic of voluntary ignorance has been a commonplace, if usually unconsciously adopted. Some of my own early writings on entrepreneurship, for example, adopted the tactic.[12] So, too, with rather more consequence, do the sciences of humanity that identify the mind with the brain. Brain science of this sort is as though close study of the physiology of Sandy Koufax's arm would give a sufficient account of his baseball pitching in 1966.

*　　*　　*

It is not reasonable to reply that North and Greif and Acemoglu and Robinson and the rest *do* admit the force of ideas in their neoinstitutionalist stories. In his *Understanding the Process of Economic Change* (2005), for example, North said repeatedly that he was interested in the source of ideas. Good on Doug. But he didn't enter the humanistic conversation since Mesopotamian cuneiform on clay and Chinese scratches on bones, which has largely been about ideas. The humanistic turns of Greek rhetoric and Chinese philosophy and Jewish Talmud were studies of the sources of the ideas. Instead, North deferred to the "brain sciences"(about which it must be said he knew next to nothing). That is, he reduced ideas to matter, brain stuff, and to the mechanical incentives surrounding matter, every time. He took the brain to be the same thing as the mind, which as I and many others have observed is the central error in the phrenological branch of the brain sciences nowadays.

The less dogmatic of the neoinstitutionalists, such as Joel Mokyr and John Nye, seem on odd days of the month to believe in the North-Acemoglu prejudgment that $N \rightarrow G$. No ideas present. On even days the lesser dogmatists call ideas, I, "culture," which is the vague way people talk when they have not taken on board the exact and gigantic literature about ideas, rhetoric, linguistics, ideology, ceremonies, metaphors, stories, and the like since the Greeks or the Confucians or the Talmudists or the Sanskrit grammarians.

Ideas, I, might have had the merely static effects I deprecated earlier. But the economic point is that ideas are intrinsically subject to economies of scale ("ideas having sex," says Matt Ridley) and that institutions are often as not deeply conservative.[13] The big change in ideas in Britain was dynamic in the technical sense. The small change in institutions was not.

Consider what can be learned from the actual humanities and the actual brain sciences, the serious study of I, tending even to a dynamic conclusion. Raymond Tallis, himself a distinguished neuroscientist, reviewed favorably *Who's in Charge? Free Will and the Science of the Brain*, by Michael S. Gazzaniga, whom he describes as "a towering figure in contemporary neurobiology." Tallis writes, sprinkling in phrases from Gazzaniga, "Crucially, the true locus of this activity is not in the isolated brain" but "in the group interactions of many brains," which is why "analyzing single brains in isolation cannot illuminate the capacity of responsibility [consider the contrast with the procedures in behavioral economics and some experimental economics]. This, the community of minds, is where our human consciousness is to be found, woven out of the innumerable interactions that our brains make possible." It is what Smith said in *The Theory of Moral Sentiments* in 1759, or what John Donne said in *Devotions upon Emergent Occasions* xvii in 1624. "Responsibility" (or lack of it), Mr. Gazzaniga says, "is not located in the brain." It is "an interaction between people, a social contract—an emergent phenomenon, irreducible to brain activity." To use the old humanistic joke, the language speaks us as much as we speak the language.

The American historian Thomas Haskell wrote in 1999 a startling essay chronicling the new prominence of the word *responsibility* in a commercial America in the eighteenth and nineteenth centuries. The *Oxford English Dictionary* gives 1787 as the earliest quotation of *responsibility* in its modern sense, as accepting ethically that one has done such and such, good or bad—used by Hamilton in *The Federalist Papers* and shortly thereafter by Edmund Burke. Haskell notes that it was used much earlier in law in the sense merely of being required to respond to a legal action. Such a "responsible" person, meaning "liable to be called to [legal] account" (sense 3a), occurs as early as 1643. The *OED's* first quotation for the favorable ethical meaning of the adjectival form, the dominant modern sense, "morally *accountable* for one's actions; capable of rational conduct" (sense 3b, emphasis added), is as late as 1836—which is Haskell's precise point. The linking of "responsibility" with the market-like word *accountability* occurs in the very first and much earlier instance of *accountability* detected by Haskell in 1794 in Samuel Williams's *Natural and Civil History of Vermont*: "No mutual checks and balances, accountability and responsibility" (the older noun is *accountableness*, dating from 1668; the adjective *accountable*, 1583; and simple *account* and *accompt* are medieval).

Haskell is wary of praising the new dignity for market participants: "my assumption is not that the market elevates morality." I suppose he is squeamish about contradicting the leftish lean of most US departments of history. But then he takes it back: "the form of life fostered by the market may entail the heightened sense of agency."[14] Just so. Surely commerce, with a Reformation that in some circles flattened church governance, increased the sense of individual and responsible agency. Earlier in the essay Haskell had attributed to markets the "escalating" sense of agency, "responsibility." So the market did elevate morality. This much we can learn from humanistic historians studying the very words.

To return to what can be learned from actual brain scientists. Tallis concludes, in his own eloquent words (he is a published poet, too), "we belong to a boundless, infinitely elaborated community of minds that has been forged out of a trillion cognitive handshakes over hundreds of thousands of years. This community is the theater of our daily existence. It separates life in the jungle from life in the office, and because it is a community of minds, it cannot be inspected by looking at the activity of the solitary brain." Human agreement or acceptance, what Michael Oakeshott called the conversation of humankind, is precisely the conjective, as against the subjective.

The Jewish theologian Martin Buber wrote in 1923, "All real living is relation" and "in the beginning is relation," that is, not the solipsism beloved of the dogmatic methodological individualist.[15] "The fundamental fact of human existence," Buber wrote in 1948 in *Between Man and Man*, "is neither the individual as such nor the aggregate as such, but 'man with man.' "[16] It is neither subjective nor objective ("Objective truth is not granted to mortals," said Buber at the treason trial of Aharon Cohen in 1958, not perhaps the best thing to have said under the circumstances). The conjective, the "between" in Buberian talk, is what we know in speech and meetings and dialogue, one human with another.

If the science of economics, as the economists Nona Martin and our Virgil Storr argued, needs meaning, it needs, deontically, not merely rules of the game or brain science but the humanities all the way up to the Department of English.[17] In short, let's get serious about "brain science" by admitting that it is not the same as "mind science," and let's acknowledge that the humanities, and the higher culture generally, can shed mind light on institutions.

*   *   *

Another example. North spoke highly of the anthropologist Clifford Geertz (1926–2006). It is hard not to. But North reads Geertz and his co-authors as supporting an economistic notion that in caravan trade, such as in Morocco around 1900, in North's formulation, "informal constraints [on, say, robbing the next caravan to pass by] . . . made trade possible in a world where protection was essential and no organized state existed."[18] North misses the noninstrumental, shame-and-honor, non–Max U language in which Geertz in fact specialized, and he misses, therefore, the dance between internal motives and external impediments to action, between the dignity of a self-shaping citizen-not-a-slave and the merely utilitarian "constraints" of a man-rat facing incentives. The toll for safe passage in the deserts of Morocco, Geertz and his coauthors actually wrote, in explicit rejection of Max U, was "rather more than a mere payment," not, that is, a mere monetary constraint, a budget line, a fence, an incentive, an "institution" in the reduced definition of Samuelsonian economics. "It was part of a whole complex," the anthropologists actually wrote, "of *moral rituals*, customs with the force of law and the weight of *sanctity*."[19]

"Sanctity" doesn't mean anything to North the economist and reformed Marxist, who, for example, in his 2005 book treats religion with an unlettered contempt worthy of Richard Dawkins or Christopher Hitchens ("Ditchkins," says Terry Eagleton 2006). Religion to North means just another "institution" in his utilitarian, subject-to-constraints sense, that is, rules for an asylum. He labels religion repeatedly as "non-rational." Religion to him is not about sanctity or the transcendent, not about faithful identity, not about giving lives a meaning through moral rituals. It is certainly not an ongoing intellectual and rational conversation about God's love, not to speak of an ongoing conversation *with* God. Religion is just another set of constraints on doing business, whether the business is in the market or in the temple or in the desert. In this North agrees with the astonishing economist Laurence Iannaccone and his followers when they come to study religion.[20] (Iannaccone, like me, is in fact a believer, but I am speaking of his Beckerian theory, not his personal religious practice; in his latest writings, though, Iannaccone is unifying the two.) Religion to the conventional Iannaccone school is a social club with costs and benefits, not an identity or a conversation. (Anyone who has actually belonged to a social club, of course, knows that it soon develops into "moral rituals, customs with the force of law and the weight of sanctity." I could instance as such a club the Chicago School of economics during its salad days in the 1970s. One of our sanctified rituals was to repeat *de gustibus non est disputandum* while passionately advocating a very particular intellectual *gustus*.) North asserts, for example, that in a prelegal stage, "religious precepts . . . imposed standards of conduct on the [business] players."[21] He spurns the worldview that goes with religious faith. His own religion of science, of course, is in fact nothing like a mere constraint. He construes it as his identity, his moral ritual, his sanctity—in short, the meaning of his life, negotiated continuously over its extraordinary course. But ethical consistency is not a strong point of Samuelsonian economics.

Avner Greif, North's ally in neoinstitutionalism, calls culture "informal institutions," and North tried to talk this way as well.[22] Greif takes every social equilibrium to amount to an informal institution, which would, I have noted repeatedly, make all social science by definition into a case of neoinstitutionalism. The informality, however, makes such "institutions" quite different from asylum-type rules of the game. One does not negotiate the rules of chess while playing it. But informality *is* indeed continuously negotiated—that is what the word *informality* means, precisely the degree of setting aside forms that distinguishes a backyard barbecue from a state dinner. How to behave at the barbecue? (Hint: do not jump naked into the bushes.) Just how far can a man go in teasing his mates? Just how intimate can a woman be with her girlfriends? The rules are constructed and reconstructed on the spot and on the fly, depending on ethos and ethics and love, which in such cases makes the Samuelsonian metaphor of constraints highly inapt.

One does not have to deny that ethos, ethics, and love are often influenced by incentives to believe that once they become part of a person's identity they have an effect independent of the very incentives. Once a woman is corrupted by life in a communist country, for example, it is hard to reset her economic ethics. She goes on relying on the "bureau" model of human interaction as against the market. Once the untouchables in India a century before independence converted to Christianity in order to get Max U advantages from the British Raj, it became part of their identity. Their descendants now fiercely defend their identity as Christians in the new circumstances, in which it is very much *not* an advantage. Likewise once you are educated in Samuelsonian economics it is hard to reset your intellectual life. You go on thinking of every social situation in terms of Max U's mechanical reaction instead of a socially constructed dance, or the Austrian term "human action" of a free will.[23] The Geertzian metaphor of negotiation and ritual often makes more sense. Yeats said it in "Among School Children": "O body swayed to music, o brightening glance, / How can we know the dancer from the dance?"

North, like numerous other economists such as Steve Levitt of freakonomics who have settled into the positivist straightjacket, talked a good deal about meaning-free incentives because that is what Samuelsonian economics can deal with. The constraints. The budget lines. The relative price. One can agree that when the price of crime goes up (i.e., the incentives change in the direction of, say, harsher punishment), less of it will be supplied (well . . . unless overpolicing erodes Black faith in the police). Yet one can also affirm that crime is more than a passionless business proposition. If you don't believe it, tune into one of the numerous prison reality shows and watch an inmate struggling with the guards with his own mad purpose, though with quasi-prudent means. Or listen to Ishmael about Captain Ahab: "in his heart, Ahab had some glimpse of this, namely: all my means are sane, my motive and my object mad."[24] If crime is more than utterly passionless calculations by Max U, then changing the ethics of criminals and their acquaintances can affect it—ethics that do change, sometimes quickly. During a big war, for example, crime rates fall on the home front. The metaphors of crime as being like employment as a taxi driver or of a marriage as being like a trade between husband and wife or of children being like consumer durables such as refrigerators have been useful. Neat stuff. But they don't do the whole job. Sometimes they are disastrously misleading, as when economists provided ammunition for conservative politicians in the 1990s for increasing punishments for crimes such as the horrible crimes of sitting peacefully smoking a joint or snorting cocaine.

Meaning, as Virgil Storr and I and other exponents of humanomics say, matters. A cyclist in Chicago writing to the newspaper in 2008 about a fellow cyclist killed when he ran a red light declared that "when the traffic light changes color, the streets of our cities become an every-man-for-himself, anything-goes killing zone, where anyone who dares enter will be caught in a stream of intentionally more-deadly, high-mass projectiles, controlled by operators who are given a license to kill when the light turns green."[25] The motorist who unintentionally hit the cyclist probably offered a different meaning to the event. A good deal of life and politics and exchange takes place in the ignoring of incentives and the assertion of meaning—the mother's love or the politician's integrity or the economist's enthusiasm, what Keynes called animal spirits and what Sen calls commitment (and after him what I call virtues and corresponding vices other than Prudence Only).

To humans, though not to rats and grass and other Max U beings, meaning matters, metaphors matter, stories matter, identity matters, ethics matter, talk matters, free will matters, the dance matters. Considering that we are humans, not grass, they matter a good deal. Let's measure them.

CHAPTER TEN

Neoinstitutionalism, in Short, Is Not a Scientific Success

The political scientist Barry Weingast wrote in 2016 a characteristically amiable and generous comment on a paper by me published in the *Scandinavian Economic History Review* and about the book that lay behind it, *Bourgeois Equality*. It is good that Weingast and I have one agreement, an important one, namely, that a new liberalism in northwestern Europe around 1800 mattered, and that it has been much neglected as an influence on the Great Enrichment that followed. "The importance of liberty and equality," he writes, "is woefully underappreciated in the literature."[1] Good. To that extent Weingast agrees with humanomics—which is, I say again, an economics in which the shifting ideas and rhetoric of humans have material consequences. The socialist prime minister in Sweden, Olof Palme, declared that "the political winds are from the left: let us set sail," and his sailing had consequences. Humanomics says that material incentives are not the sole cause of human action. "Liberty and equality are essential necessary components of an explanation for the Great Enrichment," Weingast writes.[2] Good again. And, further, "Students of development and the Great Enrichment have failed to see the critical role of these ideas."[3] I am delighted that he agrees with me to this extent, and repeatedly, and most amiably.

Yet I disagree with him on most of the rest of the what he says. Perhaps I am mistaken: he can set me straight if I am. If we are to make scientific progress in thinking about how we became so very rich—Sweden, the once-impoverished sophisticate, as Lars Sandburg put it, going from about $2 a day in 1800 per person in present-day prices to about $110 now, a factor of over fifty, we are going to need to listen, really listen to our friends' questions and objections.[4]

Weingast writes that "McCloskey begins by listing previous hypotheses that she believes are not the underlying cause. . . . The list is long: the industrial revolution, . . . technological change."[5] Yet my books, such as the present one, say over and over and over again (to the point I fear of tedium: I apologize) that the tsunami of human creativity called the Great Enrichment *was* caused by technological change. The not-unprecedented Industrial Revolution, and the utterly unprecedented Great Enrichment, did not come from routine investment or routine removal of inefficiencies in property rights. Ingenuity encouraged by liberalism, such as that of John Ericsson and Alfred Nobel and Sven Wingquist, made Sweden and the rest rich.

To put it another way, the starting point for us of the very small (yet very fine) Ideational School in economic history—Joel Mokyr, Margaret Jacob, Jack Goldstone, myself, and in some moods Eric Jones—is that the heart of economic growth *has* been radical change in technology (steam, general anesthetic, printed circuits) and to a lesser degree change in *some* economic institutions (the engineering profession, forward markets, packaging of brands, containerization; but not the formal rules of the game, which didn't much change). Our point is that the routine investment or the routine specialization or the routine betterment in property rights that bourgeois economists have been inclined to credit since the blessed Smith—not to speak of the appropriation of surplus value or the redistribution of the fruits of the struggle on the picket line that socialist economists have been inclined to credit since the masterful Marx—cannot come close. Thousands of percentage points are what we are assigned in economic history to explain, not the mere 50 percent or at a stretch 100 percent from the betterments in property rights that, I say again, North and Weingast claimed arose from England's Glorious Revolution.[6] The greatness of the Great Enrichment is what makes routine accumulation or routine redistribution or routine institutional change or routine exploitation wholly inadequate to do the scientific job. My story is that accidents of European politics led to liberalism, which led to technological ingenuity, which led to Enrichment.

Yet Weingast is not the first to assign such a bizarre *rejection* of technological change to me. My exposition must be gravely at fault. I'll try to do better.

Weingast worries me, too, in declaring in his title that the neoinstitutional economics he and North pioneered "exposes the neo-classical fallacy."[7] The "fallacy" he imagines is an alleged supposition that good laws are always already in place. To the contrary, he believes, governments are necessary and themselves must have causes, which he supposes the neo-classicals have skipped over. The neoinstitutionalists such as North and himself, he is claiming, deny such a "fallacy."

But the claim that North and Weingast improve on the silly neoclassicals is mistaken. The old neoclassicals such as Menger, Marshall, and Wicksell had a lively appreciation of institutional change, as did their students such as Fogel and Engerman on slavery and North himself on ocean transport. I complained to North over and over again that, by contrast, his neoinsti-tutional economics repeats and reinforces the other, and actual, modern neoclassical fallacy. A Samuelsonian economist—such as North himself—believes passionately in the entire sufficiency of modeling by maximizing utility under constraints. The constraints, the neoclassicals affirm, as did Doug, are constitutions and other formal rules of the game. Doug never did respond to my complaint. *This* neoclassical fallacy may be seen in We-ingast's own writings, and also in, say, I have noted, Oliver Williamson's. It is absent in the writings of the cowinner of the Nobel Memorial Prize in Williamson's year, Elinor Ostrom, or the cowinner in North's year, Robert Fogel. Both went beyond Max U toward a truly revolutionary humanom-ics. North and Weingast are faux revolutionaries against the Samuelsonian tyranny, mere Mensheviks compared with us real Bolsheviks.

The significant fallacy, I am saying, is to believe that material incen-tives (those constraints) run the show and that language is irrelevant noise emanating from the orchestra pit. Perhaps the fallacy I am identifying explains why neoinstitutionalism, claimed by North and Weingast to be so alarming and revolutionary and antineoclassical, has been received so cordially by the reigning Samuelsonian economists. The Samuelsonians can see that neoinstitutionalism is merely a reiteration of the Samuelso-nian dogma that Max U and noncooperative game theory suffice, that we can go on and on with theoretical tales in economic history with little or no quantitative or qualitative testing. Thus Acemoglu.

* * *

Weingast has formed his comment on my paper and book into a restate-ment of his own writings. I suppose I am justified, then, in going down the same path.

Proposition 1: Neoinstitutionalism is Samuelsonian. As I just said, neo-institutional economics in the hands of North, Wallis, Weingast, Williamson, Greif, Acemoglu, and others is conventionally Samuelsonian, reducing

social interactions to "incentives." In putting forward his own notion of a
"fallacy," Weingast writes that "neoclassical economics implicitly assumes:
security, hence absence of violence; a strong system of property rights and
contract enforcement; and the absence of arbitrary or predatory behavior
by the state. None of these conditions can exist without government."[8] Yet
the government that he posits arises out of a "self-enforcing" set of *incen-*
tives. That is to say, he has pushed the Samuelsonian incentives back one
step. The engine is still material incentives. No words or ideas, thank you:
we're behaviorists and materialists.

Proposition 2: Ethics matters more than governments.   Weingast's legal
centralism, though, is not justified factually. He claims, note, that "none of
these conditions [for markets] can exist without government." It is mistaken. The origin of property itself is here at issue. Kings arose, claimed
James VI of Scotland, soon to be James I of England, in *The True Law*
of Free Monarchies of 1598, "before any estates or ranks of men, before
any parliaments were holden, or laws made, and by them was the land
distributed, which at first was wholly theirs. . . . And so it follows of neces-
sity that *kings were the authors and makers of the laws*, and not the laws of
the kings."[9] In fact and in logic and in history King James, like Weingast,
was mistaken. True, property can be guaranteed by government, But the
evidence is crushing that property much more usually is taxed or stolen
by government and that anyway property arises easily and repeatedly in
history without government at all. I have mentioned the experiments and
historical inquiries by Kimbrough, Smith, and Wilson and by Wilson, Jaworski, Schurter, and Smyth. Consider the Iceland of the sagas, Israel of
the judges, or for that matter the mobile property of the hunter-gatherers.
Mainly ethics—not mainly law—holds a society together. Changes in ethics push it forward.

Proposition 3: Neoinstitutionalism is circular.   The legal centralism of
neoinstitutionalism is begging the question. Weingast's main criticism of
my emphasis on liberal ideas, such as Sweden's liberalization in the mid-
nineteenth century, is that "for ideas to have an impact, a series of conditions must hold. Ideas must—somehow—be translated from the realm
of abstraction to the realm of action; that is, they must be implemented.
Moreover, the implementation must be 'self-enforcing' in the sense that
it gives political officials the incentives [there it is again] to honor and
sustain these ideas as they become embodied in practice. Failing this

self-enforcing condition, ideas will remain abstractions or produce unintended effects."[10] Although seconded by Acemoglu and Robinson (2006,
2012, 2019), Greif (1989, 2006), and others of the neoinstitutional school,
the argument here fails in logic and in evidence. In logic it begs the question. His sentences *assume* that institutions are necessary. To be sure, if
"institutions" *mean* "social ideas," then of course the argument is the same
as mine, and I welcome Weingast to the Ideational School. But if "institutions" mean, as he does here want them to mean, incentives expressed
through the monopoly of coercion (giving "political officials the *incentives*
to honor and sustain these ideas"), the argument is quite different, and
begs the question, because the conclusion that we "must . . . must . . . must"
is inserted into the premise. QED.

Proposition 4: Mere words matter.   Words can be powerful as matters
of identity and ethics. Weingast says, "Political officials must have incentives to adhere to the rules." "Must" again. "Incentives" again. No. The
officials do not need such incentives, if we are to understand the word as
the neoinstitutionalists regularly want us to understand it as solely material incentives beyond language and ethics. Chinese officialdom during the
long reign of the examination system was surely sometimes corrupt and
self-serving or cowed by the threat of imperial punishment. But the officials
were also moved by internalized Confucian norms of probity, as one can
see in poetry written by them.[11] Materially, the state can hang an admiral
to encourage the others. But mainly the others expect themselves to do
their duty and engage the enemy more closely. Hobbes famously claimed,
erroneously, that "the bonds of words are too weak to bridle men's ambi-
tion, avarice, anger, and other passions, without the fear of some coercive
power."[12] Weingast, too, quotes Hobbes on the point: "Covenants," Hobbes
wrote, "without the sword, are but words, and of no strength to secure a
man."[13] Game theorists call talk "cheap." Confident though they are in
their no-language lemma, Weingast, Hobbes, and the game theorists and all
the "rational"-choice theorists of Samuelsonian economics are mistaken.
Words have some strength and are sometimes decisive. Consider, for example, "all men are created equal" and "government of the people, by the
people, for the people" and "I have a dream that my four little children
will one day . . . not be judged by the color of their skin but by the content
of their character" decade after decade shaming the racism of the United
States and slowly killing the monster. Consider your own motivations or
the motivations of Weingast himself to be a serious and courageous scholar.

Proposition 5: The evidence for law above all is feeble. The Weingas-
tian argument of material incentives supplied by governmental power is
mistaken in its implied sociological and historical evidence. Most social
life is (to use exactly the wrong word) governed without government and
is commonly governed by the words we habitually use. I have repeatedly
noted that Bart Wilson argues, for example, that "justice" resides as much
out in the language games we play as in the self-interest games we play
from individual utilities.[14] "Justice" is not solely within our heads, but neither is it only in the government's courts of law. And Weingast's argument
contradicts one's ordinary experience of life in any society, such as the
society of economic-historical scientists. Rules of politeness and relevance
apply there and have no governmental backing: look at the conversation
Weingast and I are having. Ordinary conversation—as the "ordinary language" philosophers and the students of linguistic pragmatics observe—
are "governed" by what they call conversational implicatures. To argue
therefore that the claim that the government's monopoly of coercion is
necessary, I repeat, is factually mistaken. Even societies with weak or absent governments, such as the tenth-century Iceland I have mentioned, are
nonetheless so governed, in Gunnar's dooming resolution to return to his
farm, in Njáll's burning, Hallgerðr's hair.

Furthermore, what is a constitution if not a language game? The North-
Wallis-Weingast "doorstep condition" number 3 is "the absence of arbitrary
or predatory behavior by the state."[15] The problem is that the government
itself is supposed to enforce the absence, which is against all we have learned
from political theory since Machiavelli and Hobbes and Buchanan.[16] The
problem forces Weingast to posit those "self-enforcing" mechanisms, which
surprisingly, he claims, did not occur to human minds before *The Federalist
Papers*. And even the government that resulted from *The Papers*, you might
note, has a habit of arbitrary and predatory behavior. Witness the Palmer
Raids and Jim Crow and the IRS tax code, even before Trump.

Proposition 6: The assumed legal and economic history is mistaken.
Weingast depends on the understanding of economic history implied or
asserted by early modern theorists such as Hobbes, Locke, Montesquieu,
Smith, and *The Federalist Papers*. It's the method used before the professionalization of history. One sees it among leftists in their belief in Marx
and Lenin and here among liberal statists (that oxymoron) in the belief
in Montesquieu and Madison *as historians*. Marx and Montesquieu and
Smith and Mill and Weber were all very great thinkers, but they read
and thought before the full professionalization of historical research and

therefore got a good deal of the history quite wrong. Weingast's method results in assertions such as "the medieval world lacked the standard neo-classical assumptions of secure property rights, contract enforcement, rule of law, and a lack of violence."[17] Few medieval economic or social historians, as I have reported above, think so. The assertion is of a piece with the North-and-Weingast notion promulgated in 1989, and now widely credited by economists such as Acemoglu who have not looked into the evidence, that 1689 was a New Day. But, as I have said before, from Pollock and Maitland in 1895 through Harold Berman in 2003, the legal historians, like the economic historians of medieval Europe, don't think so.

I do wish most economists, and even some economic historians, would stop crediting the undocumented claim by North and Weingast that English law was notably defective before the Glorious Revolution. It wasn't. The fine economic historian P. J. Hill, for example, in a recent comment on *Bourgeois Equality*, channeled North, Wallis, and Weingast. P. J. writes that "one of the characteristics of the open access order is the rule of law, an institution that is noticeably absent in the limited access orders."[18] On what evidence could one assert that the rule of law was noticeably absent in, for example, the Ottoman Empire? A book of 2016 by Metin Coşgel and Boğaç Ergene looks deeply into the matter for a portion of northern Turkey in the eighteenth century.[19] Their findings do not seem to be radically different from the bias of English law against poor people in the same century. Rich people did better in court, but not always. In the idiom of Yiddish again, so what else is new?

Proposition 7: Legal rules get reinterpreted continuously.   Language games are loose and interpretable, not mechanical and simple, which is why the United States has a Supreme Court. Recently the American columnist Fareed Zakaria, worrying about a tendency to "illiberal democracy" expressed in Trump's campaign against a free press, observed that "it turns out that what sustains democracy is not simply legal safeguards and rules, but norms and practices—democratic behavior."[20] That's right, and it undermines the salience of constitutional machinery, fascinating though it is to the neoinstitutionalists. The historian of the medieval English economy I mentioned earlier, James Davis, argued so. Rules of the game never come with their own interpretation. It is a point made by, for example, the literary critic and public intellectual I have also mentioned, Stanley Fish, who taught contracts regularly over at the law school when he was chair of English at Duke. He makes the point about legal documents as much as about John Milton's poetry. Interpretive communities impart the meaning of a law or of a poem.[21] And such communities can be called ethical (which includes bad as well as good ethics). Law is an ethical conversation. Or, I say, a tap dance that swings.

Proposition 8: Prudence Only often fails. An economics useful for economic history cannot always be reduced to Max U. It's hard to get through to economists on the point, so enamored are they of the Max U story of budget lines and incentives, which they have been taught since childhood is a complete theory of choice. For example, before about 1983 it was hard to get through to me, trained as an economist and not yet much socialized in history or in *humaniora*. I wrote economic history then solely under the notion that prudence was the only virtue that people attended to—even though it is obvious that for some economic problems the virtues such as Temperance or Love or Justice figure. Consider a country banker or a nursery school teacher or a judge on the US court of appeals. The economists like me had not read the opening pages of Aristotle's *Nicomachean Ethics*, or the *Exodus* of the Jews, or the *Mahabharata* of the Hindus, all of which exhibit choice as a painful exercise in ethical identity, by contrast with the snappy determinism of a so-called consumer facing a so-called budget line.

Proposition 9: The "door" should have opened in China, among others. The "doorsteps" are ubiquitous. North, Wallis, and Weingast in 2009, and Weingast in 2016 argue that the first stage in the transition to a liberal economy is attaining their three "doorstep conditions: (i) rule of law for elites; (ii) a perpetually lived state and organizations; and (iii) control over the various sources of violence."[22] I argue in the trilogy on the Bourgeois Era at some length to the contrary. In the present book I add numerous other points against a neoinstitutionalism lacking ideas and language, exhibited in *humaniora* since the Epic of Gilgamesh. The evidence for their doorstep conditions falls well outside the three modern nations that North, Wallis, and Weingast take as the basis for "a conceptual framework for interpreting recorded history." What was different, as they could have seen if their inquiries had done much testing beyond England (and not Scotland), France (and not the Low Countries), and the United States (and not Sweden, China, Russia, the Ottoman Empire, and the rest), was the new ideology of liberalism, peculiar to northwestern Europe after 1776. Just as Weingast said, "the importance of liberty and equality is woefully underappreciated in the literature."

The chain of Weingast's argument starts by claiming that ideas must be embodied in institutions (false, and, when they are in fact embodied in institutions, often enough they *slow* any change, which slowing Weingast on the contrary and erroneously says is characteristic of ideas, as "culture"). Then it moves on to claiming that institutions such as private property need government (false again if the claim is that they always or even very often need it). It then moves to claiming that in particular the institutions of property are rare (false yet again). In other words, the "doors" in the vocabulary of North, Wallis, and Weingast lie open all over history, as, for example, in fifth-century Athens and Republican Rome. Then why, one may ask, did they not see liberalism and a Great Enrichment? The answer I give is this: Because the liberal idea of equality, liberty, and justice *for all* was not in play. Slave societies are slow to innovate if slavery is big there. Liberal societies innovate because no one is a slave, at any rate in theory and in eventual outcome.

Weingast believes he is refuting my refutation of the rarity of the doorstep conditions when he says in a footnote that "McCloskey (2016a:8) observes that 'scores' of states have attained these conditions in history, from ancient Israel to the Roman Republic, Song China and Tokugawa Japan."[23] He is conceding, note, my main point. Then he adds, as though he thinks it confuted the point, "Yet at any given moment, the number of such states is small relative to the number of limited access orders, and none prior to 1800 created a Great Enrichment."[24] That again is my point: none prior to the idea of liberalism, unique to northwestern Europe in the eighteenth century.

If the transition to extremely high modern economic growth required some special ingredient around 1800, what was it? Economic growth and democracy had been routinely throttled or malnourished in earlier times. North, Wallis, and Weingast want to be seen as tough-guy materialists, but when they seek explanations of the "transition proper" to "open access societies," they fall naturally into speaking of a rhetorical change. Good. Two crucial pages of their 2009 book speak of "the transformation in thinking," "a new understanding," "the language of rights," and "the commitment to open access."[25] Though they appear to believe that they have a material explanation of "open access to political and economic organizations," in fact their explanation for why Britain, France, and the United States tipped into open access is ideational.[26] Ideas change, they are saying, as I am, through sweet talk as much as through material interests.

Proposition 10: Ideas dominate designs. Neoinstitutionalist mechanisms don't suffice. It is characteristic of neoinstitutionalism to make claims such as that "James Madison and his coauthors in *The Federalist Papers* . . . figured out how to design and sustain a regime of liberty and equality."[27] Weingast believes that the US Constitution somehow by its design assures that people will favor liberty and equality. I refer him to Article IV, section 4, clause 3, the Fugitive Slave Clause, even before the dismal acts of Congress in 1793 and 1850 and the Dred Scott decision in 1857. Or no article, section, or clause on women. Or to the election of Donald Trump. Remember Zakaria. Ideas such as that "a subject and a sovereign are clean different things" or that "all men created equal" matter crucially, and change.

*   *   *

Weingast concludes on a critical note, declaring that what he understands to be my position — "that liberty and equality can exist apart from institutions" — is "problematic."[28] My position, to the contrary, is that the institutions we both admire, such as rule of law for elites (consult Genghis Khan, who, I have noted, enforced it strictly among the Mongol tribes) or the separation of powers (consult the Roman Republic, the three branches, *lex curiata de imperio*, and *Senatus Populusque Romanus*), are commonplace and are themselves nothing like sufficient. Around 1800 in northwestern Europe the liberal idea, by contrast, did suffice, considering the routine enforcement of routine laws was anyway universal, to inspirit ordinary people to extraordinary creativity. Innovism.

Weingast's generous instinct is to accept my arguments into his own. "Embodied and implemented through institutions, liberty and equality imply the Smithian sources of economic growth, that is, the division of labor and capital accumulation." I showed in some detail how inadequate such a Smithian idea is to explain the Great Enrichment. "Taken together, these two ideas foster creativity by rewarding people for solving problems." I showed that liberty suffices for creativity and that institutions such as patents and internal improvements and other governmental devices are mostly obstacles when they are not outright thievery from the public purse. Or again, "Many of the hypotheses McCloskey rejects are important necessary components of the great enrichment even if none alone are sufficient to explain it."[29] Weingast does not I think entirely grasp that my claim is that capital and institutional change and even the decline in government-sponsored exploitation, such as the ending of *stavnsbånd* in Denmark or of mine slavery in Scotland or of using military conscripts to dig canals in Sweden, themselves depended, to use the Marxist word, on shifting ideology.

Or, to use the ancient word, growth depended on social and political rhetoric. It did not depend on institutions common to ancient Greece and Song China and eighteenth-century northwestern Europe.

PART III

Humanomics Can Save the Science

CHAPTER ELEVEN

But It's Been Hard for Positivists to Understand Humanomics

An issue we can converse about, and perhaps change our minds about, if we listen, really listen, is the range of this word *institutions*. Everyone seems to agree that it is a pretty baggy word. Sometimes in science bagginess is a good idea, leading eventually to the right amount of precision (e.g., "energy" and "evolution"). Sometimes, I've said, it's not ("phlogiston" and "ether").

Start with North's rules of the game. As Avner Greif and Joel Mokyr noted in criticizing an early version (2015) of my argument here, "the idea of institutions-as-rules, originally proposed by North (1981, 1990), was soon realized to be limited in scope. Yet, it was rhetorically powerful."[1] Yes, it certainly was, especially because North kept repeating it in its simplemindedness, and most economists if asked would say that just such a definition is the heart of neoinstitutionalism. Ask them. The expert practitioner of neoinstitutionalism might reply—if she for some reason wanted to save the admittedly limited definition—that rules can be written or tacit (but possible to bring to consciousness) or even irrevocably subconscious. Yet (she would then say) all such constraints involve costs and rewards—which implies thinking of institutions as relative prices, budget lines facing given tastes.

Whew! Safely back to Samuelsonian economics. Ethics, schmethics. No need to listen to the departments of philosophy, history, religion, classics, communications, anthropology, or literature. Thank whatever God there is!

The final, Samuelsonian step to Max U s.t. *C*, though, is only justified even as price theory if you slip in an additional assumption that the rules or costs or constraints or whatever cannot be affected by (to use Albert

Hirschman's humanomical vocabulary) Voice or Loyalty, or by (to use my vocabulary) the virtues of Courage, Hope, Temperance, Love, Faith, or Justice—at any rate not by enough to matter greatly to the outcome.

I'm reminded of the characteristic move that Machiavelli, Hobbes, Mandeville, Bentham, Becker, North, and others take. They declare in effect that dramatic economic betterment (or whatever behavior it is they are trying to explain: getting married, having a child, following a contract, obeying the law, not obeying the law) has an element, however minor, of that undoubted virtue, prudence, one of the seven primary virtues in the Western tradition. Therefore—non sequitur alert—the behavior is *all* prudence. *Forget about the other six virtues!* Maximize a utility function subject to constraints! "It is the great fallacy of Dr. Mandeville's book", wrote Adam Smith in 1759, "to represent every passion as wholly vicious which is so in any degree and any direction."[2] By "vicious" he meant Prudence Only, the sociopathy of Max U driven only by the costs and rewards of the rules of the game. Or not, if the suckers let you get away with it. Many men delight in thinking that they participate in the Mandevillean vice. We're tough, they say to themselves. Trumpian. Dead soldiers are suckers.

Smith, as a virtue ethicist in the precise sense of the Western tradition from Aristotle, Cicero, and Aquinas, with Chinese and South Asian versions of the same, disliked excessive reductions. "By running up all the different virtues . . . to this one species of propriety [namely, 'the most real prudence'], Epicurus indulged a propensity," he noted, "which philosophers . . . are apt to cultivate with a peculiar fondness, as the great means of displaying their ingenuity . . . to account for all appearances from as few principles as possible."[3] It is Ockham's Razor, with which so many male philosophers and economists have cut themselves shaving. Parsimony, after all, is not the *only* intellectual virtue. Smith therefore in substance avoided the utilitarian pitfall—into which his friend Hume gazed fondly and into which Bentham eagerly leapt and in which Samuelsonian economists such as my numerous neoinstitutional and behavioral friends now wallow happily. If they can think of no better justification, they assert that an economist should anyway specialize in prudence, to suit her comparative advantage. Fine. But then trade, as the argument for comparative advantage requires.

I have claimed repeatedly by now that neoinstitutionalism is Max U Redux. I'll venture to go further. I am going to make some people even more angry (for which I apologize, as the politicians say, if I offend you). But I need to make the point about neoinstitutionalism in the history of economic thought because the point is correct, and if we are going to understand what we are doing in economics, we had better get it straight.

It is that the North-Acemoglu program is deeply unoriginal, being, as I just suggested and show at length in the Bourgeois Era trilogy, deeply Samuelsonian. (My own theme, by the way, that liberalism made the modern world, is equally unoriginal, being eighteenth-century progressive political theory redux. But at least I admit it. Nay, I proudly affirm it.) North persuaded most economists on the contrary that neoinstitutionalism courageously rejects conventional Samuelsonian economics; that it is new, new, new; and that he made it up, with help from Steve Cheung and Yoram Barzel at the University of Washington; and that—here it was not North, who knew better, because he actually read the citation for the prize (which I in fact helped write), but his followers making such a claim—he got the Nobel Prize for doing so.

North achieved such a spin on intellectual history by claiming persistently, in every paper or book he wrote after about 1980, that "neoclassical" economics misses institutions. But neither it nor most other approaches to economics do. Come to think of it, some of Doug's own earlier and pathbreaking work in economic history was in fact unusually neglectful of institutions, though it is the work for which he received the Nobel. But none of the work by most of his colleagues in the field at the time neglected institutions anywhere near as much as the First North did. Stanley Lebergott or Robert Gallman or his cowinner in 1993 Robert Fogel emphasized institutions. After all, institutional analysis is as old as economics. For example: Smith's analysis of the political economy of mercantilism; Mill's and Marshall's (incorrect) analysis of sharecropping as a constraint and a social habit; Schumpeter's and Israel Kirzner's (correct) analysis of entrepreneurship embedded in social custom and psychology; Fogel's and Engerman's (probably incorrect) assignment of the gang system as an explanation of Southern productivity before the Civil War; Mokyr's and Ó Gráda's (correct) analysis of Britain's skill level for betterment in the eighteenth century; my own (very, very correct) analysis of the institutions of open fields in the fourteenth century; Sheilagh Ogilvie's (correct) analysis of medieval guilds; and on and on and on.[4] Economic history in particular—whether or not it uses, as do all cliometricians, an "English economics" (as the German historical school and American old institutionalists derisively called it)—has always been massively about institutions and their effect on the economy; for example, on economic growth.

Guido Tabellini said in the same discussion that Greif and Mokyr participated in that my characterization of what is mainly going on in neoinstitutional economics—a tale of the elimination of (mere) Harberger triangles of inefficiency—is unfair. He says, *a contrario*, that it is about good institutions that "allow the economy to exploit dynamic gains from enterprise, investment and innovation."[5] His story of what is going on in neoinstitutionalism would be nice if it were correct (though, by the way, "investment" is not to the point, being derivative from enterprise and innovation; he is making the usual move by economists of trying to lie innovation down on the procrustean bed of routine investment). But most economists in fact understand neoinstitutionalism, whether they read it or practice it or have just vaguely heard about it, as being about static efficiencies redeemed. Again, ask them. Perhaps they adopt such an understanding because they teach their students or clients relentlessly about $MC = MB$—even though the life of commercially tested betterment since 1800 has been creativity, not Max U. Whatever its psychological origin, I claim that economists have a deep confusion about the connection between efficiency (Peter Boettke, I've noted, calls it "Smith") and commercially tested betterment ("Schumpeter").[6]

The confusion is evident, for example, in the economist and economic historian Robert Allen, who mixes up—as most noneconomists do also—movements along a given production function with movements of the whole function.[7] The one is governed by routine relative scarcities, à la Samuelson. The other, which explains the great bulk of economic growth, does not in logic or in fact depend on such static scarcities. Acemoglu and Robinson, likewise, whom Tabellini claims make the dynamic point, invariably stress efficiency gains out of static incentives and do not explain how commercially tested *betterment* would come from property rights. Would property rights in slaves do so also? In government offices? In *latifundia*? In the image of Mickey Mouse after Congress passed the Mickey Mouse Protection Act in 1998? One can reduce betterment to a matter of mere efficiency (and "investment") by claiming that the (in fact disgraceful if characteristic) inventions by late medieval Venice of patents and copyrights ("intellectual property," the lawyers call it, a new market for their services) led to the optimal pursuit of knowledge. But Venice itself after the fifteenth century did not produce an industrial revolution and did not share much in the Great Enrichment until the late twentieth century.

In fact the program of neoinstitutional economics in almost all its (in the words of Greif and Mokyr) "strands that resemble one another much less than Professor McCloskey's lumping of them would suggest" preserves Max U regardless.[8] That's why I lump them. As Greif and Mokyr declare, neoinstitutional economics is wonderful at "incorporating institutional features in neo-classical economics, even without violating the rationality and self-interest assumptions central to it." Bravo. A case in point is Greif's focus in his work on a noncooperative game theory (which has repeatedly been shown in experiments, I note again, to be nothing like the whole life of humans). Mokyr is wiser in his historical work, which recently has allowed ample room for virtues other than prudence. As I said, neoinstitutionalism is Samuelsonian economics in drag.

Greif and Mokyr wax eloquent in denying that either of them is wearing a dress and high heels. They claim,

> We're not all Max U's anymore. Her criticism [of Max U] is especially otiose, however, because the literature has long recognized that rules are, well, rules and that motivation is the linchpin of institutions. One work that expresses this view is Greif (2006). He noted that rules "are nothing more than instructions that can be ignored. If prescriptive rules of behavior are to have an impact, individuals must be motivated to follow them. . . . By 'motivation' I mean here incentives broadly defined to include expectations, beliefs, and internalized norms."

But such a construal of "rules," as I have noted now several times, turns the economics into a tautology, which Greif, at least on the evidence of the passage here, does not grasp. The locution "motivation is the linchpin of institutions" says that humans are motivated. Uh-huh. If you define "incentives" so broadly that they include "expectations, beliefs, and internalized norms," then you can fit into them any evidence you wish without scientific content, at any rate if you have no believable account of expectations, beliefs, and internalized norms, insisting on a rigid behaviorism ignorant of the humanities. If "motivation" is anything that humans do, then nothing is gained scientifically by saying that they respond to motivation. Of course they do. Humans are moved to human action. Got it. If peasants in medieval open fields in fact had more plots than could be explained by the prudence of portfolio diversification, the historian can gesture to expectations, beliefs, and internalized norms and then can go home early. He can leave a note on the door saying that regrettably the actual strictly behaviorist and mechanical and antihumanistic study of expectations, beliefs, and internalized norms is in its infancy, and so he cannot, alas, be more specific. Come back in a few decades, when the brain scientists have finally found the mind in the brain, the ghost in the machine.

Yet the same is *not* true of serious scientific uses of the humanities, as I illustrated for example with the riff earlier on John Searle's analysis of institutions. Humanistic study is nothing like in its infancy. It is three or four millennia old. If we make use of it we *can* be highly specific in gathering evidence on "motivation." We learn that Antigone faced a dilemma, that King David indulged his lusts, that Iago exercised a "motiveless malignity."

Still, Mokyr and Greif are vexed that I keep giving them reading lists in the humanities. I must say I am astonished at their vexation. I myself admit that I have not read all the works in neoinstitutional economics, even confined to those that Greif and Mokyr cite — and there is much more. But I am *ashamed* that I haven't, and promise to try to do better. I thought this was the way we do things in science — giving out reading lists, testing one another, discovering our hidden presuppositions, many of which can in fact be discovered by seriously listening to literature and its literature (*Geisteswissenschaften, sciences humaines*). Science is difficult. We're not supposed to whine that it's too much *work* to listen, really listen.

A long time ago, in a group of philosophy grad students and faculty and I at the University of Iowa's intellectually narrow Department of Philosophy, I asked John Searle (whom I know a bit and whose theory of language and society I used here and whose books are on the reading lists I give out) whether he had read Hegel. John quipped, "No, and I intend never to do so," at which we all laughed (even I did, to my shame). John was signaling a purposely ignorant scorn for the whole of what is known in the trade as Continental philosophy. Shame on him.

I expected Mokyr and Greif to be better than Searle. But then I read the snarky complaint that I don't tell them precisely how they should "deploy the 'exact and gigantic literature about ideas, rhetoric, ideology, ceremonies, metaphors, stories and the like.'" They continue, saying that "it seems to advance us by very little." But I have shown in detail now for decades "precisely" how such evidence advances us — for example, in the Bourgeois Era trilogy the killer app (if I do say so myself) of explaining modern economic growth, filled with quantitative and qualitative evidence. Earlier I had shown how the study of rhetoric could expose the absurd econometric routine of null hypothesis significance testing. Two examples, merely, you say. But big ones. I have published dozens of others laying out how precisely for this or that. If we keep ignoring such evidence, we will advance very little in our human science.

*   *   *

My amiable critics from neoinstitutionalism all say that neoinstitutionalism *does* acknowledge the humanities, through something they all label *culture*. Another of my friends, the highly sophisticated economist Richard Langlois, uses the C-word. But it is so baggy that, like *institutions*, little is conveyed. Still, if I were certain that my beloved colleagues had listened, really listened to the experts on "culture" from Homer and Hillel to Rabindranath Tagore and Tennessee Williams, I would not be so resistant as I am to their use of the term.

Thus Langlois: "The principal culprits for actually stopping entrepreneurship are culture and institutions. McCloskey is now willing to admit, perhaps reluctantly, that both of these factors can be important. But the point here, and in *Bourgeois Dignity*, seems to be that culture is what does the heavy lifting." I demur, because of the vague *culture* word Langlois and the others use, a baggy error term that can be brought in at any moment to save the hypothesis. By contrast, economists have, if we will only listen, numerous precisely categorical and even ratio-scale-quantifiable or socially comparative or historically deep studies in the humanities that can help us understand how ideas, ideology, rhetoric, and ethics actually change. For example, the definition of words change, as did the word *responsibility* studied by Haskell. I myself have done research on the meaning of, say, the word *honest* and its highly suggestive change over time.[9] But we have to listen to the evidence.

The word *ethics*, for example, is much more exact than *culture* (and so are *ideas*, *ideology*, and *rhetoric*, unless we stick with a sneering positivist method that claims without listening to the evidence that they are all "vague"). In 2006 I wrote a long book about commercial ethics but finally realized, two books on the subject later, that what I was getting at was not really Ms. Jones's personal rectitude. Unhappily, that is what everybody thinks when they hear that McCloskey is talking about "bourgeois virtues." They immediately think of, say, Weber and a (mistaken) psychological hypothesis, not McCloskey and a (correct) sociological hypothesis. Even Mokyr, who should know better, falls into such a strange reading. I blame myself for not making the point clearly enough even to such a highly intelligent reader. On the contrary, the important ethical change I argue, with massed evidence on the point, was Ms. Jones's attitudes formed in the human conversation *about* the rectitude of other people, in this case bourgeois people. I call it in *Bourgeois Equality*, clumsily, "social ethics" — such as the indignation, as I have said, that is *not* expressed in Italy when *il furbo* sneaks ahead of everyone else at the ticket office in the Rome railway station.

Yes, I realize that economists since Lionel Robbins (as Langlois points out, and as I noted earlier) have fled from the mere mention of ethics.

They know nothing about it, believing it, I have noted, to be merely the *preaching* of *stupid* commandments. They don't want to learn anything about it beyond Hicks-Kaldor compensation (stay tuned). Perhaps in this matter—I think Langlois would agree—we ought to go back to our master, the Professor of Moral Philosophy at Glasgow, 1752–1764.

I don't think institutions work without a great deal of social ethics—think of the constitutions of the USSR or the Russian Federation. Read the last novel by the Soviet liberal Vasily Grossman (1906–1964), *Forever Flowing*, and stop thinking that institutional change is anything but ethical, good or bad. Think of the laws on rape, the same in Uganda and in the United Kingdom, with very different results.[10]

I can use the examples offered by Langlois to make my own and Lincoln's point. For example, Langlois says, "Chinese people I have spoken with do not see present-day Chinese culture as affirming or honoring of commercial activity. It is a culture of bald-faced pragmatism. We are all socialists (wink, wink), but it's okay to go about bettering our conditions."[11] But the "honor" I speak of does not have to be treating entrepreneurs as superheroes in the way we treated Steve Jobs (a nasty case, actually, of one sort of *lack* of social ethics in his treatment of people; though a good case of social ethics in his treatment of devices that people loved and would pay for). Such a modest "honor" sufficed in Britain in 1800 or China in 1978 to produce astounding results considering the depth of the earlier disdain. "Pragmatism" looks like an entirely new social ethic.

And so I do not understand what Langlois means by saying that "the Red sultans (mostly) stopped throwing improvers off the cliff, and the Chinese Empire is becoming rich. That's an institutional change, not a cultural one." Again the word *culture* obscures the matter. Ethics *did* change— among the elite. Langlois seems to think that "cultural" change must be widespread to have any effect. It shows how misled the thinking of even a brilliant and humane economist gets if he sticks with "culture" without really taking on board what anthropologists, philosophers, and philologists have said about it. The spread through the society is of course relevant and can be measured by the mind-scan on dead people that the humanities offer. But if enough Ben Franklins or Count Bismarcks or Vladimir Lenins change from workers to entrepreneurs or from liberals to imperialists or from law students to revolutionaries, a lot can happen to measurable events and for a while to measurable public sentiment.

Langlois does, though, understand what I am saying better than most people do (Deirdre, work on your clarity!): "McCloskey's thesis would seem to be that economic growth will take place if the system of convention (culture [Deirdre says: yuk!], ethics) makes it legitimate to take advantage of commercial entrepreneurial opportunities." Langlois quotes the astonishing book by Young Back Choi in 1993: "Of the many factors relevant in determining entrepreneurial success most notable is the role of property rights in enabling entrepreneurs to overcome envy barriers, making possible the market process of social learning."

But then Langlois extends it: "Even if the culture is against me, I have a trump card in abstract and anonymous social institutions." No you don't, dear—not if ethics, ideology, rhetoric, and the conversation of humankind is trumps against the particular anonymous social institution that would enable you to overcome envy barriers. The market, for example, doesn't *perfectly* eliminate racial prejudice. It helps, but not 100 percent. Langlois quotes Schumpeter in (1912) 1934 writing that "the only man [the entrepreneur] has to convince or impress is the banker who is to finance him—but by buying them or their services, and then using them as he sees fit." That is only true, the way Choi's claim is true, *after* the Bourgeois Revaluation, part of the egalitarianism in economic rights and social standing that by a series of happy accidents peculiar to northwestern Europe started to grow after 1517. Otherwise the property rights, the market trump cards, and the writs of bankers would be dead letters, like the American constitution was for southern Blacks before the 1960s, or to some degree for all Blacks until Black Lives Matter.

Robert Lawson in the same conversation with Mokyr, Greif, Tabellini, and Langlois doesn't like my pairing of Italy and New Zealand noted above and urges me to do the two-variable regression on a "sample" of countries he exhibits.[12] But I do not offer the Italian–New Zealand instance as the confirmation of a law, merely as an interesting falsification of such a law. Italy is notorious for public stupidity and corruption and yet does well enough in its voluntary economy to offset the stupidity and corruption. Surely it requires explanation why such a country has about the same income as New Zealand, a paragon of economic wisdom and honesty. It suggests that adopting betterments, not carrying on with wisdom and honesty, explains most of a high income.

As to the econometrics, I need to remind Lawson that his two-variable regression is probably not a correct specification of the connections between income and corruption. Doubtless a similar regression of the consumption of paper on national income would have similar results, but one would not want therefore to dump paper on poor countries to make them rich. A more profound example of the same point is William Easterly's attack, I have noted, on "capital fundamentalism": rich countries have lots of dammed-up rivers ("Iowa, land of ten lakes"); therefore, if Ghana makes such an artificial lake, it will become rich.[13] Not.

Surely high income itself independently reduces corruption for various reasons that could be explored quantitatively. Chicago was very corrupt as recently as 1960. My friend Jack Zimmerman, from southwest Chicago, tells a hilarious story how as a teenager at the time he lost a suburban girlfriend because he bragged to her father that he had bribed a Chicago traffic cop in exactly the minimum, Max U, amount, a feat that his own father had admired very much indeed. But with rising income (and education and moves to the suburbs and other correlates of income) Chicagoans grew less tolerant of the Chicago Way (*Ubi est mea*: "Where's mine?"), and the powerful and corrupt alderman Fast Eddie Vrdolyak went to prison, twice. And in any case, Lawson's point makes my own. Where would uncorruption come from? Not, as I have argued, from more laws, as again like the Soviet Constitution, but from an ethical change— the sort that caused the Great Enrichment in the first place.

The same reply can be made to all the comments by my friends the neoinstitutionalists, using their own examples to show that my argument is correct and theirs is mistaken. (I apologize for using such an aggressive trope as the *elenchus* on them. But I urge them to set aside their anger and to listen, really listen.) Greif and Mokyr, for example, give many interesting and important instances from British history during the eighteenth century. Each of the instances, contrary to what they claim, shows that I am correct about the relative rigidity of institutions during the Industrial Revolution and that a striking change in ethics about other people's behavior, not institutions such as property law or whatever, is what mattered. Greif and Mokyr praise, for example, "North and Weingast's (1989) classic and influential paper on the topic and heavily used in empirical work on institutions," which characterization of this influence is certainly correct. It is a classic, and was influential, and is heavily and uncritically used by others in neoinstitutionalism, as for example the alarming passage by Acemoglu I discussed earlier. Yet the North and Weingast paper is wholly mistaken as historical science, which I showed at length in pages 310–354 of *Bourgeois Dignity* (2010) and adumbrate in the present book. Consider just one example among many of neoinstitutionalism's startling historical and economic mistakes: the taxation by which the Stuarts are supposed to have terribly enslaved property owners, on the estimates in the paper itself, amounted to about 2 percent of English national income per year. Compared with the Dutch-imitating polity that was brought in with

BUT IT'S BEEN HARD FOR POSITIVISTS TO UNDERSTAND HUMANOMICS 143

a Dutch king and the Glorious Revolution, and compared with any modern state, the Stuarts were pikers at extraction of income to engage in economically pointless foreign wars. So much for property rights being overridden by the English state *before* 1689. (It is by the way strange of Greif and Mokyr to claim that McCloskey "never refers to the North-Weingast paper." As I say, the paper and North's other effusions were criticized in detail in forty-five pages of *Bourgeois Dignity*, a book which at least Mokyr claims to have read.)

"By the late eighteenth century, however," Greif and Mokyr write again, "contemporaries recognize the role of poor relief in fostering disruptive and labor-saving innovations." They are giving a fine example, out of a half dozen similar ones in the later pages of their piece, of precisely the change in ideology about which I wrote in the trilogy. When "contemporaries recognize," of course, it's a case of Lincoln's "public sentiment" that makes statutes and decisions possible or impossible to be executed. It's not a change in institutions—which is to say it's not something that can be ordered up by rules of the game. With such sentiment on his side, Lincoln realized, the rules of the slavery game could be changed. And, with a little help from General Grant, he did.

*　*　*

Richard Langlois wants me to engage more with Schumpeter. I think he will agree that the engagement is achieved in *Bourgeois Equality* (2016), whose text (excluding, that is, citations in footnotes and bibliography) discusses substantively the insightful Joseph Alois more than thirty times and then also in a recent paper.[14] I have become a Schumpeterian after a misspent youth assaulting his quantitatively challenged epigones such as David Landes and Peter Mathias and Derek Aldcroft.[15] I only criticize the master now for putting too much weight on bankers (for a while Schumpeter was one himself, by the way, though he didn't do well at it). Schumpeter did not know, because the historical work on primary sources had not yet been done, that banking is ancient, not something peculiar to Quattrocento Italy. And especially I still criticize Schumpeter for not having a serious sociological or historical or rhetorical account of how and why entrepreneurs were unleashed after 1800.

It is true, as Langlois says with characteristic precision, that "entrepreneurship is not a hothouse flower that blooms only in a culture supportive of commercial activity; it is more like kudzu, which grows invasively unless it is cut back by culture and institutions. McCloskey needs to tell us more about the structure of the relationship among culture, institutions, and entrepreneurship, and thus to continue the grand project begun by Schumpeter." I've followed Langlois's advice and told people a good deal along such lines in *Bourgeois Equality*. The structure I have in mind, which I recommend to others as a testable scientific hypothesis, is that ethics and rhetoric, which can be given exact content and which can be seen in action in law and literature, were hostile to entrepreneurship in every large-scale society until the Netherlands in the sixteenth century and Britain in the eighteenth century.

Langlois is spot on when he notes that "If you attend a meeting of the International Joseph A. Schumpeter Society, you can hear many papers on 'entrepreneurship policy,' which seeks an activist role for government in somehow fomenting entrepreneurship that would not otherwise take place. This is especially popular in Europe. . . . They don't want to stop doing any of the many policy things that [in fact, Langlois is saying] discourage entrepreneurship." Some years ago a few of us were at the end of an exhausting three weeks on the Free-Market Road Show, organized by Barbara Kolm to rush around the capitals of the Balkans recommending liberty for their entrepreneurs to have a go. The last meeting was in social-democratic Vienna before a small audience of bored journalists and a few members of the public. We gave our pep talks recommending liberty from the governmental programs that hobbled entrepreneurs. At the end a young man, about twenty years old, stood up and effused in excellent English, "I *loved* your talks, and *love* the idea of entrepreneurs having the liberty to have a go. *But* . . . in Austria you have to understand that we have a problem. There is *no government program for training entrepreneurs*." Gak. We didn't want to criticize such an enthusiastic young man, and so we merely sank back into our seats in despair.

Guido Tabellini praises, as North and company do, the modern state for "its ability to establish order and deter violence, to enforce contracts, to provide public goods" in aid of economic development such as "entrepreneurship policy."[16] It is startling to hear an Italian supposing that most states are in such a benevolent business. I recall the opinion of his countryman, Carlo Levi, who as an Italian and a Jew and an antifascist had little patience with the widespread modern notion of *lo stato* as savior. He wrote of the impoverished towns in Calabria to which he was banished 1935–1936: "None of the pioneers of Western civilization brought here his sense of the passage of time, his deification of the State or that ceaseless activity [by *lo stato*] which feeds upon itself [thus the obstacles to the Great Enrichment]. No one has come to this land except as an enemy, a conqueror, or a visitor devoid of understanding."[17]

*   *   *

Mokyr wrote in earlier correspondence with me that "you are of course correct in that institutions must be understood in conjunction with beliefs, that is, culture." I have said why the rush to call the very precise findings of the humanities ranging from philology to anthropology by the excessively baggy word *culture* is a scientific error. Now I want to draw attention to a widespread error in how economists think about "beliefs," especially evident in Greif/Mokyr and in Tabellini, namely the error of taking beliefs to be "information" and of a restricted sort, namely, probabilities about states of the world (though of course sometimes mistaken). Douglass North also thought of "beliefs" as "information," again reducible to budget lines or, as he liked to say late in his life, "brain science."

Beliefs are *not* merely propositional, such as my own belief that natural selection explains the origin of species. Think about it. Beliefs are also dispositional and practical, that is, matters of identity, matters of rhetoric and ethics, matters of what sorts of propositions one is willing to entertain and what ethical attitude one takes toward them. And therefore they are also "speech acts." (I have been saying this to economists—that is, mainly to deaf ears—since 1983.) Thus, "belief" in science, such as you and I possess, is not reducible to accepting propositions such as $F = ma$. It is a disposition, which in some degree changed during the seventeenth century. Here again the humanities come to our scientific aid. The word *belief* is cognate with *love*, as in the antique phrase "I would lief" do such and such, in the way that *true* is cognate with personal *troth*, as in *betrothed*. It meant in religion before "natural theology" in the eighteenth century *not* propositional belief such as affirming Snell's Law of Refraction. As the writer on religion Karen Armstrong has pointed out, it meant a loving loyalty, in troth to a person or to a way of life, the following for example of what Jesus would do, or the 613 laws of Orthodox Judaism, or the scientific program of Francis Bacon.[18] Luther explicitly denied the propositional definition of faith: "Faith does not require information, knowledge, and certainty," he wrote, "but a free surrender and joyful bet on His unfelt, untried, and unknown goodness."[19] Commitment. I pledge my troth as to the unreasonable effectiveness of mathematics in the physical sciences.[20] Greif and Mokyr are certainly correct to declare that "it would be useful to know how and why people believe what they believe and how they change their minds." But that is what the history of civilization from the Torah and the Vedas and Cicero down to John Searle and Mary Midgley and Clifford Geertz is all about.

Greif and Mokyr declare that "an institution as a system of rules, beliefs, expectations, and norms perpetuates only if it elicits behavior that is consistent with the rules, that reaffirms the associated beliefs and expectations, and that replicates its underpinning norms." If this rotund expression is understood as anything other than a tautology (achieved ex post facto by canny definitions of *reaffirms* and *replicates*, for example), it is still another instance of the materialist lemma. It looks lovely on the pages of the *Journal of Economic Theory* but looks odd coming from Mokyr—who has brilliantly shown the force of ideas, such as the mad ideas of Francis Bacon on scientific progress, though they took three centuries of failure to come close to eliciting behavior (namely, true enrichment) reaffirming the belief.

But in any case I would like to see the historical evidence that the materialist lemma is true. If you examine books of history it looks, actually, absurd. Take belief in astrology, for example. Are we saying that casting horoscopes was "reaffirmed" by the outcomes of lives and battles? Or are we saying that the resistance for fifty years by American geologists to the plausible argument of 1916 by a German meteorologist that continents moved "reaffirmed" the underpinning norms of science? Or, to use an example I have been trying to get economists to understand since the 1980s, are we saying the institution of econometrics and in particular its reliance on null-hypothesis significance testing in the absence of a substantive loss function, such as what Greif and Mokyr breathlessly call "recent cutting-edge economic research," reaffirmed the underpinning norms of science? The "underpinning norm" of econometrics is surely that we need to get magnitudes when we assert an economic effect, and we might get them from properly identified observations. Good. But, I say again, it has been shown by dozens of the leading theoretical and applied statisticians since Edgeworth that such testing does *not* replicate such a norm. Not at all.[21] Yet econometrics goes on and on and on, taught to graduate students in such a way that they are disabled from thinking quantitatively.[22] That's "perpetuates" for you.

Citing some econometric studies of US states and elsewhere that define "religion" as ignorant fundamentalism, Guido Tabellini asks, "How do we know that it is the diffusion of bourgeois ethics (and the associated appreciation of innovation with commercial value), rather than openness to innovation in general, that is responsible for rapid economic development?" How indeed? "Innovation in general"—for example, in music in seventeenth-century Italy or in poetry in Shakespearian England or in drama in the same era in England and in Spain—might be a substitute for commercially tested betterment in the economy. It probably was, as an alternative path for a creative person—though recall that Shakespeare was also a businessman. Or it can be, as Tabellini is claiming, an indicator of a general ability, like IQ. That last one I doubt and offer a good deal of evidence in *Bourgeois Equality* that it is not so. For instance, the success of overseas Chinese before 1978, at a time that their countrymen languished at home, suggests that no general "Chinese" ability was in play to explain their languishment. What all my critics miss is what I thought I made clear in *Bourgeois Dignity* (in 2010; in *The Bourgeois Virtues* [2006] I was myself half confused about it in the same way that they are): that "ethics" is to be taken as mainly *not* individual character but as the opinion about character in the society at large. It is a sociological not a psychological matter.

On the other hand, I quite agree with Tabellini that "generalized" ethics (about other people's character) is what matters for economic success. The crux, as I have just said, is to realize that the ethics that matters is not so much how people are constituted as it is how they view other people. (In Tabellini's work coauthored with Greif that he cites, though, they attribute tribalism, correctly, to China, but then do not acknowledge its gigantic role in Europe also. *All* preindustrial societies are organized tribally. A long time ago Edward Banfield, for example, characterized his village in the Mezzogiorno as running on "amoral familism."[23] It was a tribalism of an especially narrow sort, to be widened rather by the Mafia, the Camorra, and the 'Ndrangheta.) Anyway, such a generalized ethics is what *Bourgeois Equality* (2016) stresses and studies and explains. In a word, the crux was the rise of liberalism, the crazy theory that all people are created equal, not subordinated to tribal chiefs and customs.

Tabellini cannot be blamed for not reading a book by me that had when he wrote not yet come out (*Bourgeois Equality*). On the other hand he criticizes me for not reading his own works, so I suppose turnabout is fair play (*L'inversione è . . .*). It would not take much inquiry into what I was writing before 2015, even before the book came out, to discover that I have a massive answer to his "second obvious difficulty with an ideas-based explanation of economic and political development[, namely,] that ideas are endogenous. Where do these ideas come from, and why do they spread so rapidly in some places or moments in time and not others?" The blithe supposition that "ideas are endogenous," as Tabellini declares with no sense of its scientifically erroneous character, is a materialist dogma, to be sure, but not therefore obviously correct as science. One would like to know, for example, how Einstein arose as a merely superstructural result of the means of production at the base. Or more to the point here, one would like to know what the history of economics would look like without, say, Smith, Schumpeter, Samuelson, and Arrow. Or for that matter North.

But in any case, where the ideas come from and how they spread (slowly, not as Tabellini says "rapidly," though quicker than the institutions whose change is supposed to have caused the modern world), and why in some places and not in others, is the subject of *Bourgeois Equality*. Terence Kealey and Joel Mokyr have noted the liberated science of Europe, with its numerous intermediate clubs for science, and have contrasted it with the centralized control under the Manchus exercised after 1644 in China.[24] The Reformation, for example, did not have its main influence through the anxiety about predestined election that Max Weber stressed but instead through the dignifying of ordinary believers in the Radical Reformation (as against what historians call the Magisterial Reformation of Luther and Calvin and Henry VIII). (There is more to be said, about 1,700 pages more, actually, but I want you to buy and read the trilogy on the Bourgeois Era. Especially buy.)

In his strictures on my methodological points, Tabellini again retails positivist dogma rather than facts or common sense. He says, as though it were uncontroversial, that "we ought to explain social phenomena starting from the decisions of individuals." Who says? I sometimes joke about my beloved graduate school classmate Tom Sargent, who says, "We *must* base macroeconomics on microfoundations." And then in the joke I ask him, "But why?" To which he answers, "We *must* base macroeconomics on microfoundations." To which I ask again, "But why?" To which he answers ... Another example is Kant claiming on the second page of *Groundwork of the Metaphysics of Morals* that we *must* not use anthropology—that is, what we know about humans—in framing ethical principles. We *must*. *Wir müssen*. But no reason we "must" is supplied, there or anywhere else in Kant or in Tabellini.

Having repeated the usual and startlingly amateurish philosophical dogmas prevalent among economists (if Tabellini wants to get serious about the philosophy I recommend a book of 1994 called *Knowledge and Persuasion in Economics*), Tabellini outlines how the mind can be reduced to economic incentives—the materialist dogma again. He, like my other dear friends in criticism, wants us in economics to go on as before, ignoring the humanities, and refusing to learn anything from *le facoltà di lettere*—even though in Italian and every other language (if not in English since the late nineteenth century) they teach *scienza* too.

And that, my dears, is my point, fiercely denied in Samuelsonian neoinstitutionalism.

CHAPTER TWELVE

Yet We Can Get a Humanomics

Daniel Klein, another humanomical member of that admirable George Mason school of Austrian economists, wrote in 2012 a book about all this, *Knowledge and Coordination: A Liberal Interpretation*. One of the many good features of the book is its scholarship. Klein *actually reads* even the people with whom he does not agree. Amazing. George Stigler, a witty man though a terrible reader and a profoundly misleading political economist, once remarked that John Stuart Mill "was perhaps the fairest economist who ever lived: he treated other people's theories at least as respectfully as his own, a mistake no other economist has repeated."[1] Klein is fair—maybe not to Mill's standard but far above the mean. And so one gets a sense reading Klein's book what The Others were actually saying. *Audite et alteram partem.*

Klein is good, too, at the philosophical and humanistic skill of categorization (I especially admire the skill because I don't have it), distinguishing usefully, for example, "concatenate coordination" (a pleasing social order looked at from above) and "mutual coordination" (people spontaneously lining up their plans, as in Schelling Points). "Respondence," another Klein coinage, is "our rather automatic responding to new bits of information that simply rain down on us." He does not confine it to information on, say, the distribution of prices in a local market for secondhand Toyota Camrys, which Stigler said is discerned through a routine investment in gathering bits.[2] Klein distinguishes respondence on the one hand from Stiglerite "information" and on the other from epiphany, where discovery lives. Surely Klein's teacher Israel Kirzner is right in claiming that "the most impressive aspect of the market system is the tendency for [innovations] to be discovered."[3] The static efficiency beloved of Samuelsonians such as Stigler is not. (And yet the details of static efficiency, not the social habits that lead to innovation, are what we teach in microeconomics. I did in 1985, or example, in *The Applied Theory of Price*. The static details are lovely, and often useful, but we need students to learn more: price theory in humanomics.)

Klein, who as I just said was a student of Kirzner, interprets the rabbi: "Under a régime of economic liberty, substantial and socially beneficial epiphanies occur more often not only because more opportunities exist but also because interpretive faculties are more advanced and more aroused" because more practiced.[4] Though Kirzner emphasizes that discovery depends on an internal insight—the Aha! moment in which one's way of looking at the matter suddenly shifts—he also argues that laissez-faire provides a context for an "interest," as he calls it, in making innovations. Surely. The "interest" that Kirzner and Klein are taking about, though, is not merely prudential, Max U. It is not only about money. It is about the engagement of humans with their lives, illuminated by the stories we tell. The American folksinger Ani DiFranco, for example, exhibits it in a fierce opposition to commerce in music. To analyze the mix of interest and epiphany that is entrepreneurship, Klein retells Somerset Maugham's story "The Verger," in which an illiterate servant becomes an entrepreneur. (It is another merit in Klein's book that he is cordial to insights from the humanities, our stories and metaphors and the Tanakh, Mishnah, and Talmud commenting on them, taking them as serious scientific data. Klein, I am affirming, is among the practitioners of humanomics. Yet so is Kirzner, though less literary—if you overlook his mastery of Jewish holy literature [though, somewhat oddly, he never quotes it in his economics].)

A good context for the mix of interest and epiphany, it has been found, comes also from liberty of speech and action.[5] The multiple voices that the printing press, the Reformation, and the fragmentation of political power in Europe began to allow by the seventeenth century permitted a new régime of ideas having sex.[6] But the same is true within a single person: we are each a polylogue of internal interests, some articulate, some tacit—this in sharp disagreement with the single-mindedness of Max U. Klein uses the idea of multiple selves proposed by Marvin Minsky, a computer scientist at MIT, quoting him thus: "Even the ideas we 'get' for ourselves come from communities—this time the ones inside our heads."[7] "The truth," Minsky continues, "is that a person's mind holds different views in different realms."[8] Klein, in other words, is edging away from Kirzner's asocial vision of the alert entrepreneur. Klein remarks, "Going forward, rarely can [the entrepreneur] go it alone; she needs cooperators."[9] I recommend to him, and to you, the research of the management empiricist Saras Sarasvathy at the Darden Business School of the University of Virginia. She shows at work in the careers of entrepreneurs exactly such a rhetorical skill in recruiting cooperation.[10] Consider again Lord Nelson.

Another Kleinian idea among scores in the book is the self-correcting character of the profits from obstacles thrown up to innovation. "The pitfall itself generates betterment opportunities that spark entrepreneurial transcendence."[11] It is a characteristically Austrian insight that disequilibrium is necessary for profit opportunities. Yes: the obstacles to innovation make the rewards to whatever innovation *does* break through even higher (Richard Langlois, take note). Consider the innovation bursting out after the COVID-19 plague and its governmental lockdowns. By "pitfall" Klein means such governmental obstructions and monopolies. But the profit opportunities can be for the rent seekers rather than the seekers after commercially tested innovations. Thus, in Chennai in India the government favors massive—and in the long run counterproductive—projects of seawater desalinization to solve the looming drought because such projects give maximal opportunities for ribbon cutting and political glory. It is a persistent bias in governmental decision-making, whether in a democracy or in a tyranny—for example, the Brazilian decision to build Brasilia, or the Danish decision to add a glorious bridge to a perfectly adequate tunnel to the mainland of Europe, or the Chinese decision to initiate a Belt and Road Initiative to build railways across central Asia to Europe when a single New Pananax Triple E container ship handles in one go over 200 full freight trains.

There's a horrible fact here that can be analyzed with a good old Chicago School, Marshallian economics of entry and exit. I have lamented the loss of the *echt* economics (Vernon Smith calls it "ecological" economics), which has been driven out of the minds of young economists by the triumph of Samuelson's reduction to the individual level of Max U ("constructivist" economics). Because a prohibition, such as the War on Drugs, or a glorious project such as the Belt and Road Initiative, creates opportunities for rent seeking, the profit from real progress is starved. Look for the evidence in lower-class neighborhoods of African Americans. The War on Drugs is a war on poor Blacks, tempting their young men into the trade and then jailing them for long terms, destroying family life.

Humanomics, with such price theory, supports Klein's central (Smithian) liberal concern, which is to support a liberated society. Opportunities in a liberated and sensible society, he notes, are *not* crowded out by the profit from evading ill-advised prohibitions or ill-advised glories and are therefore directed to the real obstacles of error or ignorance or lack of alertness. Instead of dreaming up new ways to defeat the Drug Enforcement Agency—think of Stringer Bell in the first three seasons of *The Wire*—the alert person is invited to dream of new "socially beneficial epiphanies." Defeating the agency, of course, is also "socially beneficial," since consumers of drugs are willing to pay for the services of the skilled evader of the law. But the benefit is like that of ceasing to bang one's head against the wall. The more direct suggestion would be not to start banging one's head (for example, not to start a War on Drugs) and therefore provide a favorable context for using one's head instead to innovate in the use of oil or cell phones.

In other words, there are two margins, one of getting around a governmental obstruction and the other getting around a lack of imagination. Both yield pure profit if an epiphany detects a new way around an obstacle, an obstacle artificial or natural, the free lunch of economic growth that Kirzner talks about. Both profits are soon, and usually soon enough, driven down by entry, despite terrifying myths brought out meanwhile of "natural monopoly." The master and permanent monopoly—because armed, and hired by the monopolists—is the very government called on to attack the private and temporary monopolies—who are "armed" only metaphorically with attractive offers to consumers such as the iPhone. Getting around governmental obstructions, note, has a natural limit, namely, the point at which all the obstructions are cleared away, as in Hong Kong under the British and before Xi Jinping. No one is banging her head against the wall, and there is no social benefit remaining in advising people to stop doing it or devising profitable tricks for getting around it. But getting around lack of imagination has no limit. That ideas having sex has increasing returns to scale is a contingent fact I have asserted of the world, to be sure, and not provable a priori. But it is the source of the modern world.

* * *

So Daniel Klein is an academic entrepreneur, observing alertly new ideas and pursuing them with energy. One may ask, though, in what market he is testing his ideas. In other words, are we persuading anyone? I join Klein, for example, in being unhappy with my good friends the Samuelsonians and their misleading obsession with Max U and equilibrium in neoinstitutionalism and other fancies. (That I was once a Samuelsonian myself merely makes me wish more fervently that I could persuade the Samuelsonians to change their minds. Like the Kropotkinite anarchists or the left Democrats or the social engineers or the socialist Episcopalians, they have all at one time or another been My People, too, misled though they all are.)

The Samuelsonian obsession with a methodological-individualist, mechanical model of Max U ("That's what a 'model' *is*," the Samuelsonian declares, and walks away well satisfied) leads the economist into a position I have noted, that if any of the market conditions shown to be *necessary* for equilibrium in some imagined Max U world are violated (an infinite number of traders, information symmetry, honesty on all sides, fully "rational" consumers), then Markets Don't Work. The argument is undeniably illogical, because, as I have said, necessary conditions are not the same as sufficient conditions. Vernon Smith, Bart Wilson, and other experimenters on *markets* (as against the behavioral economists overstudying *individual* behavior, in line with the Max U program and its dogmatic attachment to methodological individualism) have shown how quickly humans achieve efficiency, especially if they talk to each other. The sufficiency-to-necessity move, however illogical, has been immensely powerful since A. C. Pigou and then Paul Anthony Samuelson first articulated it. The crudest version, which even noneconomists have heard about, turns as I have noted on the unhappy vocabulary of "perfect" markets, which economists have been conjuring with for about a century. "Well," says the Samuelsonian determined to propose new governmental regulation of markets, a new Belt and Road violating the most obvious test of cost and benefit, "*nothing's* perfect. So we must have regulation and fresh projects by [a presumptively perfect] government."

Kenneth Arrow was someone I knew a little and admire. Like his brother-in-law, Samuelson, he was a tolerant, amiable, and extremely intelligent economist. Yet Daniel Klein finds without much trouble a bizarre assertion by Arrow, writing in 1974, typical of the line of Pigou-Samuelson-Arrow-Hahn-Stiglitz: "Trust and similar values, loyalty or truthtelling, are examples of what the economist would call 'externalities.' . . . They are not commodities for which trade on the open market is technically possible or even meaningful."[12] Huh? Oh, Ken, Ken. Klein proceeds in a chapter on "The Integrity of You and Your Trading Partners" to give with ease, of course, scores of examples of markets, such as the old Marshall Field's department store in Chicago, providing trust, loyalty, truth telling, in bulk. How, I worry, are we to persuade *anyone* of the merits of a truly liberal society if so intelligent an economist as Kenneth Arrow overlooks the relevance to the performance of markets of such obvious assurance mechanisms as hired inspectors, brokers, branding, franchising, *Consumer Reports*, Yelp, and gossip?

Something therefore is terribly wrong scientifically with the Samuelsonian approach to innovation. What is wrong, Klein argues, is that a quasi-Kirznerian entrepreneurship is left out, even in some moods by such wise heads as Frank Knight. The leaving out is a piece with the narrowing of economics to Max U players who already know all the rules of the game. A particularly ignorant and dogmatic exponent of this view is by Kenneth Binmore (Binmore was trained, by the way, as a mathematician, not an economist; but unlike another math PhD in economics, Steve Landsburg, Binmore never paused to learn Good Old Price Theory[13]). "Game theorists usually assume," Binmore writes with lordly assurance, "that the rules of the game and the preferences of the players are common knowledge."[14] Goodness. It's the Northian assumption, and it is Samuelsonian, and it is, well, pretty silly. The rules of the human game are always under discussion, moment by moment, in the courts or in Congress, and anyway in the agora, and therefore the analogy in game theory of society to a game of checkers, while once in a while is a little bit illuminating, is very far from an all-purpose social science.

"Economists and game theorists typically assure closure," Klein remarks, "by assuming that agents interpret things in a definite and final way. . . . Models teach much. . . . But overexposure to [Max U] models . . . can impair our ability to see . . . that there is much that is *not* known, even knowable," such as the differential equations that keep a bicycle rider upright, for which see Michael Polanyi (Karl's smarter brother).[15] "We forget that the knowledge we articulate," such as North's rules of the game, "rests on knowledge that is personal and tacit."[16] Thus humanomics.

*   *   *

But how to sell such an anti-Samuelsonian idea? Klein and I face a problem of persuasion. How can we change the minds of at least the thirty-something junior versions of Paul Samuelson and Kenneth Arrow or Douglass North? Klein's tactic is to cite Hayek or Kirzner and then to back up their theoretical claims by appealing to the new tradition of empirical Austrianism—thus, among his teachers Don Lavoie and Lawrence

White and among other of his colleagues Donald Boudreaux and Peter Boettke and Boettke's students, such as Emily Chamlee-Wright and Virgil Storr (although it is odd that not one of these are cited in Klein's book). Klein lists some striking case studies of the free-market provision of roads, for example, including his own study of historical turnpikes in colonial North America with John Majewski.[17]

But consider another Hayekian theme, of the contrast between two of the ideals of the Enlightenment. The one is that of liberty, which Klein and Hayek and Adam (and I say again Vernon) Smith and I admire, a liberty under which people innovate and find themselves in mostly good spontaneous orders, like those of language or art or of science itself. Such a pragmatic ideal is the characteristic goal of the *Scottish* Enlightenment, although France had a century earlier provided its leading phrase: *Laissez-faire, laissez-passer*. The "Smithian allegory," Klein writes, "could be further deployed to give better formulation to economic talk of market communication, social cooperation, and other basic ideas."[18] True.

The *French* Enlightenment, by contrast, admired rationality extravagantly and therefore the rule of experts, a rule which Adam Smith so deprecated. The modern descendants of the confident French are Pigou, Samuelson, Arrow, and Stiglitz. Their ideal is theoretical, not pragmatic. For example, Arrow's Impossibility Theorem arises from the Frenchman Condorcet (Ken was fluent in French), insisting on Perfection or Nothing, and ignoring the pragmatic compromises in a Mueller-style "pretty good" democracy. For another example, the left-Samuelsonian's pursuit of equality, or "social justice," comes with rational social engineering, because that is how such good things are to be achieved according to the "new" welfare economics of the 1930s exposited in *The Foundations of Economic Analysis*. It is utilitarianism on mathematical steroids. Take from Peter and give to Paul, if Paul is a better pleasure machine, or just better, from the expert tyrant's point of view. As Klein observes in one of his numerous vivid metaphors, if one ran a skating rink on social-engineering principles "to prevent collisions, [the planner] would have to. . . . [make the skating] slow and simple. . . . [The skaters] would not find the joy and dignity that come from making one's own course."[19] "Making one's own course" is saved from its apparent selfishness by a spontaneous order in a world in which there are many opportunities for mutually advantageous exchange — and to be sure occasional collisions. As Klein explains, "An important quality of collision is mutuality," just as in an exchange in a market. "If I don't collide with you, then you don't collide with me." If I don't succeed in getting you to agree to a bargain that hurts you, then you don't get hurt by the bargain we do in the end arrive at. "In promoting my interest in avoiding collision with you, I also promote your interest in avoiding collision with me."[20] And so the obvious and simple system of natural liberty, as Smith said, is expected to perform pretty well, like Ralph's Pretty Good Grocery.

The Samuelsonians want to *direct* society to an ideal performance in the style of French rationalism and are confident that they are just the people to do the directing. They are in this respect like lawyers rather than economists. They expect black-letter law together with the state's monopoly of coercion to determine, say, economic incidence, and they talk a good deal about laws "designed" to achieve such and such. I recalled earlier here how in the sixties we young economists at places like Harvard and MIT and Stanford were confident that the economy could be designed, that is, "fine-tuned." What killed such chutzpa—aside from the evident failure of designing and fine tuning in another sphere at the time, the war in Vietnam—was its *quantitative* failure. When, for example, even the stodgy old US of A, never mind Israel or Brazil, was experiencing in the late 1970s inflation rates of 13.3 percent per year, the magnitude was enough to kill off, say, the wage-price spiral of my first teacher of economics, Otto Eckstein.

*   *   *

And that's my point. I have been suggesting throughout this book, as an alternative tactic to Klein's Hayekian-Kirznerian narratives and case studies, that we undertake to criticize the Rationalists on *quantitative* grounds. It just might have success against the Samuelsonians. They are obsessed with pointless existence theorems and meaningless tests of statistical significance (Arrow, incidentally, emphatically agreed that statistical significance is meaningless, and said so in print early[21]). But they *believe* they adhere also to another rhetoric that developed mightily in the eighteenth and especially in the nineteenth century: Quantity, Calculation, Accounting, Oomph, Order of Magnitude. Boswell says to Johnson, "Sir Alexander Dick tells me that he remembers having a thousand people in a year to dine at his house; that is, reckoning each person as one each time he dined there."

JOHNSON: That, Sir, is about three a day.
BOSWELL: How your statement lessens the idea.
JOHNSON: That, Sir, is the good of counting. It brings every thing to a certainty, which before floated in the mind indefinitely.

BOSWELL: But . . . one is sorry to have this diminished.

JOHNSON: Sir, you should not allow yourself to be delighted with error.[22]

To persuade the Samuelsonians to move to a truly liberal society, I am suggesting here, use the attachment they think they have to Quantity.

"How things work *by and large*," correctly attributed by Klein to Marshallian thinking, is the crux.[23] You have to *measure*, *nationally*, if you want to establish that something is "by and large" true. Case studies, unless presumptively extreme bounds, won't persuade. You have therefore in your measurement to attend to possible biases and errors (and not only sampling errors). For this reason, I have noted, existence theorems are irrelevant to economic science. It is on/off, not "how much, by and large."

A sensitivity to approximation in former days was heavily reinforced by dependence on slide rules for multiplication. You can't get sensible results using a slide rule unless with every slip and slide you remind yourself about the order of magnitude you are calculating, because only then will you correctly locate the decimal point. Orders of magnitude were drilled into your head. With startling swiftness in the 1970s the slide rule became wholly obsolete, and the kids started thinking in eight- or sixteen-digit "exact" results instead of orders of magnitude. (We of the slide-rule generation also walked to and from school through six-foot drifts of snow, uphill both ways.)

For example, one can show that the existing governmental programs to help the poor are too small to do their job. Consider the statistics in the distributive-justice argument. If the one third and more of national income taxed by all levels of American government, summed, actually went to the poor, there wouldn't be any American poor. Here's how I know, engineering, slide-rule style. Suppose as much as a quarter of the one third went to the poor—well below the fraction people have in mind when defending governments as "helping the poor." The result is of course ⅓ × ¼ = ¹⁄₁₂ of gross domestic product, earmarked on the hypothesis for transfers to the poor. It would be about $1 trillion in 2006 terms (when I first made the calculation, in *The Bourgeois Virtues*, pp. 44–45). According to the official definitions for living in poverty, thirty-four million Americans did in 2006, over 10 percent of the population. The poverty figure, though in absolute terms has fallen dramatically since Presidents Kennedy and Johnson drew sharp attention to it in the 1960s, appalls. But whatever the dimensions of the problem, government doesn't seem to be the solution. If it were, then each poor person would be getting, according to the ¼ of ⅓ hypothesis, goods and services from the government equal to one trillion dollars divided by thirty-four million souls. That's about $30,000 for every man, woman, and child in poverty. And although $30,000 is still below the average gross domestic product per capita in 2006, which was about $40,000, no one would have called a family with two adults and two children getting goods and services in the amount of $120,000 a year "poor." With such an income, no poor. But there *were* poor, namely, those thirty-four million souls. It must not be true that the government's taxes and corresponding benefits go mainly, or even very much, to the poor. Well below one quarter. Hmm. Could it be that the benefits are going mainly to the middle class, which votes, not to the poor, which does not? Such a political economy would result in subsidized college educations, jobs in government for college graduates, roads outside the single-family houses of college graduates, police who treat college graduates with respect. Could be.

And of course the biggest instance is that the Great Enrichment cannot be explained by unions or governmental regulations. The productivity of the economy in 1900 was very low, and in 1800 lower. The only way that the bulk of the people were going to be made better off was by making the economy vastly more productive. Innovism did. The share going to the workers was roughly constant (it was rising for a long time during the nineteenth and early twentieth century, as land rents fell in share), though it fell by a few percentage points in the 1990s and 2000s. Labor's share was determined by the marginal productivity of workers and by competition. It didn't change all that much. Therefore, even the poorest workers shared in the rising productivity.

Put all the humanomics together—leaving off neoinstitutionalism and other illiberal behaviorisms—and you get the argument for a true liberalism of life, liberty, and the pursuit of happiness. Yes.

CHAPTER THIRTEEN

And Although We Can't Save Private Max U

B ecause orthodox economists of the illiberal left or right no longer
study philosophy in graduate school or because the philosophy they
might have studied as undergraduates is itself fiercely anti-ethical—a
course in symbolic logic, say, or a course in social-science methodology beginning and ending with logical positivism about 1920—they are thought-
less about ethics. Remember Erhard and Jensen.

Or, as the economist-philosopher Mark White observes in an essay
in a recent collection on the subject of the ethical formation of economists, they have merely two thoughts: Pareto and Kaldor-Hicks.[1] Pareto:
if *all* relevant people are bettered by a project, it should go through. (But
which people are relevant?). Or, much more weakly, Kaldor-Hicks: if the
winners *could* hypothetically compensate the losers, it should go through.
(But why "could" compensate? Why not actual compensation?) Kaldor-
Hicks, formulated in the 1940s, says, in other words, that if GDP per head
goes up, we should celebrate. A lucid exposition of the orthodox argument
is a classic article by A. C. Harberger in 1971.[2]

I am not so indignant against the orthodox argument as are many of
my leftish friends. The leftists say, "Look at who is hurt by your so-called
progress!" An extended example of the left's complaint is the collection of
their illuminating newspaper articles by the historians Kenneth Pomeranz
and Steven Topik, *The World That Trade Created: Society, Culture, and the
World Economy 1400 to the Present* (2006). Pomeranz and Topik, honorable men of the left, tell skillful tales of the losers from scores of historical
rises in GDP that might satisfy Kaldor-Hicks if not Pareto. But the book
is never about the winners, always about the losers, such as the exploited

Central American workers who harvested the fiber used to bind bales in US midwestern agriculture. It never mentions that the Great Enrichment 1800 to the present has increased income per head of the poorest, in Central America, too, not by 100 percent or even 500 percent, but by thousands of percentage points.

Unlike my leftish friends, I am very willing, as was the great Hans Rosling in his posthumous volume *Factfulness* (2008), to praise such a commercially tested betterment arising from economic liberalism considering that it achieved thousands of percentage points for the poor.[3] Yes, buggy-whip manufacturers and their skilled workers were hurt by the invention of the automobile. To which I reply, with my beloved friend and former colleague Harberger, "Not to worry. And if to worry, not to worry too much."

Mark White points out that Kaldor-Hicks is a utilitarian criterion and therefore violates the Kantian rule against using up others against their will. Utilitarianism in its crudest form, much favored by economists, merely adds up the dollars . . . uh, the interpersonally comparable utils of utility . . . of the community and then goes to lunch. No worries about distribution. But of course, as the economist Donald Boudreaux regularly points out, it is ethically crazy to assert, for example, that the dollar loss to people unemployed by a rise in the minimum wage, such as the people left by the law earning zero dollars instead of positive dollars, is offset in dollars by the lovely gains to the people who go on holding the now higher-paid minimum-wage jobs. Under what ethical system is it acceptable to damage *very* poor people, who are very unskilled, in aid of *somewhat* poor people, who are somewhat skilled? The extreme case is South Africa, in which a high minimum wage sponsored by the Congress of South African Trade Unions leaves millions of nonunionists in unemployment, upward of 50 percent of the Black population, sitting in huts in the uplands of Kwa-Zulu Natal. Yet one hears daily from leftish economists just such a calculation of the alleged net benefit from the minimum wage—when the inconsistent leftists are not busy denying outright the law of demand for hired labor (though affirming it for purchases of cigarettes or sugary drinks). About the unethical outcomes of the minimum wage they say, "Not to worry."

In the movie *Saving Private Ryan*, a company of seven or so US army rangers in the precarious weeks after the 1944 Normandy invasion are put in jeopardy going into a highly contested area in order to seek out and send home a Private James Ryan, all of whose three remaining brothers have just been reported killed in action. As one of the company points out diffidently, the expedition makes no utilitarian sense. Seven to one.

Around 1978 the Department of Economics at the University of Chicago was having its weekly luncheon at the Episcopal Theological Seminary cafeteria (the irony of such a pairing did not escape us; but a greater irony came a few decades afterward, when the expanded Department of Economics took over the churchy main building of the by then defunct seminary, making God truly into mammon). A student of Gary Becker's had determined by regression analysis across US states that each execution of a convicted murderer prevented seven other murders. Gary over lunch was telling us about it. I objected—admittedly without the ethical clarity I now claim to have achieved—that the government's official execution was not the same thing as a private murder. By permitting executions, among other coarsenings of our society, we honor an all-powerful government. After all, we could deter overparking by executing the offenders, at maybe one thousand to one. But execution is not in the same ethical coin as overparking. Gary turned contemptuous, as he often did in argument. As he strode away carrying his lunch tray he repeated angrily to me over his shoulder, "Seven to one! Seven to one!" Decades later Alex Tabarrok had the identical encounter with him over the same issue.[4] Gary's ethical thinking had not advanced.

True, as in the "Trolley Problem" in ethical philosophy, sometimes seven to one is ethically decisive. Do you pull the switch between two tracks to divert a runaway trolley to kill the seven people strapped to Track A or to kill the one person strapped to Track B? By itself in isolation, of course, with no other information about the victims (e.g., no information that the seven are assuredly mass murderers as against the one saint), you choose to kill one, not seven.

Or to kill a dog rather than a child. Simple. I remember listening on the BBC in 1967 to an interview with an animal-rights advocate of an extreme sort. (Britain has long had such people. The Royal Society for the Prevention of Cruelty to Animals was founded in 1824. The Royal Society for the Prevention of Cruelty to *Children* was not founded until 1884. Don't beat your horse. Do beat your child.) The interviewer sought to entrap the animal-rights advocate by saying, "Suppose you are speeding in your auto through a country lane on a dark night, impenetrable hedgerows on either side, and you come round a bend at top speed to find to your horror an infant child sitting on one lane of the road and a dog on the other. You have to kill one [thus the Trolley Problem]. Which do you kill?" There was a long silence. Very long. At last the advocate replied, "I hope I never have to face such a choice."

Or consider the example of protection. When the Trump administration imposed tariffs on imported steel because the secretary of commerce had once been a flack for the steel industry and because Trump's main adviser on trade is an economist who never quite got what he was supposed to learn in Econ 101, we savvy economists are likely to complain that the jobs saved in steel are far outweighed by the jobs lost in steel-using industries. Seven to one. Kaldor-Hicks. Though utilitarian, it is not an entirely silly argument, rhetorically speaking, considering that the protectionists like Peter Navarro are the ones who introduced the idea of the number of American jobs protected as an allegedly relevant ethical criterion.

In just such a Kaldor-Hicks manner, for example, the economist Maximiliano Dvorkin of the Federal Reserve Bank of St. Louis reckoned that from 2000 to 2007, the United States lost about 800,000 jobs to competition from China. (It was a tiny fraction, by the way, of the jobs "lost" from what we all agree were desirable technological changes, such as the demise of video stores and the other jobs moved or made obsolete. Such jobs amounted in the seven years out of a total labor force of 140 million to *scores* of millions, not a mere 0.8 million.) But according to Dvorkin, the trade with China *gained* on the same account a similar number of *other* US jobs for a net effect on jobs of zero. (The same is true on a much larger scale of the technological unemployment I just mentioned, or else we would at present [setting aside grossly mismanaged COVID-19 lockdowns, that is] almost all be unemployed.) But as a result of the lower prices from such reallocation and competition in the China trade, "U.S. consumers gained an average of $260 of extra spending per year for the rest of their lives."[5] Expressed as a capital sum discounted to the present, the free trade with China was like every consumer getting a onetime check for about $5,000. Good, not bad.

Yet Dvorkin's ethical logic is seven to one. In *Saving Private Ryan* the problem is solved quite differently. It is not solved outside of our ethical cultures with recourse to a merely utilitarian calculation of seven to one. The Tom Hanks leader and the rest of the company—and, to the present point, we the audience watching the film—understand that more is at stake. For example, the mission is about the definition of ourselves as humans deeply sympathetic with the soon-to-be-grieving mother. It is about our willingness to risk even death in order to honor such a sympathy. Additionally, it is about being an honorable soldier and obeying honorable orders unto death—orders such as for example in 1995 at Srebrenica the Dutch battalion charged by NATO with defending the Muslims most disgracefully did not. Honor is about identity. Seven to one is not.

*   *   *

I have noted that the more usual remark against Kaldor-Hicks from the economic left and middle (the illiberal right says simply, "To hell with the losers") is that after all Kaldor-Hicks is unethical if the compensation to the losers is not actually paid. Leftist literature is rich with such remarks, the better to undermine a market economics and its claimed fruit of progress, which like Pomeranz and Topik the authors regard as unethical and unreal.

All right, but the biggest problem with a Kaldor-Hicks, utilitarian defense of a project—to build, say, a new underground railway in London— lies in the very definition of a "project." (Note the prequantitative scientific work here, done necessarily by the humanities.) Every human action is a "project." White concludes that "if compensation is to be taken seriously, it should be incorporated into any proposal submitted to a Kaldor-Hicks test." But he notes that "externalities arise from almost any social interaction with overlapping interests." Yes: indeed, *every* social interaction entails overlapping interests. If Henry David Thoreau invents new methods to make high quality pencils, as he in fact did during the 1840s in his father's business, he harms the other makers. If actual compensation is to be paid to them, then *every* project of every person requires such payment. The Victoria Line, after all, has repercussions, however tiny, on the Isle of Mull.

The absurdity of such a procedure is evident. The point might be called the Boudreaux Reductio ad Absurdum, after the Austrian economist I have mentioned, Donald Boudreaux of George Mason University, who uses it often in criticizing schemes of trade protection. Start with the paradox of marketed bread. As John Donne famously put it, "No man is an island, / entire of itself. / Each man is a piece of the continent, / a part of the main." That is to say, *every* person's action to buy or not buy, to offer for sale or not, to enter a trade or not, to improve pencil-making machinery or not, affects someone else for better or for worse. If I buy a loaf of bread, someone else cannot have it. Or to put the point another way, my decision to buy the loaf will very, very slightly raise the price faced by every other buyer to the exact extent, when summed over all of them, of the price I paid. That's market economics (the particular point is one I first learned from the great Chinese price theorist S. N. S. Cheung).

Now the Boudreaux Reductio. Under actual compensation à la Kaldor-Hicks you should be stopped from buying bread because you impose a tort on others in buying it. Everyone should compensate everyone else for everything, for every human action. You can see there is a problem here. As Boudreaux puts the defense to the Reductio: "What no person is free to do is to oblige *others* to subsidize his or her choices. I, for example, should be free to work as a poet but not empowered to force you either directly to buy my poetry or to obstruct your freedom to spend your money on mystery novels, movies, and other items that compete with my poetry."[6] Compensation entails personal or governmental power against liberty. It is not a voluntary choice within a framework of individual rights. Such compensation, if carried out logically, is unethical.

The terrifying phrase of Sombart's popularized by Schumpeter, "creative destruction," arouses the same fears and the same proposals for protection. Yet it is not "capitalism" that requires creative destruction, *but any progressive economy*. If you don't want betterment to happen and don't want poor people to get rich by the 3,000 percent that they have in Japan and Finland and the rest since 1800, then fine, we can stick with the old jobs, keeping in their former employment the peasants, elevator operators and telephone operators, the armies of typists on old mechanical Underwoods, grocery stores with a clerk in an apron handing you the can of baked beans over the counter. But if innovation is to happen—Piggly Wiggly in Memphis in September 1916 initiating the self-service grocery store, or a North Carolina tobacco trucker initiating in 1956 the shipping container—then people, and also the machines and factories owned by the bosses and their stockholders, have to lose their old jobs. Human and physical capital has to reallocate. Of course.

How much? The startling truth according to the US Department of Labor statistic is fully 14 percent of jobs per year.[7] That's *every year*, in a progressing economy. The monthly labor reports you get on the news give the *net* US figure—in a good month two hundred thousand, that being the net of new jobs gained from moving or innovation or (a minor matter this one) import substitution minus the old jobs lost from the same. The startling gross figure should be more widely known. An improving economy requires the workers and the machines to move, to reallocate, to retrain, to shift, to innovate on a very large scale, about one in seven jobs a year. Another seven to one.

So the crudely practical problem with compensation and protection and schemes of subsidized retraining by government bureaucrats who do not actually know what the new jobs will be in five years is that we cannot "afford" to compensate one in seven of the workforce every year. In a few years half the workforce would be on the dole, or kept in their old jobs at the old pay, or trained in the wrong new jobs. For that matter we could try to keep physical capital, too, where it began, directing subsidies to factories and neighborhoods rather than letting the people and factories move as creative destruction requires. Such is the peculiar ethics of giving aid to geographical places—"Keep jobs in Springfield" instead of "Help Homer Jay Simpson to move." Carried out with philosophical consistency, the Boudreaux Reductio would require us to keep shoe manufacturing in Massachusetts as much as coal mining in West Virginia, economy wide, or for that matter traditional agriculture before the Green Revolution forever. Startlingly, the left in India in response to the Green Revolution argued exactly that.

The deeper philosophical problem is that the unethical logic of actual compensation and protection violates the rights of others. The problem is that ethics in economics has been thoughtlessly attached to Rousseau's notion of a general will. Deep in left-wing thought about the economy, and in a good deal of right-wing thought, too, is the premise, as Isaiah Berlin once put it with a sneer, that government can accomplish whatever it rationally proposes to do. As has been often observed about leftists even as sweet as was John Rawls, the left has no theory of the behavior of the government. It assumes that the government is a perfect expression of the will of The People. So goes the welfare economics in the 1930s of Abram Bergson and Paul Samuelson and the public finance in the 1950s of Richard Musgrave and behind them the (mathematically incoherent) goal of the 1820s of the greatest happiness of the greatest number, to be achieved by wise utilitarians in government, said Jeremey Bentham.

The liberals such as James Buchanan (1919–2013) do have a theory of government and a good deal of empirical work to back it up. Liberalism has always been a theory against and therefore about coercion. When my left-wing friends, of whom I have many, claim with a knowing smirk that in admiring markets I am "ignoring power," I have a way of replying: no, dear, it is you who are ignoring power, the power of the monopoly of coercion called a government.

More generally, indeed, the ethical problem among economists is the entire program of social engineering. The economist James Morgan is right to note that a peculiar "sense of mission and of entitlement are built into economics, and this contrasts with sociology and political science."[8] One could take the view that Adam Smith did say that it is in fact the "greatest impertinence" to proliferate policies. It is not at all controversial among most economists (but should be) to assume that they should be unsleepingly active in devising new ones.

*   *   *

In any case we need something to prevent the Boudreaux Reductio from being ethically required, with the ending of all human progress in science, the arts, or the economy. The usual guard rail is the notion of "rights." As John Stuart Mill put it in *On Liberty*, "society admits no right, either legal or moral, in the disappointed competitors to immunity from . . . suffering [from successful competition]; and feels called on to interfere only when means of success have been employed which it is contrary to the general interest to permit—namely, fraud or treachery, and force."[9] An ill-advised and undercapitalized pet store into which the owner pours his soul goes under. But he does not get compensation by way of Kaldor-Hicks. A little independent office for immediate health care opens half a block from a branch of the largest hospital chain in Chicago and seems doomed to fail the test of voluntary trade. The testing of business ideas in voluntary trade is obviously necessary for betterment in the economy—as it is too by nonmonetary tests for betterment in art and science and scholarship and would be in a wholly planned socialist economy too. But such failures are deeply sad if you have the slightest sympathy for human projects, or for humans. Yet we cannot admit a right to subsidy or protection or compensation. A pet store, the health-treatment office, the Edsel, Woolworth's, Polaroid, and Pan American Airlines face the same democratic test by trade: Do the customers keep coming forward voluntarily? That's all you as the pet store owner or as Boudreaux's imagined poet have a right to—the right to let the customers choose you or not, which is why commercially tested betterment is in its actual practice the most altruistic of systems. The customers, in line with the core principle of liberalism, get to say No.

Without such liberal rights to trade with whom we wish, we would all, by governmental compulsion backed by the monopoly of coercion, remain in the same jobs perpetually "protected." Or, with taxes taken by additional state coercion, we would subsidize new activities without regard to a commercial test by voluntary trade, "creating jobs" as the antieconomic rhetoric has it, venturing into the high frontier of space, for example, at enormous expense "because no private entity will do it."

Such schemes assume that the government knows better than profit-dependent businesspeople about what customers want or should have. It is the declared premise of Marianna Mazzucato's book of 2013. But consider the possibility that the reason no private entity will venture into the high frontier of, say, the Anglo-French Concorde airplane is that it makes no sense. If the assumption of governmental wisdom is mistaken, the effect of such venturing is to lower national income, which is a bad thing by the very assumption of the ethical system being applied. And the schemes assume that there is nothing objectionable about the coercion required in taxation and regulation to do the venturing in the first place.

Anyway, to descend again to crude practical problems, the protective schemes and governmental entrepreneurship seldom work for the welfare of the poor, not to speak of the rest of us. Considering how a government of imperfect people actually behaves in practice, the job "protection" and job "creation" regularly fail to achieve their gentle, generous, infantilizing purpose. The political decision-making means that the protections and creations get diverted to favorites, such as jobs for the boys and girls running poverty programs. Or spending on useless military jets, spread over every congressional district. Or premature ventures into the high frontier such as, Mazzucato's favorite, the Concorde. In a society of lords or clan members or Communist Party officials or even voters restricted by inconvenient voting times and picture IDs, the unequal and involuntary rewards generated by sidestepping the commercial test are seized by the privileged. The privileged are good at that.

No, we can't save Private Max U as ethics. We need the guide rails of rights, especially the liberal right to say No.[10]

A striking example of unethical behavior by economists arising from utilitarianism and seven to one is not the orthodox and Kaldor-Hicks-besotted development economists whom many criticize from the left but the science-besotted, field-experiment economists. They are to be criticized not from left or right—both of which are enthusiasts for big government and therefore big coercion in differing forms—but from the viewpoint of a liberalism in a society of liberated people having what Kant called equal dignity.[11] Mark White mentions at one point that the criterion of all-around win-win, that is, Pareto improvement, is ethically inadequate if lacking an answer to the question *which* people are the alleged winners.

But it is seen as the "gold standard" of tests of welfare by economists. Similarly, experiment economists such as Esther Duflo at MIT argue that double-blind experiments on other people not volunteers is the gold standard in medical research and therefore should be so in economics. After all, we need above all to be scientific, understood as exposited in high school chemistry. We are authorized to hurt one group to help another if seven to one—though of course we do not subject *ourselves* to the experiment. Shades of the minimum wage. The ethical contrast is sharp with the long history of *self*-experimentation in medicine, such as the courageous junior doctors and other volunteers under Dr. Walter Reed (though not Reed himself) in the 1900 confirmation that yellow fever is spread by mosquitos.[12] In the dismal, if brief, history of field experiments in economics, the worst case so far is described by Ziliak and Teather-Posadas.[13] The field experimenters gave out eyeglasses to Chinese children randomly to "test" whether being able to see Chinese characters affects the speed with which the children learn to read them—as though we didn't already know that children who can't discern characters can't learn to read them.[14] Any normally ethical person regards such an experiment as hideously unethical, using up other people (yet not our masterful academic selves) in anti-Kantian fashion. The ethical course is to not do the experiment at all and instead give away the money collected to provide glasses to as many needful Chinese children as you can find. The using up of the near-sighted children who do *not* get the glasses ("the control group") is justified by Kaldor-Hicks, at best, seven to one. And most especially it is justified by the juiced-up record of scientific publications by professors of economics at MIT or the University of Minnesota. In medicine the history of unethical field experiments on involuntary subjects is long. The economists propose now to initiate their own Tuskegee syphilis experiments, sacrificing one for seven.

A test: an economist actually, ethically, deeply believes in free international trade when she accepts that *her* ox may be gored, that she may lose some advantage. It is to experiment on oneself, in the style of the junior doctors under Walter Reed or Amartya Sen's "commitment"—that is, an act that *loses* utils or money, which registers thereby its genuine character.

CHAPTER FOURTEEN

We Can Save an Ethical Humanomics

A s Mark White summarizes the guard rail of rights, we object to a loss "particularly [he must mean 'only'] if those losses, or harms, involve violations of their rights, and are therefore wrongful, regardless of the net utility generated."[1] He quotes Richard Posner (who like him misunderstands Ronald Coase's eponymous theorem): "But when transaction costs are prohibitive, the recognition of absolute rights is inefficient." Well, not always.

What exactly are the "rights" that Boudreaux, McCloskey, White, Coase, Posner, and Mill find so lovely? "The homeowner who does not take as much care of his lawn as his neighbors do," says White, "is lowering their well-being and possibly their home values, but is not violating any widely recognized right of theirs."[2] Well, maybe, but not always.

Note: *widely recognized*. That's the key. The notion of rights is not technological but entirely social (which was Coase's *actual* point). We decide what are rights and what are not. In some societies I have the right to wear a dress that exposes my arms. But in Saudi Arabia and among orthodox Jews I do not, because of a socially formulated externality, the sexual temptation that such exposure is supposed to generate among men. We decide what is an externality. Or to put it the other way, we decide what are "widely recognized" rights that cannot be infringed. White says, "individuals are free to act in ways that do not necessarily increase total welfare, and may even lower it; this is the sense in which, as [the legal philosopher Ronald] Dworkin said, 'rights trump welfare.' "[3] Yes, I am free so to act. I can kill my cow just for the fun of it. But wait. Rights do *not* trump welfare in an ethical person—"widely recognized"—a person for example raised on a farm who views killing cows for no reason as evil. You have a right to falsify your economic research, at least in black-letter law, for example by sprinkling the fairy dust of instrumental variables on your regressions. You won't go to jail for it. But as an ethical person you will not let yourself do it.

We need to raise up people like that. That's the obvious and simple solution to the ethical formation of economists—not codes or formulas in an act of utilitarianism or constitutional constraints in black-letter law. Neither side, neither the professor of economics standing for absolute utility nor the law professor standing for absolute rights, speaks of the raising up of people. It is the characteristic vice of Western ethical philosophy since Descartes that it takes the individual to be a fully formed, male, Western, and philosophically inclined adult and pays no attention to how people are raised up to consider others or themselves or the transcendent, ethically speaking. Modern Western moral philosophy is peculiarly masculinist and, so to speak, adultist, taking an autonomous, finished adult, preferably a middle-aged and childless bachelor, as the site for philosophizing. Feminists such as Carol Gilligan and her many followers and critics do not forget that we were all once children, and feminists such as Nel Noddings and Annette Baier do not forget that we all came from families.[4]

Some men also do not forget it. Adam Smith did not, and Kenneth Boulding, and a few other precursors of humanomics.[5] The philosophy of the Scholastics and of the Greeks and Romans—and of Confucians in China and of Hindus and Buddhists in South Asia—treat raising up as crucial. The hero of the *Mahabharata*, the virtuous if flawed Yudhishthira, is asked by the mother of the Pandavas, "Why be good?" He replies, "Were *dharma* ['virtue,' among other meanings] to be fruitless . . . [people] would live like cattle."[6] Precisely. To be raised up as human is to put on the vestments of ethics. The cynical economist will sneer and believe he can get along with without any ethical vestments, "with no normative aspects whatsoever." But in his actual human life he puts them on without thinking. Yudhishthira's reply is exactly paralleled by Cicero lambasting the Epicureans—the ancient Mediterranean's version of Max U, Jensenite economists—as "those men who in the manner of cattle [*pecudum ritu*, literally, 'by the cattle's rite'] refer everything to pleasure" and who "with even less humanity . . . say that friendships are to be sought for protection and aid, not for caring."[7] Consult Gary Becker. Seven to one.

The method of ethical philosophy since Hobbes has been to abandon the ancient tradition of the virtues and its program of raising up a child to become an ethical adult, and instead to judge the goodness or badness of actions from afar by rule and formula developed in the seventeenth and eighteenth centuries among Western philosophers. A formula elevating one virtue to cover all the virtues became the master trick. For example, utilitarians in the train of Hobbes and Bentham and then the modern positivists such as Jensen and Becker fell for the theoretical impulse to collapse everything into prudence. The collapsing is as old as Mo-zi in China in the fifth century BCE, or the Epicurean school of the Greeks and Romans, or Machiavelli, or Hobbes, or Bernard Mandeville in the *Fable of the Bees* (1705, 1714, 1723). What Hobbes overlooked, and has been overlooked since by every ethicist eager to stand in judgement of actions, is that character matters and is more than a calculation of cost and benefit, even socially. Thus also humanomics.

Carol Gilligan long ago pointed out the masculinist character of stories of ethical development.[8] A standard story in tests of ethical development is the dying wife. A man's wife is dying of a treatable disease, but he does not have the money to buy the drug that can save her. Is it ethical for him to break into the drugstore and steal it? The male way of answering the question is to turn to an ethical formula, such as the one Kant proposed—in which case, no, he would not break in. It would violate Kant's categorical imperative that any act must be judged by its ability to be made into a general maxim. Stealing cannot be a general maxim, or the social world disintegrates. Yet girls and women answer in a more richly narrative way. They want to know what relationship the man and wife had, what kind of a person the druggist is, what the surrounding society is like. It's not the slam-bang rules such as the categorical imperative.

We need ethical raising up, not more ruminations on slam-bang formulas.

*   *   *

What sort of ethical raising up? Not Max U and Trumpism. People also have identities (faith) and projects (hope) for which they need courage and temperance, those self-disciplining virtues. And they all have some version of transcendent love—the connection with God, the traditional object, though modern substitutes are the worship of science or humanity or the revolution or the environment or art or rational-choice models in political science.

Mark White in an earlier essay had arrived at a similar conclusion. He said that a Kantian ethical theory posits a prudential and an ethical self, the choice between them being determined by a probability, p, that one has the strength of character to follow the ethical self. This seems to fit

Kant, and as White pointed out it also fits John Searle's notion of a "gap" in decision-making or free will. But White realized that something is fishy. "Is the probability distribution, representing one's character, exogenously given? Though that would make things much simpler, I should think not; it is crafted by our upbringing, and even to adulthood one can act to improve his character. Of course, this . . . [suggests] the question: to what goal or end does one improve character?" His reply was that "in the Kantian model . . . we assume that a rational agent's true goal is to be moral."[9] But that is the goal of being a virtuous person. His argument begs the question. It is circular (though in this field we are going to find that good is good, pretty much every time).

*　*　*

What to do, then for economics? Answer: raise up ethical men and women, some of whom become economists, and at best they will practice humanomics. We are not doing so now in the education of economists. The naive understanding of Friedman's 1970 essay on business ethics to the contrary, graduate students, and undergraduates, too, need to be told to be as ethically driven as Milton actually was as a man and an economist. What's needed is an ethical change of attitude, or character, as the economist George DeMartino puts it, "a practice of critical inquiry into the myriad ethical questions that arise in the context of and as a consequence of economic practice."[10] "Professional ethics" he continues, "is not in the first instance about preventing crooks, frauds and charlatans from acting badly." It's about ordinary life. It's not about incentives, as many economists instinctively suppose. It's about ethics at home. Shame. As teachers of writing put it, "Be good, and then write naturally." Or as Cato the Elder said, the rhetorician is "the good man speaking skillfully." The good economist is the good person speaking intelligently about the economy.

All right, how? Wim Groot and Henriette van den Brink in a recent essay quote Daniel Hamermesh, who noted that "professors in public universities—the large majority of economists [he may on this be wrong: nonacademic economists are numerous]—have a direct obligation to use their knowledge on a broader stage: They are paid by the public, and it behooves them to try to educate the entire public."[11] (Note the ethical evocation of the cash nexus even in the profession itself.) The responsibility is taken more seriously by Continental professors. I remember seeing once a complete bibliography for the great Swedish economists of a century ago—Wicksell, Heckscher, Ohlin, Cassel, as I recall—and being startled by how much educating of the entire public they all did, each publishing over their careers a journalistic piece once every fortnight or so. The responsibility should not be about "incentives." University professors in countries like the United States or the Netherlands or Sweden make enough to put that consideration aside. The fellow Dutch economist of Groot and van den Maassen, Arjo Klamer—another student of the humanistic economist at the University of Amsterdam, Joop Klant (1919–1994)—does so and contributes deeply and eloquently to the public conversation.[12] The point is professional responsibility, not vanity or Max U. After a dozen or so appearances on the national stage, the vanity and gratification wear out. One does it for the good of one's fellow citizens.

The medieval motto, I have noted, was "listen even to the other side." It is especially the ethical responsibility of a scholar and scientist to listen to the other side, though most, disgracefully, do not. An example of not listening, in this case to any side, is Anne Krueger's startlingly careless and slanted review in the *Journal of Economic Literature* of *The Oxford Handbook of Professional Economic Ethics* (2016) (edited by DeMartino and me: mainly, I report, by DeMartino).[13] (Anne, whom I admire very much as an economist, later partially apologized.) So, yes, the bourgeois, orthodox economists should listen.

But the left needs to follow its own advice. I have long observed that many heterodox economists do not actually know price theory, the core of liberal economics. They think they do—because they are clever, and have graduated from the New School (a place I wish I had taught at, to save such clever kids from this particular ignorance). But they don't. I invite them to open *The Applied Theory of Price* randomly (available free on my website: no excuses) and see whether they can answer any of the five hundred worked problems there. A less embarrassing way to get the price theory and the thinking like an economist straight is to read in Austrian economics. In recent decades (after many earlier decades of *not* getting Austrian economics), I have been trying to persuade my friends on the left that Austrian economics is also heterodox, though promarket. Except for the remarkable Ted Burczak at Denison University, who urges Marxists to read Hayek, they aren't biting.[14] If you ask me to listen open-mindedly to Marx or Myrdal or Mirowski, dears, it is only fair that you listen open-mindedly to Mill and Menger and Mises.

George DeMartino, a man of the left, does. He emphasizes the "irreparable ignorance . . . [economists face as they] try to understand, predict, and control inherently complex systems," and then immediately earns his pluralistic street cred by pointing out that that Austrians (he cites Hayek) and Knightians and Shackleites know it too.[15] The economist James Morgan has noted that "the elimination of philosophy, methodology, history of economic thought and ethics from the education of the economist [means that they miss that] . . . both Austrians who follow Hayek and structural and post-Keynesians. . . . [emphasize] cumulative causal processes."[16] Yet aside from Morgan and George and Ted and some of my friends at *Rethinking Marxism*, together with once upon a time Herb Gintis and Sam Bowles, few on the heterodox left listen to the heterodox liberals of the Austrian tradition, even those presently flourishing at George Mason.

White speaks of Kant's notion of "a *dignity*, an incalculable and incomparable worth, due to their capacity for autonomous choice—that is, the ability of make ethical choices despite inclinations or preferences to the contrary."[17] Note the last clause, "despite preferences." I suggest that the economics should focus on the Austrian notion of "human action," which is emphatically about autonomous, real, difficult choice but not about mechanical pseudochoice. The utilitarians focus on *re*action, instead of action. They focus on the utils gathered from a faux "choice" literally predetermined by taste and constraints instead of the dignity achieved by reflecting on the choice in the first place.

Not rules, constraints, institutions, but ethics. What we really need is not a social, eighth-floor criterion but a ground-level one, which is to say a continuously renegotiated agreement among actual people trying to be good, down at the level of individual ethics, to participate in a liberal society willing to accept 3,000 percent enrichments of the poor. White properly attacks merely "potential Pareto improvements" when they are not defended by anything more than 10 > 9. We need an ethic or ideology of innovism, 3,000 > 1 in the long run rather than 10 > 9, or even 7 > 1, in the short. The locus of ethics is not the society but the person. "Social justice," as the Austrians say all the time, to the puzzlement of their colleagues left and right, is meaningless.

What concretely to do? DeMartino speaks of internships, residencies, and immersions, an approach to economic science that my friend Richard Weisskoff of the University of Miami has long advocated in economics, and practiced. I've often thought that such fieldwork would be good, especially for graduate students, though I myself am typical of academic economists in having done none of it myself. But before sending the kids out, they have to told to be good and then to discover economic truth naturally by reading widely. The good economist speaking skillfully. Reinstate as a required course in graduate programs the history of economic thought. That way the economists can learn what Mill and Pareto and Wicksteed actually said, largely favorable to a liberal regime of commercially tested betterment. Have one less econometrics course, say. Turn one of the remaining econometrics courses into a course on the numerous ways other than regression analysis that we can measure the social world.

*   *   *

Language as ethics: that is what we need. DeMartino envisions the economics initiate taking a ceremonial oath.[18] It is an excellent idea. Economists sneer at such "mere rhetoric."

Craig Duckworth in a recent essay expresses a desire to haul conscience over into institutions and incentives, à la Oliver Williamson: "the taking of an oath functions, in intention, as an institutional device. The responsibilities it entails, structure behaviour so as to achieve objectives towards which professions may not be naturally inclined, and that are not easy to incentivise."[19] Compare Douglas Allen's book discussed earlier. Duckworth finds it "difficult to be convinced that, in this context, the act of commitment itself provides the basis of the normativity of a professional code of conduct."

I am surprised. Duckworth doubtless runs his own professional life ethically from the man within. If his college dean would say, "Cheat to get promotion," he wouldn't do it. Duckworth says, strangely, "commitment (being voluntary) can be withdrawn ad libitum." So he seems to fall for Hobbes. In Hobbes, and Duckworth, and most economists, promises are not promises, commitments are not commitments, responsibility is not responsibility, ethics is not ethics. As someone put it recently, truth is not truth.

Well, no. Or rather, yes, we need ethics, expressed in words, which will get us to as much of a worthwhile scientific truth as we need. Which, after all, is the point of saving private Ryan and of saving economic science and making a humanomics.

Acknowledgments

All the chapters originating in previously publications by me have been more or less heavily revised and rearranged. Hints to the original sources are given below.

The Argument in Brief. New.

Chapter 1. New.

Chapters 2, 3, 4. "The Two Movements in Economic Thought, 1700–2000: Empty Economic Boxes Revisited," *History of Economic Ideas* 26, no. 1 (2018): 63–95.

Chapter 5. "The Ethical and Scientific Offences of Erhard and Jensen." A comment on Erhard and Jensen, "Putting Integrity into Finance: A Purely Positive Approach." *Capitalism and Society* 12, no. 1 (May): art. 5.

Chapter 6. "A Neo-Institutionalism of Measurement, Without Measurement: A Comment on Douglas Allen's *The Institutional Revolution*." *Review of Austrian Economics* 26, no. 4 (2013): 262–373.

Chapter 7. "Getting beyond Neo-Institutionalism: Virgil Storr's Culture of Markets." *Review of Austrian Economics* 27 (2014): 463–72.

Chapters 8 and 9. From chapters in *Bourgeois Dignity* (2010) and *Bourgeois Equality* (2016), both University of Chicago Press.

Chapter 10. "Neo-Institutionalism Is Not Yet a Scientific Success: A Reply to Barry Weingast." *Scandinavian Economic History Review* 65 (2017): 116–23.

Chapter 11. "The Humanities Are Scientific: A Reply to the Defenses of Economic Neo-Institutionalism" (by Greif, Mokyr, Langlois, Lawson, and Tabellini). *Journal of Institutional Economics* 12, no. 1 (2015): 63–78.

Chapter 12. "Austrians, Anti-Samuelson, and the Rhetoric of Quantification: A Comment on Daniel Klein's *Knowledge and Coordination.*" *Studies in Emergent Order* 7 (2014): 15–29.

Chapters 13 and 14. "Conclusion: Raising Up Private Max *U.*" In *The Ethical Formation of Economists*, edited by Wilfred Dolfsma and Iona Negru, 164–83. London: Routledge, 2019.

Notes

Introduction

1. DeMartino (2011), DeMartino and McCloskey (2016), and a brilliant attempt to square true liberalism with economics, Altman (2020).

2. Popper 1945.

3. Rorty 1983.

4. Lavoie 1990.

5. Smith and Wilson 2018.

6. On some of the problems with such behaviorism, see McCloskey (2018).

7. For which see McCloskey and Mingardi (2020).

8. Altman 2020; Langlois 1994, 2002; Klamer 2007, 2017; Wilson 2010, 2020; Smith and Wilson 2018; DeMartino 2011; DeMartino and McCloskey 2016. And numerous economic sociologists.

9. Kelling and Wilson 1982

10. Feynman 1974.

11. Doyle 1886, chap. 3.

12. Novick (1988) on American history. Novick told me that in Ranke's phrase, *eigentlich* should actually be translated "essentially," which gives the phrase a less naively Baconian sound.

13. McCloskey 1998a.

14. Koopmans 1957, viii.

15. On Bergman, McCloskey (1998b) and Orcutt (1961).

16. A popular discussion of this undoubted scientific fact about humans, bonobos (not other chimps), elephants, and whales is Christakis (2019).

17. Smith (1776), 1.22, first and second paragraphs

Chapter One

1. Harris (1995) tells of Chomsky's war against heresy. In case you need to know,

Samuelson (whom I never knew personally) was my mother's mixed-doubles tennis partner.

2. Acemoglu and Robinson 2006, 2012.

3. Wilson 2020.

4. Umbeck (1977) and Radford (1945), and extensions and generalizations in Stringham 2015 and Bell 2018. David Skarbeck notes the puzzle of order in prisons and solves it brilliantly—though too much along neoinstitutionalist lines.

5. 1 Samuel 8.

6. Weatherford 2004.

7. Weatherford 2004, 224.

8. *Brennu-Njáls Saga*, 70 kalfi. Njál is speaking to Mord at the Althing, the Icelandic gathering for trade and law reading and dispute settling: In the translation in the Gutenberg Project it is in chapter 69, not 70.

9. All the learning here is extracted from http://forum.wordreference.com/threads /icelandic-proverb.788627.

10. Compare Robert Higgs's ([2012] 2015, intro.) argument that families and neighborhoods could enforce most laws better than a remote state.

11. Kimbrough, Smith, and Wilson 2010; Wilson et al. 2012.

12. Kimbrough, Smith, and Wilson 2010, 208.

13. See Hazlett 2017.

14. A brilliant discussion of the role of Arrow's Impossibility Theorem in political science is Saucedo (2021).

15. Bourne 2019.

16. For example, again, Harberger (1954).

17. Epstein 2009, xii–xiii.

18. Boaz 2015, 1.

19. Smith 2002, 2007.

20. Mazzucato 2013; Mingardi 2015; McCloskey and Mingardi 2020.

21. Ostrom 1990, 215.

22. Diamond 2019.

23. Spender (1989, intro.), and also Spender (2014), the preface of which calls it "a second shot at the same target." Spender found that the lawyer, banker, and philosopher Alfred Schlitz used the same word, *recipe*, thinking of it as flexible, modified by the master chef in practice.

24. DeMartino and McCloskey 2016

25. On guilds, against the statist and neoinstitutionalist fantasy of their benevolence, see Ogilvie (2019).

26. Shultziner et al. 2010, 123–24.

Chapter Two

1. Veblen 1898.

2. A51/B76. See the lucid discussion of this famous remark by Robert Hanna in "The Togetherness Principle, Kant's Conceptualism, and Kant's Non-conceptualism," in *Stanford Encyclopedia of Philosophy*, http://plato.stanford.edu /entries/kant-judgment/supplement1.html.

3. Clapham 1922.

4. A point suggested to me by Wei Shuangda of Zhejiang University.

5. Smith 1776, 7.9.3.

6. Wasserstein and Lazar 2016.

7. Quoted in Hodges (1983), 154.

8. Philosophers habitually use on-off qualitative categories to recommend, for example, reducing to quantities the psychology of risk-taking. Lining up qualitative arguments with a *qualitative* theory of probability, by contrast, is described in two articles by Stefánsson (2016a, 2016b).

9. McCloskey 2012.

10. "Aus so krummem Holze, als woraus der Mensch gemacht ist, kann nichts ganz Gerades gezimmert werden" is from Kant's "Idea for a Universal History on a Cosmopolitan Plan" (1784), sixth thesis. The remark was made famous among English speakers by Isaiah Berlin. Kant took it from the Bible, in Ecclesiastes 1:15,"That which is crooked cannot be made straight." One stands amazed that many secular students of Kant insist that his upbringing as a German Pietist had no influence on his thinking.

11. Sowell (2015), 114. Donald Boudreaux drew my attention to the passage.

12. Giovannoni (2014), fig. 8, p. 21. The "property" complement of the share of income accruing to employees, with an attribution of the laboring part of mixed incomes (such as those of proprietors such as farmers), rises from 16 percent in 1960 to 22 percent in 2012. Enterprise profit should exclude rents, which are included here. But because rents are also absorbed by socialist states, the category (determined by the humanities) here is about right.

13. I treat that particular, and troubled, humanistic definition in chap. 13.

14. Folbre 2001.

15. Jouvenel (1961) 1999.

16. Clapham 1922, 305, 311–12.

17. McCloskey 1989.

Chapter Three

1. Waterman (2012), 425. I have slightly modified the punctuation.

2. Peart and Levy 2005.

3. McCloskey and Mingardi (2020) explores the point.

4. Stiglitz interview in the *International Herald Tribune*, October 11, 2006.

5. Baran and Sweezy (1966). It is significant that Sweezy's prize-winning PhD thesis in the Harvard Economic Series (1938) was on the early monopolization of the English coal trade.

6. Harberger (1954) on allocative monopoly; Tullock (1967) on rent seeking; H. Gregg Lewis (1963, 1986) on trade union success; McCloskey (1970) on overinvestment abroad.

7. Solow 1956.

8. R. Sato (1963, 1966). Amusingly, another Japanese Sato, one K. Sato, immediately questioned the claim, bringing it down to thirty years. But thirty years still makes steady-state analysis mistaken as policy. A treatment of the state of play is Reiss (2000).

9. Briggeman 2015.

10. Fukuyama 1989, 1992; McCloskey 2020a.

11. Hobsbawm 2011, 416.

12. Simon 1947; Shackle (1972) 1992; Coase 1960; Kirzner 1979.

13. An analysis of the offending passage in its original French is in McCloskey (2014).

14. See, for example, the short essays on various books over the years by Robert Reich in McCloskey (2020b).

Chapter Four

1. Again, Hazlett (2017).

2. Nordhaus 2004.

3. Telser (2007). I came to it from my friend the economist David Haddock of the Northwestern Law School, who was a student of Telser's.

4. See, for example, the astonishing chart in Braudel and Spooner (1967). Subsequent studies have not improved on their chart by marshaling meaningless tests of statistical "significance."

5. For the popular case, McCloskey and Carden (2020).

6. That I do not give citations for the assertions in the paragraph does not mean the evidence for their truth does not exist. For each it does, though of course there are contrary findings too. We are dealing with science, not holy writ. But I cannot resist citing one theoretical essay showing the illogic, at least, of my teacher Chamberlain: McCloskey (1985), chap. 20, sec. 1.

7. Feynman (1965) 2017, 156, 160.

Chapter Five

1. MacIntyre 1981, 11, his emphasis.

2. Hobbes, *Leviathan* (1651) 1914, pt. 1, chap. 6, p. 24; chap. 15, p. 82.

3. Robbins (1932), 134. Amartya Sen (1987) says that such a view was "quite unfashionable then." Not I think among the reigning *fashionistas* of 1932.

4. Blaug 1980, 132–33.

5. Wilson 2010.

6. Quoted in McEvoy (2001), 291. The provenance of the remark is a little hazy, but it is very well known. In Danish, the philosopher Hans Siggaard Jensen informs me, it was something like "Fysik er ikke om hvordan verden er, men om hvad vi kan sige om den."

7. "Am Anfang / war das Wort / und das Wort / war bei Gott / Und Gott gab uns das Wort / und wir wohnten / im Wort / Und das Wort ist unser Traum / und der Traum ist unser Leben." From Rose Äuslander, *Gedichte von Rose Ausländer*, http://www.deanita.de/buecher19.htm.

8. Ziliak 2008.

9. Duhem 1914, 281; 1954, 185.

10. Feynman 1963, 1:22–21.

11. The story is from Reid (1986).

12. Wilson 2010.

Chapter Six

1. Allen 2011, 218. "Holding the weather gage" means arranging that your ship is to windward of the ship you are attacking, which gives you the advantage of being able to attack when he other ship would have to tack into the wind to do so.

2. For a recent collection of examples, see McCloskey (2020b), *Historical Impromptus*. For bigger cases before the trilogy on the Bourgeois Era, see Ziliak (2001).

3. O'Brien 1993, 2011a, 2011b; Greenfield 2001, 2012; Parthasarathi 2011; Mazzucato 2013.

4. Allen 2011, p. 79.

5. Cannadine 1990, app. B, p. 711, and discussion pp. 206–22.

6. North, Wallis, and Weingast 2009.

7. Allen 2011, 65.

8. Ó Gráda 2009.

9. North and Weingast 1989.

10. Mokyr 2009.

11. For detailed justifications for what follows, see McCloskey (1985), chaps. 22–25.

12. Mokyr 2009; Boldrin and Levine 2008.

13. Allen 2009.

14. Again, Smith (1776), 7.9.3.

15. Kirzner 1976, 79.

16. Kirzner, 84.

17. Allen 2011, 4.

18. North and Thomas 1973, 157.

19. Broadberry and Bishnupriya 2005; Allen 2009; Zanden 2009.

20. Jones 2010, 27–29.

21. Jones, 29.

22. Jones, 245.

23. Allen 2011, 219, 226.

24. Allen, 248n12.

25. Allen, 220.

26. McCloskey 2001.

27. Allen 2011, 107.

28. Allen, 21.

29. Allen, 19.

30. Allen, 110.

Chapter Seven

1. Battalio and Kagel 1975, 1981.

2. Sen 1977.

3. Quoted in Storr (2012), 26.

4. Quoted in Storr, 24, emphasis added.

5. Storr, xiii.

6. Storr, 98.

7. Ingram and Roberts 2000.

8. Storr 2012, 25.

9. Klamer 2007, 2017; Zelizer 2005; Smith and Wilson 2018; Chamlee-Wright and Storr, 2010; Chamlee-Wright 2010.

10. Greif (1989), quoted in Storr (2012), 1.

11. Storr 2012, 3.

12. Storr, 9.

13. Storr, 48

14. David (1985), but see Lewin, (2002); the point about easy adoption of non-QWERTY keyboards is mine, from a blog before blogs.

15. Storr (2012), 48.

16. Storr, 25.

17. Storr, 33.

18. Hyde 1998.

19. Easterly 2001; McCloskey 2010, 125–67.

20. Storr 2012, 57.

21. Simon (1981) 1996.

22. Chamlee-Wright and Lavoie (2000), quoted in Storr (2012), 47.

23. Nee and Swedberg 2007, 4–5.

24. Weber (1904–1905). It is one of the numerous crazy consequences of the

author-date system, by the way, that Storr refers to this throughout as "Weber 2011," based on the 2011 translation.

25. Storr 2012, 59.

26. Storr 2012, 66–69

27. Weber (1958 [translation of Weber 1904–1905]), 79, emphasis removed.

28. Searle 2010, 95.

29. Searle (2010), 95–96, emphasis added, and my additions in brackets. Compare Sen on "commitment," or for that matter my own articulation of commitments as virtues (McCloskey 2006).

30. Searle 2010, 115.

31. Searle, 113.

32. Searle, 122.

33. McCloskey 2016, chaps. 25, 26.

34. Searle 2010, 10.

35. Searle, 12, 17.

36. Fish 1980.

37. Searle 2010, 8.

38. Oakeshott (1933) on modal verbs (e.g., *ought, may, would*) entailed in all thought, including science; and Putnam (1990), 115.

39. Searle 2010, 7.

40. Searle, 9.

41. Searle, 105.

42. Searle, 106.

43. Boettke 2012, 12.

44. Kiesling 2011; Boettke 2011.

45. North and Weingast 1989.

46. The "others" are admittedly a small bunch, so enchanted have people been by North and Weingast, but it would include Peter Murrell (2009).

47. Acemoglu (2008); compare Acemoglu, Johnson, and Robinson (2005), citing R. H. Tawney, unaware, it seems, that such Fabian views of a century ago have been overturned by historical science.

48. Miller 1951, 131.

49. Campbell 2005, 8.

50. Campbell, 10.

51. Raftis 1996, 4.

52. McCloskey 1975a, 1975b, 1976.

53. Raftis 1996, 118.

54. Raftis, 7, 9–10; Berman 1983.

55. Raftis 1996, 214n40.

56. O'Brien 1993, 126, table 6.1.

57. Clark (2007) is good on this, pp. 10, 212.

58. Chaucer (ca. 1400) 1992, "General Prologue," lines 276–77.

Chapter Eight

1. Parks 2013, 8–9, 18, 143–44.
2. Davis 2012, 453–55.
3. Rossi and Spagano 2014.
4. Mueller (1985). Remarkably, it is the same Mueller who does political science.
5. McCloskey (1998b, 2008). And while we're speaking of price theory, McCloskey (1985), available as a pdf free at deirdremccloskey.org.
6. Carlos and Lewis 1999, 726.
7. Adams 1994.
8. Zamagni 2010, 63.
9. Das 2009, p. xxxiii–xxxiv.
10. http://www.transparency.org/cpi2012/results.
11. World Bank, "Doing Business," http://www.doingbusiness.org/rankings; real income, Penn Tables for 2010.
12. Razafindrakoto, Roubaud, and Wachsberger 2013, English abstract.
13. Acemoglu and Robinson 2012, 450.
14. Coate 2010, 15.
15. Chamlee-Wright and Storr, eds. 2010; Chamlee-Wright 2010.
16. Williamson 1999, 322.
17. Williamson, 324.

Chapter Nine

1. Personal correspondence, February 6, 2021.
2. North and Weingast 1989.
3. I owe my colleague Joseph Persky for the idea of adding $f(N, I)$.
4. Will 2019, 236.
5. Will, 227.
6. Will, 235.
7. Will, 236.
8. Gilomee 2003.
9. Lincoln (1858) 1894, 298.
10. "The Garden," at https://www.poetryfoundation.org/poems/44682/the-garden-56d223dec2ced.
11. McCloskey 2016.
12. For which see some of the articles in McCloskey 2020b.
13. Ridley 2010.
14. Haskell 1999, 10.
15. Buber 1937, 4, 18.
16. Buber 1967, 202.

17. Nona and Storr 2012.

18. North 1991, 103.

19. Geertz, Geertz, and Rosen (1979), 137, quoted in North (1991), 104, emphasis added.

20. Iannaccone 1998.

21. North 1991, 99.

22. Greif 2006, 9, 71, 115, 154, 187.

23. McCloskey 2020a.

24. Melville, *Moby-Dick*, chap. 41.

25. Keuhn 2008, 20.

Chapter Ten

1. Weingast 2016, 190.

2. Weingast, 199.

3. Weingast, 199.

4. Sandburg 1979.

5. Weingast 2016, 189.

6. North and Weingast 1989.

7. Weingast 2016, 190.

8. Weingast, 190.

9. James Stuart, James VI of Scotland (1598) 1996], 69, emphasis added.

10. Weingast 2016, 190.

11. For example, Lyou Dzung-Ywan in the Tang dynasty (in Whincup 1987, 161). In Whicup's translation, the top-scoring bureaucrat Lyou writes, "Fortunate now / This banishment to the southern wilds," giving him time to become, in Whincup's judgment, "one of Tang China's greatest prose masters."

12. Hobbes (1651) 1914, chap. 14.

13. Hobbes, chap. 17.

14. Wilson 2010.

15. Weingast 2016, 190.

16. McCloskey 2006.

17. Weingast 2016, 191.

18. Hill 2016.

19. Coşgel and Ergene 2016.

20. Zakaria 2019.

21. Fish 1980, 2001, 47, 57, 92.

22. Weingast 2016, 191.

23. Weingast, 191n2.

24. Weingast, 191n2.

25. North, Wallis, and Weingast 2009, 192–193.

26. North, Wallis, and Weingast, 194.

27. Weingast 2016, 191.

28. Weingast, 195.

29. Weingast, 199.

Chapter Eleven

1. Greif and Mokyr (2015), 30; the "early version" was the article in the *Journal of Institutional Economics*, McCloskey (2015a).

2. Smith (1759) 1790, 7.2.4.12, p. 312.

3. Smith, 7.2.4.12, p. 299.

4. Kelly, Ó Gráda, and Mokyr 2013; McCloskey 1976; Ogilvie 2019; etc.

5. Tabellini 2015.

6. Boettke (2011), quoted in Kiesling (2011).

7. Allen 2009; McCloskey 2010, 188–91.

8. Greif and Mokyr 2015, 30.

9. McCloskey 2016, chaps. 25, 26.

10. Lincoln (1858) 1894, 298.

11. Langlois 2015.

12. Lawson 2015.

13. Easterly 2001.

14. McCloskey, "Schumpeter the Incomplete Rhetorician." Unpublished. Available at deirdremccloskey.org.

15. For which see the little papers and reviews collected in McCloskey 2020b.

16. Tabellini 2015.

17. Levi (1945) 1947.

18. Armstrong (2009) 2010.

19. Luther, Sermon 25:7, quoted in Armstrong (2009) 2010, 171.

20. Wigner 1960.

21. Ziliak and McCloskey 2008, 2.

22. Ziliak and McCloskey 2019.

23. Banfield 1958.

24. Kealey 1996, 2008; Mokyr 2016.

Chapter Twelve

1. Stigler 1987, 90.

2. Klein 2012, 12; Stigler 1961.

3. Kirzner 1985, 30.

4. Klein 2012, 119.

5. Klein, 87–89, gives an illuminating exposition.

6. Ridley 2010, 1, 270.

7. Minsky, *The Society of Mind* (1986), 66, quoted in Klein (2012), 92.

8. Minsky, 302, quoted in Klein (2012), 92.

9. Klein (2012), 142.

10. Sarasvathy 2013.

11. Klein (2012), 113.

12. Arrow (1974), 23, quoted in Klein (2012), 180.

13. Landsburg 2017.

14. Binmore (1992), 150. It is indicative of a trivializing attitude among some theorists in economics toward the field that Binmore titled his textbook "Fun and Games." If you ask theorists what their scientific purpose is, they will often reply, "Fun." That's nice. Society pays an economist-mathematician a good deal of money to indulge his fun.

15. Polanyi 1958.

16. Klein (2012), 10. Klein is referring in *tacit* and *personal* to the words introduced into science studies in the 1950s by Polanyi (a chemist of Hungarian origin at the University of Manchester, eminent just below the level of the Nobel; his son won it in chemistry).

17. Klein (2012), 173

18. Klein, 31.

19. Klein, 5.

20. Klein, 4.

21. Arrow 1959 (1960). I got him to say so to a big audience at the American Economic Association meetings in Chicago around 2000, and he did. But then I turned to him and asked him to also foreswear meaningless existence theorems. No go.

22. Boswell (1791) 1949, 2:456.

23. Klein 2012, xiii.

Chapter Thirteen

1. White 2019.

2. Harberger 1971.

3. Rosling, Rosling, and Rosling Rönnlund 2018, 47–74.

4. Tabarrok 2015.

5. Dvorkin 2017; see also Caliendo, Dvorkin, and Parro 2015.

6. Boudreaux 2018.

7. See Diamond 2019; Haltiwanger 2011; McCloskey 2017b.

8. Morgan 2019.

9. Mill (1859) 2001, 86–87.

10. Schmidtz 2011, 784–85.

11. Alice Nicole Sindzingre (2019) gives in the same volume in which White wrote an excellent survey of the numerous ethical problems involved.

12. Weisse 2012; Mehra 2009.

13. Ziliak and Teather-Posadas 2019.

14. Glewwe, Park, and Zhao 2012.

Chapter Fourteen

1. White 2019, 78.

2. White, 88.

3. White, 84.

4. Gilligan 1982; Noddings 1984; Baier 1994.

5. Boulding 1956, 1973.

6. Das 2009, 73.

7. Cicero (44 BCE) 1923, 32.

8. Gilligan 1982.

9. White 2006, in the manuscript of 2005, p. 15.

10. DeMartino 2019, 9.

11. Groot and Maassen van den Brink 2019, 136.

12. Klamer 2007.

13. Krueger (2017), and our reply, DeMartino and McCloskey (2018).

14. Burczak 2006.

15. DeMartino 2019, 11.

16. Morgan 2019, 155.

17. White 2019, 79.

18. DeMartino 2011.

19. Duckworth 2019, 181.

Works Cited

Acemoglu, Daron. 2008. "Growth and Institutions." In *The New Palgrave Dictionary of Economics*, 2nd ed., edited by S. N. Durlauf and L. E. Blume. London: Palgrave Macmillan.

Acemoglu, Daron, Simon Johnson, and James Robinson. 2005. "The Rise of Europe: Atlantic Trade, Institutional Change, and Economic Growth." *American Economic Review* 95:546–79.

Acemoglu, Daron, and James A. Robinson. 2006. *Economic Origins of Dictatorship and Democracy*. Cambridge: Cambridge University Press.

Acemoglu, Daron, and James A. Robinson. 2012. *Why Nations Fail: The Origins of Power, Prosperity, and Poverty*. New York: Crown Business.

Acemoglu, Daron, and James A. Robinson. 2019. *The Narrow Corridor: States, Societies, and the Fate of Liberty*. New York: Penguin.

Adams, John. 1994. "Economy as Instituted Process: Change, Transformation, and Progress." *Journal of Economic Issues* 28 (June): 331–55.

Allen, Douglas W. 2012. *The Institutional Revolution: Measurement and the Emergence of the Modern Economic World*. Chicago: University of Chicago Press.

Allen, Robert C. 2009. *The British Industrial Revolution in Global Perspective*. Cambridge: Cambridge University Press.

Altman, Morris. 2020. *Why Ethical Behavior Is Good for the Economy: Towards Growth, Well-Being and Freedom*. Cheltenham: Edward Arnold.

Armstrong, Karen. (2009) 2010. *The Case for God*. New York: Knopf/Anchor Books.

Arrow, Kenneth J. (1959) 1960. "Decision Theory and the Choice of a Level of Significance for the *t*-Test." In *Contributions to Probability and Statistics: Essays in Honor of Harold Hotelling*, edited by Ingram Olkin et al., 70–78. Stanford, CA: Stanford University Press.

Arthur, W. Brian. 1994. Increasing *Returns and Path Dependence in the Economy*. Ann Arbor: University of Michigan Press.

Baier, Annette C. 1994. "Ethics in Many Different Voices." In *Moral Prejudices: Essays on Ethics*. Cambridge, MA: Harvard University Press.

Banfield, Edward C. 1958. *The Moral Basis of a Backward Society.* New York: Free Press.

Baran, Paul, and Paul Sweezy. 1966. *Monopoly Capital.* New York: Monthly Review Press.

Battalio, R. C., and John Kagel. 1975. "Experimental Studies of Consumer Demand Behavior Using Laboratory Animals." *Economic Inquiry.* 13 (March): 22–38.

Battalio, R. C., and John Kagel. 1981. "Commodity Choice Behavior with Pigeons as Subjects." *Journal of Political Economy* 89 (1): 67–91.

Bell, Tom W. 2018. *Your Next Government? From the Nation State to Stateless Nations.* Cambridge: Cambridge University Press.

Berman, Harold J. 1983. *Law and Revolution: The Formation of the Western Legal Tradition.* Cambridge, MA: Harvard University Press.

Binmore, Ken G. 1992. *Fun and Games: A Text on Game Theory.* Lexington, MA: D. C. Heath.

Blaug, Mark. 1980. *The Methodology of Economics; or, How Economists Explain.* Cambridge: Cambridge University Press.

Boaz, David. 2015. *The Libertarian Mind.* New York: Simon and Schuster.

Boettke, Peter. 2011. "Why the Great Stagnation Thesis Is the Most Subversive Libertarian Argument of Our Age." *The Coordination Problem* (blog), July 15. http://www.coordinationproblem.org/2011/07.

Boettke, Peter J. 2012. *Living Economics: Yesterday, Today, and Tomorrow.* Oakland, CA: Independent Institute.

Boldrin, Michele, and David K. Levine. 2008. *Against Intellectual Monopoly.* Cambridge: Cambridge University Press.

Boswell, James. (1791) 1949. *The Life of Samuel Johnson, LL. D.* 2 vols. London: J. M. Dent.

Boudreaux, Donald. 2018. "Letter to Amanda Crossland." *Cafe Hayek* (blog), August 23. https://cafehayek.com/2018/08/us-embrace-freedom.html.

Boulding, Kenneth E. 1956. *The Image: Knowledge in Life and Society.* Ann Arbor: University of Michigan Press.

Boulding, Kenneth E. 1973. *The Economy of Love and Fear.* Belmont, CA: Wadsworth.

Bourne, Ryan. 2019. "How 'Market Failure' Arguments Lead to Misguided Policy." *Policy Analysis* 863 (January 22). Washington, DC: Cato Institute.

Braudel, Fernand, and Frank Spooner. 1967. "Prices in Europe from 1450 to 1750." In *The Cambridge Economic History of Europe,* vol. 4, *The Economy of Expanding Europe in the Sixteenth and Seventeenth Centuries,* edited by E. E. Rich and C. H. Wilson, 374–486. Cambridge: Cambridge University Press.

Briggeman, Jason. 2015. "Search for Justification of the Policy of Pre-market Approval of Pharmaceuticals." PhD diss., George Mason University. http://mars.gmu.edu/bitstream/handle/1920/9656/Briggeman_gmu_0883E_10872.pdf.

Broadberry, S. N., and G. Bishnupriya. 2005. *The Early Modern Price Divergence: Wages, Prices and Economic Development in Europe and Asia, 1500–1800.* CERP Discussion Paper 4947. London: Centre for Economic Policy Research.

Buber, Martin. 1937. *I and Thou*. Translated by Ronald Gregory Smith. Edinburgh: T. and T. Clark. Originally published in German as *Ich und Du*, 1923.

Buber, Martin. 1967 *Between Man and Man*. Translated by R. G. Smith. New York: Macmillan. Originally published in German, 1948.

Burczak, Theodore. 2006. *Socialism after Hayek: Advances in Heterodox Economics*. Ann Arbor: University of Michigan Press.

Caliendo, Lorenzo, Maximiliano Dvorkin, and Fernando Parro. 2015. "Trade and Labor Market Dynamics." Working Paper 2015–009C, Federal Reserve Bank of St. Louis, August.

Campbell, Bruce M. S. 2005. "The Agrarian Problem of the Early Fourteenth Century." *Past and Present* 188:3–70.

Cannadine, David. 1990. *The Decline and Fall of the British Aristocracy*. New Haven, CT: Yale University Press.

Carlos, Ann M., and Frank D. Lewis. 1999. "Property Rights, Competition, and Depletion in the Eighteenth-Century Canadian Fur Trade: The Role of the European Market." *Canadian Journal of Economics/Revue canadienne d'economique* 32 (3): 705–28.

Chamlee-Wright, Emily. 2010. *The Cultural and Political Economy of Recovery: Social Learning in a Post-disaster Environment*. New York: Routledge.

Chamlee-Wright, Emily, and Don Lavoie. 2000. *Culture and Enterprise: The Development, Representation and Morality of Business*. New York: Routledge.

Chamlee-Wright, Emily, and Virgil Henry Storr, eds. 2010. *The Political Economy of Hurricane Katrina and Community Rebound*. Cheltenham: Edward Elgar.

Chaucer, Geoffrey. (ca. 1400) 1992. *The Canterbury Tales*. Everyman ed. New York: Knopf.

Choi, Young Back. 1993. *Paradigms and Conventions: Uncertainty, Decision-Making and Entrepreneurship*. Ann Arbor: University of Michigan Press.

Christakis, Nicholas A. 2019. *Blueprint: The Evolutionary Origins of a Good Society*. New York: Little, Brown.

Cicero, Marcus Tullius. (44 BCE) 1923. *Laelius de amicitia*. Trans. W. A. Falconer. Loeb ed. Cambridge, MA: Harvard University Press, 1923.

Clapham, John H. 1922, "Of Empty Economic Boxes." *Economic Journal* 22 (3): 305–14.

Clark, Gregory. 2007. *A Farewell to Alms: A Brief Economic History of the World*. Princeton, NJ: Princeton University Press.

Coase, Ronald H. 1960, "The Problem of Social Cost." *Journal of Law and Economics* 3 (October): 1–44.

Coate, Douglas. 2010. "Disaster and Recovery: The Public and Private Sectors in the Aftermath of the 1906 Earthquake in San Francisco." Working paper, Rutgers University, Newark, New Jersey.

Cook, Earnshaw. 1964. *Percentage Baseball*. Cambridge, MA: MIT Press.

Coşgel, Metin, and Boğaç Ergene. 2016. *The Economics of Ottoman Justice: Settlement and Trial in the Sharia Court*. Cambridge: Cambridge University Press.

Cowen, Tyler 2011. *The Great Stagnation: How America Ate All the Low-Hanging Fruit of Modern History, Got Sick, and Will (Eventually) Feel Better.* New York: Dutton.

Das, Gurcharan. 2009. *The Difficulty of Being Good: On the Subtle Art of Dharma.* Oxford: Oxford University Press.

David, Paul A. 1985. "Clio and the Economics of QWERTY." *American Economic Review* 75, no. 2 (May): 332–37.

Davis, James. 2012. *Medieval Market Morality: Life, Law and Ethics in the English Marketplace, 1200–1500.* Cambridge: Cambridge University Press.

Davis, Lance E., and R. A. Huttenback. 1986. *Mammon and the Pursuit of Empire: The Political Economy of British Imperialism, 1860–1912.* Cambridge: Cambridge University Press.

DeMartino, George F. 2011. *The Economist's Oath: On the Need for and Content of Professional Economic Ethics.* New York: Oxford.

DeMartino, George F. 2019. "Training the 'Ethical Economist.' " In *The Ethical Formation of Economists*, edited by Wilfred Dolfsma and Ioana Negru, 7–23. London: Routledge.

DeMartino, George F., and Deirdre Nansen McCloskey, eds. 2016. *The Oxford Handbook of Professional Economic Ethics.* New York: Oxford University Press.

DeMartino, George F., and Deirdre Nansen McCloskey. 2018. "Professional Ethics 101: A: Reply to Anne Krueger's Review of *The Oxford Handbook of Professional Economic Ethics.*" *EconJournal Watch*, January 31.

Diamond, Arthur M., Jr. 2019. *Openness to Creative Destruction: Sustaining Innovative Dynamism.* New York: Oxford University Press.

Doyle, Arthur Conan. 1886. *A Study in Scarlet.* Wikisource.org. https://en.wikisource .org/wiki/A_Study_in_Scarlet.

Duckworth, Craig. 2019. "Social Connection and the Responsible Economist." In *The Ethical Formation of Economists*, edited by Wilfred Dolfsma and Ioana Negru, 61–76. London: Routledge.

Duhem, Pierre. 1914. *La théorie physique son objet et sa structure.* 2nd ed. Paris: Chevalier et Rivière.

Duhem, Pierre. 1954. *The Aim and Structure of Physical Theory.* Princeton, NJ: Princeton University Press.

Dvorkin, Maximiliano. 2017. "What Is the Impact of Chinese Imports on U.S. Jobs?" *Regional Economist.* Federal Reserve Bank of St. Louis. May 15.

Eagleton, Terry. 2006. "Lunging, Flailing, Mispunching: Review of Dawkins, *The God Delusion.*" *London Review of Books*, October 19, 32–34.

Easterly, William 2001. *The Elusive Quest for Growth: Economists' Adventures and Misadventures in the Tropics.* Cambridge, MA: MIT Press.

Edelstein, Michael. 1982. *Overseas Investment in the Age of High Imperialism: The UK, 1850–1914.* New York: Columbia University Press.

Epstein, Richard A. 2009. Foreword to *Law, Liberty and the Competitive Market*, by Bruno Leoni. Edited by Carlo Lottieri. New Brunswick, NJ: Transaction, 2009.

Erhard, Werner, and Michael C. Jensen, 2016. "Putting Integrity into Finance: A Purely Positive Approach." *Capitalism and Society* 12, no. 1 (May): art. 1.

Feynman, Richard P. 1963. *The Feynman Lectures on Physics*. Caltech Division of Physics, Mathematics and Astronomy and The Feynman Lectures Website. http://www.feynmanlectures.caltech.edu/.

Feynman, Richard P. (1965) 2017. *The Character of Physical Law*. Cambridge: MIT Press, 2017.

Feynman, Richard P. 1974. "Cargo Cult Science." *Engineering and Science* 37 (7). http://www.sealevel.info/feynman_cargo_cult_science2.html.

Fish, Stanley. 1980. *Is There a Text in This Class? The Authority of Interpretive Communities*. Cambridge, MA: Harvard University Press.

Fish, Stanley. 2001. *How Milton Works*. Cambridge, MA: Harvard University Press.

Fleishacker, Samuel 2014, "Adam Smith and the Left." In *Adam Smith: A Princeton Guide*, edited by Ryan Hanley, 478–93. Princeton, NJ: Princeton University Press.

Folbre, Nancy. 2001. *The Invisible Heart: Economics and Family Values*. New York: New Press.

Friedman, Milton. 1953. "The Methodology of Positive Economics." In *Essays in Positive Economics*, 3–16. Chicago: University of Chicago Press.

Friedman, Milton. 1970. "The Social Responsibility of Business Is to Increase Its Profits." *New York Times Magazine*, September 13, sec. SM, p. 12.

Fukuyama, Francis. 1989. "The End of History?" *National Interest* 16 (Summer): 3–18.

Fukuyama, Francis. 1992. *The End of History and the Last Man*. New York: Free Press.

Galbraith, John Kenneth. 1958. *The Affluent Society*. Boston: Houghton Mifflin.

Gazzaniga, Michael S. 2011. *Who's in Charge? Free Will and the Science of the Brain*. New York: Harper-Collins.

Geertz, Clifford, Hildred Geertz, and Lawrence Rosen. 1979. *Meaning and Order in Moroccan Society*. New York: Cambridge University Press.

Gilligan, Carol. 1982. *In a Different Voice: Psychological Theory and Women's Development*. Cambridge, MA: Harvard University Press.

Gilomee, Hermann. 2003. *The Afrikaners: Biography of a People*. Cape Town: Tafelberg.

Giovannoni, Olivier 2014, "What Do We Know about the Labor Share and the Profit Share? Part III. Measures and Structural Factors." Levy Economics Institute, Bard College, Working Paper 805. Annandale-on-Hudson, NY: Levy Economics Institute. http://www.levyinstitute.org/pubs/wp_805.pdf.

Glewwe, P., Park A., Zhao M. 2012. "Visualizing Development: Eyeglasses and Academic Performance in Rural Primary Schools in China." Working Paper

WP12–2, Center for International Food and Agricultural Policy, University of Minnesota. St. Paul, MN: Center for International Food and Agricultural Policy.

Goldstone, Jack A. 2002. "Efflorescences and Economic Growth in World History: Rethinking the 'Rise of the West' and the Industrial Revolution." *Journal of World History* 13, no. 2 (Fall): 323–89.

Gordon, H. Scott. 1954. "The Economic Theory of a Common-Property Resource: The Fishery." *Journal of Political Economy* 62:124–42.

Gordon, Robert J. 2016. *The Rise and Fall of American Growth: The U.S. Standard of Living since the Civil War*. Princeton, NJ: Princeton University Press.

Greenfeld, Liah 2001. *The Spirit of Capitalism: Nationalism and Economic Growth*. Cambridge, MA: Harvard University Press.

Greenfield, Liah. 2012. *Nationalism: Five Roads to Modernity*. 2nd ed. Cambridge, MA: Harvard University Press.

Greif, Avner. 1989. "Reputation and Coalitions in Medieval Trade: Evidence on the Maghribi Traders." *Journal of Economic History* 49 (December): 857–82.

Greif, Avner. 2006. *Institutions and the Path to the Modern Economy: Lessons from Medieval Trade*. Cambridge: Cambridge University Press.

Greif, Avner, and Joel Mokyr. 2015. "Institutions and Economic History: A Critique of Professor McCloskey." *Journal of Institutional Economics* 12 (1): 29–41.

Groot, Wim, and Henriette Maassen van den Brink. 2019. "Economists, Their Role and Influence in the Media." In *The Ethical Formation of Economists*, edited by Wilfred Dolfsma and Ioana Negru, 132–44. London: Routledge.

Haltiwanger, John C. 2011. "Job Creation and Firm Dynamics in the United States." *NBER Innovation Policy and the Economy* 12:17–38.

Harberger, Arnold C. 1954, "Monopoly and Resource Allocation." *American Economic Review* 44 (2): 77–87.

Harberger, Arnold C. 1971. "Three Basic Postulates for Applied Welfare Economics: An Interpretive Essay." *Journal of Economic Literature* 9 (3): 785–97.

Harris, Randy Allen. 1995. *The Linguistics Wars*. Oxford: Oxford University Press.

Haskell, Thomas L. 1999. "Responsibility, Convention, and the Role of Ideas in History." In *Ideas, Ideologies, and Social Movements: The United States Experience since 1800*, edited by P. A. Coclanis and S. Bruchey, 1–27. Columbia: University of South Carolina Press.

Hazlett, Thomas W. 2017. *The Political Spectrum: The Tumultuous Liberation of Wireless Technology, from Herbert Hoover to the Smartphone*. New Haven, CT: Yale University Press.

Higgs, Robert. (2012) 2015. "Freedom: Because It Works or Because It Is Right?" *The Beacon*, December 27. http://blog.independent.org/2012/12/27/freedom-because-it-works-or-because-its-right/. Reprinted in *Taking a Stand: Reflections on Life, Liberty, and the Economy*. Oakland, CA: Independent Institute.

Hill, Peter J. 2016. "Dining with Deirdre." *Faith and Economics* 68 (Fall): 21–27.

Hobbes, Thomas. (1651) 1914. *Leviathan*. Everyman's Library 691. London: J. M. Dent.

Hobsbawm, Eric. 2011. *How to Change the World: Reflections on Marx and Marxism*. New Haven, CT: Yale University Press.

Hodges, Andrew. 1983. *Alan Turing: The Enigma*. New York: Simon and Schuster.

Hovenkamp, Herbert. 1990. 'The First Great Law and Economics Movement." *Stanford Law Review* 42:993–1058.

Hyde, Lewis. 1998. *Trickster Makes This World: Mischief, Myth, and Art*. New York: Farrar, Straus and Giroux.

Iannaccone, Lawrence. 1998. "Introduction to the Economics of Religion." *Journal of Economic Literature* 36 (September): 1465–95.

Ingram, Paul, and Peter Roberts. 2000. "Friendship among Competitors in the Sydney Hotel Industry." *American Journal of Sociology* 106 (2): 387–423.

James Stuart, James VI of Scotland. (1598) 1996. *The True Law of Free Monarchies; and, Basilikon doron*. Edited by Daniel Fischlin and Marl Fortier. Toronto: Centre for Reformation and Renaissance Studies.

Jones, Eric L. 1988. *Growth Recurring: Economic Change in World History*. New York: Oxford University Press.

Jones, Eric L. 2010. *Locating the Industrial Revolution: Inducement and Response*. London: World Scientific.

Jouvenel, Bertrand de. (1961) 1999. "A Better Life in an Affluent Society." Translated by H. Krall. *Diogenes* 33 (Spring 1961): 50–74. Reprinted in *Economics and the Good Life: Essays in Political Economy*, edited by Dennis Hale and Marc Landry, 97–118. New Brunswick, NJ: Transaction, 1999.

Kealey, Terence. 1996. *The Economic Laws of Scientific Research*. London: Macmillan.

Kealey, Terence. 2008. *Sex, Science and Profits*. London: William Heinemann.

Kelly, Morgan, Cormac Ó Gráda, and Joel Mokyr. 2013. "Precocious Albion: A New Interpretation of the British Industrial Revolution." Annual Reviews of Economics, School of Economics, University College Dublin, July.

Kelling, George L., and James Q. Wilson. 1982. "Broken Windows: The Police and Neighborhood Safety." *Atlantic* 249 (March): 29–38.

Keuhn, Aaron. 2008. Letter to the editor, *Chicago Tribune*, March 7.

Kiesling, Lynne. 2011. "Boettke on Cowen, Smith, Schumpeter, and Stupidity." *Knowledge Problem*, July 19. https://knowledgeproblem.com/2011/07/19/boettke -on-cowen-smith-schumpeter-and-stupidity/.

Kimbrough, Erik O., Vernon L. Smith, and Bart J. Wilson. 2010. "Exchange, Theft, and the Social Formation of Property." *Journal of Economic Behavior and Organization* 74, no. 3 (June): 206–29.

Kirzner, Israel M. 1976. "Equilibrium versus Market Processes." In *The Foundations of Modern Austrian Economics*, edited by Edwin Dolan, 114–25. Kansas City: Sheed and Ward. https://oll.libertyfund.org/titles/dolan-the-foundations -of-modern-austrian-economics-1976/simple#lf0724_head_027.

Kirzner, Israel M. 1979. *Perception, Opportunity and Profit Studies in the Theory of Entrepreneurship*. Chicago: University of Chicago Press.

Kirzner, Israel M. 1985. *Discovery and the Capitalist Process*. Chicago: University of Chicago Press.

Klamer, Arjo. 2007. *Speaking of Economics: How to Get in the Conversation*. London: Routledge

Klamer, Arjo. 2017. *Doing the Right Thing: A Value Based Approach*. London: Ubiquity Press.

Klein, Daniel B. 2012. *Knowledge and Coordination: A Liberal Interpretation*. Oxford: Oxford University Press.

Klein, Daniel B., and Gordon J. Fielding. 1992. "Private Toll Roads: Learning from the Nineteenth Century." *Transportation Quarterly* 46, no. 3 (July): 321–41.

Klein, Daniel B., and John Majewski. N.d. "Turnpikes and Toll Roads in Nineteenth-Century America." EH.net. http://eh.net/encyclopedia/turnpikes-and-toll-roads-in-nineteenth-century-america/.

Koopmans, Tjalling C. 1957. *Three Essays on the State of Economic Science*. New York: McGraw-Hill.

Krueger, Anne O. 2017. Review of *The Oxford Handbook of Professional Economic Ethics*. *Journal of Economic Literature* 55:209–33.

Kuhn, Thomas S. 1962. *The Structure of Scientific Revolutions*. Chicago: University of Chicago Press.

Kuhn, Thomas S. 1977. *The Essential Tension: Selected Studies in Scientific Tradition and Change*. Chicago: University of Chicago Press.

Khurana, Rakesh. 2007. *From Higher Aims to Hired Hands: The Social Transformation of American Business Schools and the Unfulfilled Promise of Management as a Profession*. Princeton, NJ: Princeton University Press.

Kolko, Gabriel. 1965. *Railroads and Regulation, 1877–1916*. Princeton, NJ: Princeton University Press.

Landsburg, Stephen E. 2017. "McCloskey at Chicago." In *Humanism Challenges Materialism in Economics and Economic History*, edited by Roderick Floud, Santhe Hejeebu, and David Mitch, chap. 10. Chicago: University of Chicago Press.

Langlois, Richard. 1994. Review of *Business Organization and the Myth of the Market Economy*, by William Lazonick. *Journal of Economic Behavior and Organization* 23:244–50.

Langlois, Richard N. 2002. "Schumpeter and the Obsolescence of the Entrepreneur." Economics Working Papers 200219. http://digitalcommons.uconn.edu/econ_wpapers/200219.

Langlois, Richard N. 2015. "Institutions for Getting Out of the Way." *Journal of Institutional Economics* 12:53–61. https://www.cambridge.org/core/journals/journal-of-institutional-economics/article/institutions-for-getting-out-of-the-way/EAEEBCBFEED9FC2A541661DBC7996D91/core-reader.

Lavoie, Don C., ed. 1990. *Economics and Hermeneutics*. London: Routledge.

Lawson, Robert A. 2015. "Can Two Observations Confirm a Theory? A Comment on Max U versus Humanomics." *Journal of Institutional Economics* 12 (1): 49–51.

Levi, Carlo. 1947. *Christ Stopped at Eboli: The Story of a Year.* Translated by Frances Frenaye. New York: Farrar, Strauss. Originally published in Italian as *Cristo si è fermato a Eboli*, 1945. http://archive.org/stream/christstoppedate013078mbp/christstoppedate013078mbp_djvu.txt.

Lewin, Peter, ed. 2002. *The Economics of QWERTY: History, Theory, and Policy; Essays by Stan J. Liebowitz and Stephen E. Margolis.* New York: New York University Press.

Lewis, H. Gregg. 1963. *Unions and Relative Wages in the United States.* Chicago: University of Chicago Press.

Lewis, H. Gregg. 1986. *Union Relative Wage Effects: A Survey.* Chicago: University of Chicago Press.

Lincoln, Abraham. (1858) 1894. "First of the Lincoln-Douglas Debates." Ottawa, Illinois, August 21. In *Abraham Lincoln: Complete Works, Comprising His Speeches, Letters, State Papers, and Miscellaneous Writings*, vol. 1, edited by John G. Nicolay and John Hay. New York: Century.

Lipsey, Richard G., and Kelvin Lancaster. 1956. "The General Theory of Second Best." *Review of Economic Studies* 24 (1): 11–32.

MacIntyre, Alasdair. 1981. *After Virtue: A Study in Moral Theory.* Notre Dame, IN: University of Notre Dame Press.

Martin, Nona P., and Virgil Henry Storr. 2012. "Talk Changes Things: The Implications of McCloskey's *Bourgeois Dignity* for Historical Inquiry." *Journal of Behavioral and Experimental Economics* 41 (6): 787–91.

Mas-Colell, A., M. D. Whinston, and J. R. Green. 1995. *Microeconomic Theory.* New York: Oxford University Press.

Mazzucato, Mariana. 2013. *The Entrepreneurial State: Debunking Public vs. Private Sector Myths.* London: Anthem Press.

McCloskey, Deirdre Nansen. 1970. "Did Victorian Britain Fail?" *Economic History Review* 23 (December): 446–59.

McCloskey, Deirdre Nansen. 1975a. "The Economics of Enclosure: A Market Analysis." In *European Peasants and Their Markets: Essays in Agrarian Economic History*, edited by Eric L. Jones and William Parker, 123–60. Princeton, NJ: Princeton University Press.

McCloskey, Deirdre Nansen. 1975b. "The Persistence of English Common Fields." In *European Peasants and Their Markets: Essays in Agrarian Economic History*, edited by Eric L. Jones and William Parker, 73–119. Princeton, NJ: Princeton University Press.

McCloskey, Deirdre Nansen. 1976. "English Open Fields as Behavior Towards Risk." *Research in Economic History* 1 (Fall): 124–70.

McCloskey, Deirdre Nansen. 1985. *The Applied Theory of Price.* 2nd ed. New York: Macmillan.

McCloskey, Deirdre Nansen. 1989. "Formalism in Economics, Rhetorically Speaking." *Ricerche economiche* 43 (1/2): 57–75.

McCloskey, Deirdre Nansen. 1990. *If You're So Smart: The Narrative of Economic Expertise.* Chicago: University of Chicago Press.

McCloskey, Deirdre Nansen. 1994. *Knowledge and Persuasion in Economics*. Cambridge: Cambridge University Press.

McCloskey, Deirdre Nansen. 1998a. *The Rhetoric of Economics*. Rev. 2nd ed. Madison: University of Wisconsin Press.

McCloskey, Deirdre Nansen. 1998b. "Simulating Barbara." *Feminist Economics* 4, no. 3 (Fall): 181–86.

McCloskey, Deirdre Nansen. 2001. "Women's Work in the Market, 1900–2000." In *Women in Twentieth-Century Britain: Economic, Social, and Cultural Change*, edited by Ina Zweiniger-Bargielowska. London: Longmans.

McCloskey, Deirdre Nansen. 2006. *The Bourgeois Virtues: Ethics for an Age of Commerce*. Chicago: University of Chicago Press.

McCloskey, Deirdre Nansen. 2008. "Not by *P* Alone: A Virtuous Economy." *Review of Political Economy* 20 (2): 181–97.

McCloskey, Deirdre Nansen. 2010. *Bourgeois Dignity: Why Economics Can't Explain the Modern World*. Chicago: University of Chicago Press.

McCloskey, Deirdre Nansen. 2012. "Happyism: The Creepy New Economics of Pleasure." *New Republic*, June 28, 16–23.

McCloskey, Deirdre Nansen. 2014. "Measured, Unmeasured, Mismeasured, and Unjustified Pessimism: A Review Essay of Thomas Piketty's *Capital in the Twenty-First Century*." *Erasmus Journal for Philosophy and Economics* 7 (2): 73–115.

McCloskey, Deirdre Nansen. 2015a. "The Humanities Are Scientific: A Reply to the Defenses of Economic Neo-Institutionalism" (by Greif, Mokyr, Langlois, Lawson, and Tabellini). *Journal of Institutional Economics* 12 (1): 63–78.

McCloskey, Deirdre Nansen. 2015b. "Max U versus Humanomics: A Critique of Neo-Institutionalism." *Journal of Institutional Economics* 12 (1): 1–27.

McCloskey, Deirdre Nansen. 2016. *Bourgeois Equality: How Ideas, Not Capital or Institutions, Enriched the World*. Chicago: University of Chicago Press.

McCloskey, Deirdre Nansen. 2017a. "The Ethical and Scientific Offences of Erhard and Jensen." A comment on Erhard and Jensen, "Putting Integrity into Finance: A Purely Positive Approach." *Capitalism and Society* 12, no. 1 (May): art. 5.

McCloskey, Deirdre Nansen. 2017b. "The Myth of Technological Unemployment." *Reason* August/September. https://reason.com/2017/07/11/the-myth-of-technological-unem/.

McCloskey, Deirdre Nansen. 2018. "The Applied Theory of Bossing People Around: Thaler's Nobel." *Reason*, March, 8–9.

McCloskey, Deirdre Nansen. 2019. *Why Liberalism Works: How True Liberal Vales Produce a Freer, More Equal, Prosperous World for All*. New Haven, CT: Yale University Press.

McCloskey, Deirdre Nansen. 2020a. "Fukuyama Was Correct: Liberalism *is* the Telos of History." "1938 Colloque Walter Lippmann," special issue of *Journal of Contextual Economics — Schmollers Jahrbuch* 139: 285–304.

McCloskey, Deirdre Nansen. 2020b. *Historical Impromptus: Notes, Reviews, and Responses on the British Experience and the Great Enrichment*. Great Barrington, MA: American Institute for Economic Research.

McCloskey, Deirdre Nansen. 2021. "The Liberty of the Will in Theology Permits the Liberated Markets of Liberalism." *Journal of Economics, Theology and Religion* 1 (1): 81–108.

McCloskey, Deirdre Nansen, and Art Carden. 2020. *Leave Me Alone and I'll Make You Rich: The Bourgeois Deal*. Chicago: University of Chicago Press.

McCloskey, Deirdre Nansen, and Alberto Mingardi. 2020. *The Illiberal Myth of the Entrepreneurial State*. London: Adam Smith Institute: American Institute for Economic Research.

McEvoy, Paul. 2001. *Niels Bohr: Reflections on Subject and Object*. San Francisco: Microanalytix.

Mehra, Akhil. 2009. "Politics of Participation: Walter Reed's Yellow-Fever Experiments." *AMA Journal of Medical Ethics* 11 (4): 326–30.

Mill, John Stuart. (1859) 2001. *On Liberty*. Kitchener: Batoche Books.

Miller, Edward. 1951. *The Abbey and Bishopric of Ely*. Cambridge: Cambridge University Press.

Mingardi, Alberto. 2015. "A Critique of Mazzucato's Entrepreneurial State." *Cato Journal* 35, no. 3 (Fall): 603–25.

Mokyr, Joel. 2009. "Intellectual Property Rights, the Industrial Revolution, and the Beginnings of Modern Economic Growth." *American Economic Review* 99 (2): 349–55.

Mokyr, Joel. 2016. *A Culture of Growth: Origins of the Modern Economy*. Princeton, NJ: Princeton University Press.

Morgan, James. 2019. "Intervention, Policy, and Responsibility: Economics as Over-Engineered Expertise?" In *The Ethical Formation of Economists*, edited by Wilfred Dolfsma and Ioana Negru, 145–63. London: Routledge.

Mueller, John D. 1985. *Astaire Dancing: The Musical Films of Fred Astaire*. New York: Knopf.

Mueller, John D. 1999. *Capitalism, Democracy, and Ralph's Pretty Good Grocery*. Princeton, NJ: Princeton University Press.

Mulkay, Michael. 1985. *The Word and the World: Explorations in the Form of Sociological Analysis*. London Boston: Allen and Unwin.

Murrell, Peter. 2009. "Design and Evolution in Institutional Development: The Insignificance of the English Bill of Rights." SSRN. http://ssrn.com/abstract=1522864.

Nee, Victor, and Richard Swedberg. 2007. Introduction to *On Capitalism*, edited by Victor Nee and Richard Swedberg, 1–18. Stanford, CA: Stanford University Press.

Noddings, Nel. 1984. *Caring: A Feminine Approach to Ethics and Moral Education*. Berkeley: University of California Press.

Nordhaus, William D. 2004, "Schumpeterian in the American Economy: Theory and Measurement." SSRN. https://papers.ssrn.com/sol3/papers.cfm?abstract_id =537242.

North, Douglass C. 1991. "Institutions." *Journal of Economic Perspectives* 5 (Winter): 97–112.

North, Douglass C. 2005. *Understanding the Process of Economic Change.* Princeton Economic History of the Western World. Princeton, NJ: Princeton University Press.

North, Douglass C., and Robert Paul Thomas. 1973. *The Rise of the Western World: A New Economic History.* Cambridge University Press, Cambridge.

North, Douglass C., John Joseph Wallis, and Barry R. Weingast. 2009. *Violence and Social Orders: A Conceptual Framework for Interpreting Recorded Human History.* Cambridge: Cambridge University Press.

North, Douglass C., and Barry R. Weingast. 1989. "Constitutions and Commitment: The Evolution of Institutions Governing Public Choice in Seventeenth-Century England." *Journal of Economic History* 49 (4): 803–32.

Novick, Peter. 1988. *That Noble Dream: The "Objectivity Question" and the American Historical Profession.* Cambridge: Cambridge University Press.

Oakeshott, Michael. 1933. *Experience and Its Modes.* Cambridge: Cambridge University Press.

O'Brien, Patrick K. 1993. "Political Preconditions for the Industrial Revolution." In *The Industrial Revolution and British Society,* edited by Patrick K. O'Brien and Ronald Quinault, 124–55. Cambridge: Cambridge University Press.

O'Brien, Patrick K. 2011a. "The Contributions of Warfare with Revolutionary and Napoleonic France to the Consolidation and Progress of the British Industrial Revolution". Department of Economic History, London School of Economics Working Papers No. 150/11.

O'Brien, Patrick K. 2011b. "The History, Nature and Significance of an Exceptional Fiscal State for the Growth of the British Economy." *Economic History Review* 64 (2): 408–46.

Ogilvie, Sheilagh. 2019. *The European Guilds: An Economic Analysis.* Princeton, NJ: Princeton University Press.

Ó Gráda, Cormac. 2009. *Famine: A Short History.* Princeton, NJ: Princeton University Press.

Olney, Martha L. 1991. *Buy Now, Pay Later: Advertising, Credit, and Consumer Durables in the 1920s.* Chapel Hill: University of North Carolina Press.

Olson, Mancur. 1982. *The Rise and Decline of Nations: Economic Growth, Stagflation, and Social Rigidities.* New Haven, CT: Yale University Press.

Orcutt, Guy H., et al. 1961. *Microanalysis of Socioeconomic Systems: A Simulation Study.* New York: Harpers.

Ostrom, Elinor. 1990. *Governing the Commons: The Evolution of Institutions for Collective Action.* Cambridge: Cambridge University Press.

Parks, Tim. 2013. *Italian Ways: On and Off the Rails from Milan to Palermo*. New York: Norton.

Parthasarathi, Prasannan. 2011. *Why Europe Grew Rich and Asia Did Not: Global Economic Divergence 1600–1850*. Cambridge: Cambridge University.

Peart, Sandra J., and David M. Levy. 2005. *The "Vanity of the Philosopher": From Equality to Hierarchy in Postclassical Economics*. Ann Arbor: University of Michigan Press.

Persky, Joseph. 2016. *The Political Economy of Progress: John Stuart Mill and Modern Radicalism*. Oxford: Oxford University Press.

Piketty, Thomas. 2014. *Capital in the Twenty-First Century*. Translated from the 2010 French edition by A. Goldhammer. Cambridge, MA: Harvard University Press.

Polanyi, Karl. 1944. *The Great Transformation*. Boston: Beacon Press.

Polanyi, Michael. 1958. *Personal Knowledge: Towards a Post-Critical Philosophy*. Chicago: University of Chicago Press.

Pollock, Frederick, and F. W. Maitland. 1895. *The History of English Law before the Time of Edward I*. 2nd ed. Cambridge: Cambridge University Press.

Pomeranz, Kenneth. 2000. *The Great Divergence: China, Europe, and the Making of the Modern World Economy*. Princeton, NJ: Princeton University Press.

Pomeranz, Kenneth, and Steven Topik. 2006. *The World That Trade Created: Society, Culture, and the World Economy 1400 to the Present*. London: M. E. Sharpe.

Popper, Karl. 1945. *The Open Society and Its Enemies*. London: Routledge.

Porter, Michael E. 1990. *The Competitive Advantage of Nations*. New York: Free Press.

Putnam, Hilary. 1990. *Realism with a Human Face*. Cambridge, MA: Harvard University Press.

Radford, R. A. 1945. "The Economic Organisation of a P.O.W. Camp." *Economica*, n.s. 12, no. 48 (November): 189–201.

Raftis, Fr. J. Ambrose. 1996. *Peasant Economic Development within the English Manorial System*. Montreal: McGill-Queens University Press.

Razafindrakoto, Mireille, François Roubaud, and Jean-Michel Wachsberger. 2013. "Institutions, gouvernance et croissance de long terme à Madagascar: L'énigme et le paradoxe." Unpublished essay, Université Paris-Dauphine, UMR DIAL (Developpement Institutions et Mondialisation).

Reid, Constance. 1986. *Hilbert-Courant*. New York: Springer.

Reiss, J. Philipp. 2000. "On the Convergence Speed in Growth Models." FEMM Working Paper 22/2000, Otto von Guericke University of Magdeburg. http://io.econ.kit.edu/downloads/Reiss_OnTheConvergenceSpeedInGrowthModels.pdf.

Ridley, Matt. 2010. *The Rational Optimist: How Prosperity Evolves*. London: HarperCollins.

Robbins, Lionel. 1932. *An Essay on the Nature and Significance of Economic Science*. London: Macmillan.

Rorty, Amélie Oksenberg. 1983. "Experiments in Philosophical Genre: Descartes' *Meditations.*" *Critical Inquiry* 9 (March): 545–65.

Rosling, Hans, Ola Rosling, and Anna Rosling Rönnlund. 2018. *Factfulness: Ten Reasons We're Wrong about the World—And Why Things Are Better Than You Think.* London: Hodder and Stoughton.

Rossi, Guido, and Salvatore Spagano. 2014. "From Custom to Law: Hayek Revisited." Unpublished essay, Edinburgh School of Law and Department of Economics and Business, University of Catania. http://mpra.ub.uni-muenchen.de /56643/.

Samuelson, Paul A. 1947. *The Foundations of Economic Analysis.* Cambridge, MA: Harvard University Press.

Sandburg, Lars G. 1979. "The Case of the *Impoverished Sophisticate*: Human Capital and *Swedish* Economic Growth before World War I." *Journal of Economic History* 39 (1): 225–41

Sarasvathy, Saras D. 2013. "Causation and Effectuation: Toward a Theoretical Shift from Economic Inevitability to Entrepreneurial Contingency." *Academy of Management Review* 26 (2): 243–88.

Sato, Ryuzo. 1963a. "Fiscal Policy in a Neo-Classical Growth Model: An Analysis of Time Required for Equilibrating Adjustment." *Review of Economic Studies* 30, no. 1 (February): 16–23.

Sato, K. 1966. "On the Adjustment Time in Neoclassical Growth Models." *Review of Economic Studies* 33 (3): 263–68.

Saucedo, Alfred. 2021. "Narrative in the Prisoner's Dilemma and Arrow's Impossibility Theory." Unpublished manuscript. Department of Political Science, University of Chicago.

Schmidtz, David. 2011. "Nonideal Theory: What It Is and What It Needs to Be." *Ethics* 121 (4): 772–96.

Schor, Juliet B. 1993. *The Overworked American: The Unexpected Decline of Leisure.* New York: Basic.

Schumpeter, Joseph A. 1934. *The Theory of Economic Development.* Translated from the 1926 German edition of the 1912 original. Cambridge, MA: Harvard University Press.

Scott, Anthony. 1955. "The Fishery: The Objectives of Sole Ownership." *Journal of Political Economy* 63:116–24.

Searle, John R. 2010. *Making the Social World: The Structure of Human Civilization.* Oxford: Oxford University Press.

Sen, Amartya. 1977. "Rational Fools: A Critique of the Behavioral Foundations of Economic Theory." *Philosophy and Public Affairs* 6, no. 4 (Summer): 317–44.

Sen, Amartya. 1987. *On Ethics and Economics.* Oxford: Blackwell.

Shackle, George L. S. (1972) 1992. *Epistemics and Economics: A Critique of Economic Doctrines.* Cambridge: Cambridge University Press.

Shultziner, Doron, Thomas Stevens, Martin Stevens, Brian A. Stewart, Rebecca J. Hannagan, and Giulia Saltini-Semerari. 2010. "Causes and Scope of Political

Egalitarianism during the Last Glacial: A Multi-Disciplinary Perspective." *Biology and Philosophy* 25 (3): 319–46.

Simon, Herbert A. 1947. *Administrative Behavior: A Study of Decision-Making Processes in Administrative Organization*. New York: Macmillan.

Simon, Julian. (1981) 1996. *The Ultimate Resource 2*. Princeton, NJ: Princeton University Press.

Sindzingre, Alice Nicole. 2019. "Experiments in Economics and Their Ethical Dimensions: The Case of Developing Countries." In *The Ethical Formation of Economists*, edited by Wilfred Dolfsma and Ioana Negru, 114–31. London: Routledge.

Smith, Adam. (1759) 1790. *The Theory of Moral Sentiments*. Edited by D. D. Raphael and A. L. Macfie. Oxford: Oxford University Press. Reprint, Indianapolis: Liberty Classics, 1976, 1982.

Smith, Adam. 1776. *An Inquiry into the Nature and Causes of the Wealth of Nations*. 2 vols. London.

Smith, Vernon L. 2002. "Constructivist and Ecological Rationality in Economics." Nobel Prize Lecture, December 8. In *Les prix Nobel: The Nobel Prizes 2002*, edited by Tore Frängsmyr, 502–61. Stockholm: Nobel Foundation, 2003. http://www.nobelprize.org/uploads/2018/06/smith-lecture-2.pdf.

Smith, Vernon L. 2007. *Rationality in Economics: Constructivist and Ecological Forms*. Cambridge: Cambridge University Press.

Smith, Vernon L., and Bart J. Wilson. 2018. *Humanomics: Moral Sentiments and the Wealth of Nations for the Twenty- First Century*. Cambridge: Cambridge University Press.

Solow, Robert M. 1956. "A Contribution to the Theory of Economic Growth." *Quarterly Journal of Economics* 70, no. 1 (February): 65–94.

Sowell, Thomas. 2015. *Basic Economics: A Common Sense Guide to the Economy*. 5th ed. New York: Basic Books.

Spender, J.-C. 1989. *Industry Recipes: An Enquiry into the Nature and Sources of Managerial Judgement*. Oxford: Blackwell.

Spender, J.-C. 2014. *Business Strategy: Managing Uncertainty, Opportunity, and Enterprise*. Oxford: Oxford University Press.

Stefánsson, H. Orri. 2016a. "On the Limits of the Precautionary Principle." *Risk Analysis* 39, no. 6 (June): 1204–22.

Stefánsson, H. Orri. 2016b. "What Is 'Real' in Probalism?" *Australian Journal of Philosophy*, September, 2016.

Stigler, George J. 1961. "The Economics of Information." *Journal of Political Economy* 69, no. 3 (June): 213–25. Reprinted in *The Organization of Industry*, 171–90. Homewood, IL: Irwin, 1968.

Stigler, George J. 1971. "The Theory of Economic Regulation." *Bell Journal of Economics and Management Science* 2 (Spring): 3–21.

Stigler, George J. 1987. *The Theory of Price*. 4th ed. New York: Macmillan.

Stigler, George, and Gary Becker. 1977. "De gustibus non est disputandum." *American Economic Review* 67, no. 2 (March): 67–90.

Storr, Virgil. 2012. *Understanding the Culture of Markets*. London: Routledge.

Stringham, Edward. 2015. *Private Governance: Creating Order in Economic and Social Life*. Oxford: Oxford University Press.

Tabarrok, Alex. 2015. "What Was Gary Becker's Biggest Mistake?" *Marginal Revolution* (blog), September 16. https://marginalrevolution.com/marginalrevolution/2015/09/what-was-gary-beckers-biggest-mistake.html.

Tabellini, Guido. 2015. "Ideas or Institutions? A Comment." *Journal of Institutional Economics* 12, no. 1 (March): 43–48.

Tallis, Raymond. 2011. "Review of Deacon and Gazzanga." *Wall Street Journal*, November 12.

Telser, Lester G. 2007. *The Core Theory in Economics: Problems and Solutions*. London: Routledge.

Tullock, Gordon. 1967. "The Welfare Costs of Tariffs, Monopolies, and Theft." *Western Economic Journal* 5, no. 3 (June): 224–32.

Umbeck, John. 1977. "The California Gold Rush: A Study of Emerging Property Rights. *Explorations in Economic History* 14, no. 3 (July): 197–226.

Veblen, Thorstein. 1898. "Why Is Economics Not an Evolutionary Science?" *Quarterly Journal of Economics* 12, no. 4 (July): 373–97.

Wasserstein, Ronald L., and Nicole A. Lazar. 2016. "The ASA Statement on *p*-Values: Context, Process, and Purpose." *American Statistician* 70 (2): 129–33. https://www.tandfonline.com/doi/full/10.1080/00031305.2016.1154108?scroll=top&needAccess=true.

Waterman, Anthony M. C. 2012. "Adam Smith and Malthus on High Wages." *European Journal of the History of Economic Thought* 19 (3): 409–29.

Weatherford, Jack. 2004. *Genghis Khan and the Making of the Modern World*. New York: Crown.

Weber, Max. (1904–1905). *Die protestantische Ethik und der Geist des Kapitalismus*. Tübingen: Mohr.

Weber, Max. 1958. *The Protestant Ethic and the Spirit of Capitalism*. Translated by Talcott Parsons. New York: Scribner.

Weingast, Barry R. 2016. "Exposing the Neoclassical Fallacy: McCloskey on Ideas and the Great Enrichment." *Scandinavian Economic History Review* 64 (3): 189–201.

Weisse, Allen B. 2012. "Self-Experimentation and Its Role in Medical Research." *Texas Heart Institute Journal* 39 (1): 51–54. https://www.ncbi.nlm.nih.gov/pmc/articles/PMC3298919.

Whincup, Greg. 1987. *The Heart of Chinese Poetry*. New York: Anchor.

White, Mark D. 2006. "A Kantian Critique of Neoclassical Law and Economics." *Review of Political Economy* 18: 235–52.

White, Mark D. 2019. "More Harm Than Benefit: The Ramifications of the Neglect of Rights in Economics." In *The Ethical Formation of Economists*, edited by Wilfred Dolfsma and Ioana Negru, 77–91. London: Routledge.

Wigner, Eugene. 1960. "The Unreasonable Effectiveness of Mathematics in the Natural Sciences." *Communications in Pure and Applied Mathematics* 13 (February 1960): 1–14.

Will, George. 2019. *The Conservative Sensibility*. New York: Hachette.

Williamson, Oliver E. 1999. "Public and Private Bureaucracies: A Transaction Cost Economics Perspective." *Journal of Law, Economics and Organization* 15, no. 1 (March): 306–42.

Wilson, Bart J. 2010. "Social Preferences Aren't Preferences." *Journal of Economic Behavior and Organization* 73 (2): 77–82.

Wilson, Bart J. 2020. *The Property Species: Mine, Yours and the Human Mind*. New York: Oxford University Press.

Wilson, Bart J., Taylor Jaworski, Karl E. Schurter, and Andrew Smyth. 2012. "The Ecological and Civil Mainsprings of Property: An Experimental Economic History of Whalers' Rules of Capture." *Journal of Law, Economics and Organization* 28, no. 4 (October): 617–56.

Zakaria, Fareed. 2019. "America's Democracy Has Become Illiberal." *Washington Post*, December 30.

Zamagni, Stefano. 2010. "Catholic Social Thought, Civil Economy, and the Spirit of Capitalism." In *The True Wealth of Nations: Catholic Social Thought and Economic Life*, edited by Daniel K. Finn, 63–93. Oxford: Oxford University Press.

Zanden, Jan Luiten van. 2009. *The Long Road to the Industrial Revolution: The European Economy in a Global Perspective, 1000–1800*. Leiden: Brill.

Zelizer, Viviana A. 2005. *The Purchase of Intimacy*. Princeton, NJ: Princeton University Press.

Ziliak, Stephen T., ed. 2001. *Measurement and Meaning in Economics: The Essential Deirdre McCloskey* (Economists of the Twentieth Century series). Cheltenham, UK: Edward Elgar.

Ziliak, Stephen T. 2008. "Guinnessometrics: The Economic Foundation of 'Students' *t*." *Journal of Economic Perspectives* 22 (4): 199–216.

Ziliak, Stephen T., and Deirdre Nansen. McCloskey. 2008. *The Cult of Statistical Significance: How the Standard Error Costs Us Jobs, Justice, and Lives*. Ann Arbor: University of Michigan Press.

Ziliak, Stephen T., and Deirdre Nansen McCloskey. 2019. "What Quantitative Methods Should We Teach to Graduate Students? Comment on Swann's 'Is Precise Econometrics an Illusion?'" *Journal of Economic Education* 50 (2019): 356–61.

Ziliak, Stephen T, and Edward R. Teather-Posada. 2019. "The Making of an Ethical Econometrician." *The Ethical Formation of Economists*, edited by Wilfred Dolfsma and Ioana Negru, 114–31. London: Routledge.

Index